Emerging Asian Economies and MNCs Strategies

NEW HORIZONS IN INTERNATIONAL BUSINESS

Series Editor: Peter J. Buckley, *Centre for International Business, University of Leeds (CIBUL), UK*

The New Horizons in International Business series has established itself as the world's leading forum for the presentation of new ideas in international business research. It offers pre-eminent contributions in the areas of multinational enterprise – including foreign direct investment, business strategy and corporate alliances, global competitive strategies, and entrepreneurship. In short, this series constitutes essential reading for academics, business strategists and policy makers alike.

Titles in the series include:

Emerging Asian Economies and MNCs Strategies

Edited by

Robert Taylor

University of Sheffield, UK

Bernadette Andreosso-O'Callaghan

University of Limerick, Ireland and Ruhr Universität Bochum, Germany

NEW HORIZONS IN INTERNATIONAL BUSINESS

Edward Elgar
PUBLISHING

Cheltenham, UK • Northampton, MA, USA

Published by
Edward Elgar Publishing Limited
The Lypiatts
15 Lansdown Road
Cheltenham
Glos GL50 2JA
UK

Edward Elgar Publishing, Inc.
William Pratt House
9 Dewey Court
Northampton
Massachusetts 01060
USA

A catalogue record for this book
is available from the British Library

Library of Congress Control Number: 2016931778

This book is available electronically in the **Elgar**online
Business subject collection
DOI 10.4337/9781785364068

ISBN 978 1 78536 405 1 (cased)
ISBN 978 1 78536 406 8 (eBook)

Typeset by Servis Filmsetting Ltd, Stockport, Cheshire

Contents

Contributors

Bernadette Andreosso-O'Callaghan holds the Jean Monnet Chair of Economic Integration at the Kemmy Business School of the University of Limerick (UL) (Ireland), and she is also Visiting Professor of East Asian Economics at the Ruhr University Bochum (Germany). She is the co-founder of the Euro-Asia Centre at UL, the first research centre dealing with contemporary Asian Studies in Ireland. She has published extensively in the following areas: comparative Europe-Asia economic integration, and economic growth and structural change in Asian countries, with a focus on East-Asian countries. Her latest publication is 'Trade and Investment Drivers – Qualifying the Type of Economic Integration in a Historical Perspective', in Louis Brennan and Philomena Murray (eds) (2015) *Drivers of Integration and Regionalism in Europe and Asia*, Routledge, London and New York (chapter 13).

Nigel Callinan is a PhD graduate from the University of Limerick and a lecturer at Pusan National University. He has been living in Korea on and off since 2002, working in the private sector and at a number of Korean Universities including Pohang University of Science and Education and Hannam University. His research interests are government-led innovation and the use of technical barriers to trade.

Christopher Dathe is a graduate from the University of Potsdam where he received a masters degree in economics in 2013. He is a research associate at the Euro-Asia Centre of the University of Limerick, and his main research area falls in the area of European integration and structural change. In this context, he does research on the impact of the financial crisis as well as on the influence of Chinese direct investment.

Sam Dzever is Professor of Management at Télécom Ecole de Management, France. His research in the fields of marketing, supply chain management, industrial organization and Asia-Pacific business has appeared in noted international academic journals, including *Industrial Marketing Management, Journal of Business and Industrial Marketing, Journal of Marketing and Communication, European Journal of Purchasing and Supply Management, Supply Chain Management: An International Journal, Journal of the Asia Pacific Economy, Asian Business* *and Management, Indian Journal of Science and Technology*, among others. He has also authored 12 books, research monographs, and edited collections, including *The Economic Relations Between Asia and Europe: Organisations Trade and Investment* (co-edited with Bernadette Andreosso-O'Callaghan, Jean-Pascal Bassino, Jacques Jaussaud), Chandos Publishing, Oxford, 2007); *Evolving Corporate Structures and Cultures in Asia: The Impact of Globalization* (co-edited with Jacques Jaussaud and Bernadette Andreosso-O'Callaghan, ISTE and Wiley, London and New Jersey, 2008).

Feng Wei is a second-year PhD student at the University of Pau, France. She received her masters degree in international management from the University of Pau in 2012. Her research is in the domain of international human resources management, especially on Chinese expatriation management.

Bhumika Gupta is Associate Professor of Human Resource Management and Program Director of the MSc in International Management at Télécom Ecole de Management (Paris, France). Her research explores a comparison of motivation levels in management practice between traditional and virtual project teams. Other research projects fall into the category of organization behaviour, strategic human resource management, corporate social responsibility, international human resource management, and innovation and change management. She has published several articles in peer-reviewed academic journals.

Jacques Jaussaud is Professor of Management, University of Pau, France, and Director of its CREG Research Team in Management. His research interests are in the areas of business strategy, organization, control, and human resources management, with a particular focus on Japan, China and other Asian countries. He has published widely in these areas, including in the following academic journals: *Management International Review, The International Journal of Human Resource Management, Journal of International Management, Asian Business and Management, Asian Pacific Business Review, Transition Studies Review*. He has also co-edited several books, including *Economic Dynamism and Business Strategy of Firms in Asia: Some Recent Developments* (China Publishing Economic House, Beijing, 2006), *Evolving Corporate Structures and Cultures in Asia* (ISTE Publishing, London, 2008) and *Economic Integration in Asia: Towards the Delineation of a Sustainable Path* (Palgrave Pivot, 2014).

Jean-Louis Mucchielli is Professor of Economics, School of Economics, University of Paris 1, Panthéon Sorbonne, France. His main research interests are international trade, foreign direct investment and agglomeration theory. He is author, co-author or editor of more than 20 books in French, English and Japanese, and has published more than 70 academic papers.

Françoise Nicolas is a senior researcher and Director of the Center for Asian Studies at the French Institute of International Relations (IFRI), Paris. She teaches at Paris-East University (Marne-la-Vallée), at Langues O' Paris and at Sciences Po, Paris. She is also an occasional consultant to the Directorate for Financial, Fiscal and Enterprise Affairs (DAF) of the OECD. Her research focuses on development strategies in East Asia; FDI and growth; regional economic integration; emerging economies and globalization. Her latest publications include 'Economic Regionalism in East Asia: The End of an Exception', in Sarah Tong (ed.) (2014) *Globalization, Development and Security in East Asia* (Volume Two: *Trade, Investment and Economic Integration*), World Scientific Publishing, pp. 105–30; 'Lessons from Investment Policy Reform in Korea' (with Stephen Thomsen and Mi-Hyun Bang) (2013), *OECD Working Papers on International Investment*, No. 2013/02, OECD.

Jeayaram Subramanian is currently pursuing his doctoral studies under the direction of Dr Bhumika Gupta at Télécom Ecole de Management, Evry, France, and his area of research includes employee job satisfaction, personality factors and the relationship between both in the aviation sector. He is also a faculty associate with Amrita Vishwa Vidyapeetham University, Amritapuri Campus, India. His areas of teaching include human resources management, global human resources management, leadership and team building, performance management and compensation. Jeayaram has published several articles in leading journals under the guidance of Dr Bhumika Gupta.

Robert Taylor was formerly Director of the Centre for Chinese Studies and Reader in Modern Chinese Studies at the University of Sheffield. His research interests focus on China's domestic and foreign policy, especially Chinese business management and foreign economic relations as well as Sino-Japanese relations. He has published widely in such academic journals as the *Asia-Pacific Business Review* and *Asian Business and Management*. He has contributed to media programmes relating to contemporary Asia. His publications include *China's Intellectual Dilemma* (University of British Columbia, 1981) and *Greater China and Japan* (Routledge, 1996). He edited *International Business in China* (Routledge, 2012) and *The Globalisation of Chinese Business* (Chandos, 2014). He also engages in management consultancy.

Utai Uprasen is an associate professor of the division of international and area studies, Pukyong National University in South Korea. His research interests are in international economic integration and in Asia-Europe economic relations.

Pei Yu is Associate Professor of International Business, School of Economics, Wuhan University of Technology, China. She obtained her PhD in economics at the University of Paris 1, Panthéon Sorbonne, France. Her main research interests are strategies of MNCs, FDI and agglomeration theory. She has published more than 20 academic papers.

Zhao Guoqin is a researcher at the Institute of Finance and Economics, Central University of Finance and Economics, Beijing, China. His research interests include regional governance, international trade and public management. He has published a large number of articles in domestic mainstream journals and he has also undertaken several research projects under the auspices of the National Social Science Fund and the Beijing Social Science Fund.

M. Bruna Zolin is Professor of Economics – Rural Development and Commodity Markets – at the Department of Economics Ca' Foscari University of Venice. Previously, she was Deputy Head of the School of Asian Studies and Business Management at Ca' Foscari University. She has served as an expert for the Food and Agriculture Organization (FAO, Rome) and she has been a visiting professor at several universities.

Acknowledgements

This volume brings together a collection of selected original pieces presented at the 19th International Euro-Asia Research Conference on 'Economic Change and Asian Business Management' at Yokohama National University, Japan, from 30 May to 1 June 2014. The editors would like to acknowledge the valuable contributions to discussions of all participants at this international seminar. We are also immensely grateful to the teams of both the Université de Pau et des Pays de l'Adour (France) and of Yokohama National University, and in particular we would like to thank Professors Hiroyuki Nakamura and Shuji Mizoguchi, Vice President of Yokohama National University, as well as Professor Jacques Jaussaud from Pau. Thanks are also due to Aoife O'Callaghan for proofreading large sections of the manuscript.

Abbreviations

ABF	Associated British Food
ADB	Asian Development Bank
ADF	Augmented Dickey-Fuller test
AEC	ASEAN Economic Community
AIIB	Asian Infrastructure Investment Bank
APAEC	ASEAN Plan of Action for Energy Cooperation
APE	Average Probability Elasticity
APEC	Asia Pacific Economic Cooperation
APSC	ASEAN Political Security Community
APT	ASEAN Plus 3
ASCC	ASEAN Social-Cultural Community
ASEAN	Association of Southeast Asian Nations
BBC	British Broadcasting Corporation
BEC	Broad Economic Categories
BMI	Body Mass Index
BRI	One Belt One Road
BRICS	Brazil, Russia, India, China and South Africa
CBD	Central Business District
CCG	Center for China & Globalization
CCPIT	China Council for the Promotion of International Trade
CEPEA	Comprehensive Partnership for East Asia
CGIT	China Global Investment Tracker
CIC	China Investment Corporation
CLM	Conditional Logit Model
CNOOC	China National Offshore Oil Company
CODI	Chinese Outward Direct Investment
COSCO	China Ocean Shipping Company
CPI	Consumer Price Index
EAFTA	East Asia Free Trade Agreement
EAS	East Asia Summit
ECFA	Economic Cooperation Framework Agreement
EU	European Union
FAO	Food and Agriculture Organization
FDI	Foreign Direct Investment

FGM	Flying Geese Model
F&B	Food and Beverage (Industry)
FTA	Free Trade Agreement
FTAAP	Free Trade Area of the Asia Pacific
FYP	Five Year Plan
GDP	Gross Domestic Product
GFC	Global Financial Crisis
GVC	Global Value Chain
HBA	Home-based Augmenting
HBE	Home-based Exploiting
HHI	Herfindahl-Hirschman Index
HQs	Headquarters
HRM	Human Resource Management
HS	Harmonized System
ICT	Information and Communications Technology
IFS	International Financial Statistics
IIA	Independence of Irrelevant Alternatives
IMF	International Monetary Fund
INTRAF	Intra-firm co-location
ITA	Information Technology Agreement
JBIC	Japan Bank for International Cooperation
JETRO	Japan External Trade Organization
KITA	Korea International Trade Association
LLL	Linkage, Leverage, Learning
LQ	Location Quotient
M&A	Mergers and Acquisitions
MNCs	Multinational Corporations
MOFCOM	Ministry of Commerce of the People's Republic of China
MOFTEC	Ministry of Foreign Trade and Economic Cooperation of the People's Republic of China
MPAC	Master Plan on ASEAN Connectivity
MRAs	Mutual Recognition Agreements
MSR	Maritime Silk Road
NBER	National Bureau of Economic Research
NER	Malaysian National Employment Return
NIE	New Institutional Economics
NLM	Nested Logit Model
ODI	Outward Direct Investment
ODMs	Original Design Manufacturers
OECD	Organisation for Economic Co-operation and Development
OFDI	Outward Foreign Direct Investment
PCM	Product Life Cycle Model

PRC   People's Republic of China
RCEP   Regional Comprehensive Economic Partnership
RMB   Renminbi
R&D   Research and Development
SCP   Structure-Conduct-Performance
SEZ   Special Economic Zone
SITC   Standard International Trade Classification
SMEs   Small and Medium-sized Enterprises
SOE   State-Owned Enterprise
S&T   Science and Technology
SWF   Sovereign Wealth Fund
TAFTA   Transatlantic Free Trade Area
TPP   Trans-Pacific Partnership
TTIP   Transatlantic Trade and Investment Partnership
UNCTAD   United Nations Conference on Trade and Development
US   United States
USD   US Dollars
VAR   Vector Autoregression
VEC   Vector Error Correction
VER   Voluntary Export Restraint
WB   World Bank
WHO   World Health Organization
WTO   World Trade Organization

1. Introduction and overview

Robert Taylor

ECONOMIC BACKGROUND

The chapters in this volume, most of which are revised versions of papers presented at the 19th International Euro-Asia Research Conference, held in Yokohama from 30 May to 1 June 2014, focus on the apparent key drivers of global economic growth in the early 21st century, the emerging Asian economies, which present multinational traders and investors with unparalleled market opportunities, given demographic change and a middle class with increasing discretionary income. There have been, however, as will be discussed later, only tentative moves towards regional economic integration, since to date areas like trade facilitation, uniform customs clearance, removal of non-tariff barriers and labour deployment issues have not been adequately addressed.

Depending on terms of association, closer union could benefit trade and investment both from within and beyond Asia (Letchumanan, 2015). Nevertheless trade within the Association of Southeast Asian Nations (ASEAN) accounted for 25 per cent of their trade in 2013, rising from 19.2 per cent in 1993. Significantly, China has become a major player in regional economic growth; trade within the region and that with China accounted for 37 per cent of the total in 2013 (Desker, 2015b). China's role becomes even more stark when considered in relation to individual nations; in recent years trade volume with Malaysia, its largest partner in Southeast Asia, has exceeded US$100 billion (Oh, 2015). Asian regional trade is necessarily linked to industrial division of labour and specialization and this is exemplified by China's conclusion of free trade agreements, an integral part of the country's globalization policy. China is certainly the world's second largest economy, biggest trader and greatest manufacturer but it is not the most technologically advanced industrial power in Asia (Luo and Xue, 2013). Thus the promotion of innovation, because of the pressing need to raise productivity and thereby avoid the middle income trap, demands greater openness of the domestic economy to accord with the terms of free trade agreements such as those with ASEAN and South Korea, the latter concluded during the Asia Pacific Economic Cooperation (APEC) summit in Beijing in November 2014. Moreover just as Japanese government leaders did in the latter decades of the 20th century, China's Premier, Li Keqiang, and his cohorts are using pressure from outside agreements to effect reform at home. The objective is to move up the technological value-added chain. Currently China has been investing in and exporting subcomponents, a case in point being China's trade with South Korea. Thus while most Chinese electronic goods exported by China to South Korea have been low-end integrated chips, those in the opposite direction have been high-end products like signal devices and semi-conductors. The resulting high-end electronic goods have then been sold to customers in China (Hu, 2015). Nevertheless, as China ascends the high-end value chain through investment, for example, by merger and acquisition, moves towards internationalization of the Chinese currency, the RMB, proceed apace, as shown in its use in cross-border trade in neighbouring countries. The Chinese leaders' role in deliberations regarding Asian regional economic integration will intensify (Liu, 2014).

China's influence in Asia, however, is not unchallenged, and the region is riven by political rivalries and economic disparities, not to mention territorial and maritime disputes in the South China Sea and Northeast Asia, which continue to impede integration. The potential parallel is the European Union (EU) and advocates point out the benefits accruing to a single market. Lessons may perhaps be learned from the EU in the areas of surrender of sovereignty and the adoption of a common currency. It is clear, for instance, how, in the case of the EU, a viable common currency is only possible with the institution of a community-wide fiscal and financial system, currently lacking. At present, however, the key barriers to Asian union are diversity of political systems in addition to economic differences. For instance, while Singapore is an authoritarian style democracy and Indonesia, Thailand and the Philippines have parliamentary systems, Vietnam and Laos are one-party states. Myanmar (Burma) is only tentatively emerging from military dictatorship. As examined later in this chapter, a bureaucracy without corruption is a '*sine qua non*' of effective implementation of and continuing adherence to community agreements relating to foreign direct investment (FDI) and labour deployment policies. Currently, for example, Singapore in those regards is vastly superior to the Philippines and Laos. Moreover a single market would be greatly affected by per capita income differentials, with Singapore again in a position of leadership. There are also contrasting demographic trends. China, in part because of its one child policy, and an aging Japan, facing labour shortages, stand in stark contrast to much of Southeast Asia, where 53 per cent of the population is younger than 30 years old, offering a continuing supply of younger workers. Consequently, the Chinese and the Japanese are attempting to provide for an aging population. Resource endowments also vary, Indonesia being rich in coal and Thailand being a rice exporter. Of course, not all these factors are negative. They could provide complementarity, thereby aiding marketing efforts; advanced technologies could balance resources like energy and grain, including rice reserves (Sheridan, 2012).

TOWARDS ASIAN REGIONAL INTEGRATION: INSTITUTIONAL MECHANISMS

It is now necessary to examine the moves to date through a main driver of economic integration, ASEAN, even though these are taking place against a background of national initiatives emanating from both within and outside the region. Economic cooperation among the nations of the region has been evolving into a process of gradual integration, and general social and political stability has proved attractive to foreign investors offering capital and technology during the past five decades, resulting in higher living standards (Kesavapany, 2015).

On a diplomatic front institutions sponsored under ASEAN have furthered regional security by facilitating relationships with external powers. Examples include the East Asia Summit (EAS), composed of the ASEAN 10 in addition to the United States, China, Japan, South Korea, Australia, New Zealand, Russia and India. Similarly, the ASEAN Plus 3 (APT) brings together the ASEAN 10 plus China, Japan and South Korea.

In spite of these successes ASEAN has undoubted weaknesses which are reflected in a diversity of multilateral institutions with overlapping institutions and decision-making powers. One issue has involved competing approaches to regional economic integration, with the EAS promoting the Comprehensive Partnership for East Asia (CEPEA) and the APT proposing the East Asia Free Trade Agreement (EAFTA). One solution, however, could be agreement on a Regional Comprehensive Economic Partnership (RCEP) discussed below. These divergences underline the absence of an ASEAN mindset, a notion which as yet means little to the population of the body's ten nation states, divided by diverse political, economic and legal systems. Likewise there is a nebulous mindset at best among politicians, bureaucrats and the intelligentsia, and even business leaders. While determined to defend their own domestic markets, manufacturers seek eased entry to other economies. Additionally, ASEAN policymakers in individual countries protect their own sectoral prerogatives and fail to coordinate with other sectors, either nationally or regionally (Desker, 2015a).

There is a sense, however, in which deliberations in these bodies may be seen as culminating in the conception of an ASEAN community, its establishment brought forward to the end of 2015 from the original deadline in 2020. In accordance with the ASEAN Charter and other earlier key initiatives, ASEAN leaders have outlined the goals and strategies of the proposed community. The ASEAN leaders have stated that the 2009–2015 Road Map, through which the body has been conceived, consists of three blueprints, the ASEAN Economic Community (AEC), the ASEAN Political Security Community (APSC) and the ASEAN Social-Cultural Community (ASCC), and on that basis further rule making will be based, although the achievement of, for example, regional and national economic goals will also be addressed through individual national and community level institutional mechanisms. On the economic front the AEC is designated to eliminate regional tariffs on most goods by the end of 2015 and increase intra-regional trade and investment, with the ultimate goals of a single market and production base. There is also ongoing cooperation in specific economic sectors, for instance, energy, witness the ASEAN Plan of Action for Energy Cooperation (APAEC), 2010–2015, which envisages a collective target where renewable energy will represent 4.5 per cent of total power installed capacity, to be achieved in 2015. In terms of security the region has been relatively peaceful, even though terrorism and territorial disputes could hinder economic cooperation. If social and cultural issues are broadly defined, the already operational ASEAN Intergovernmental Commission on Human Rights may be cited. Additionally, there are coordinating efforts in response to natural disasters and pandemics, while there have been limited attempts to enact legislation and ensure enforcement in relation to pollution induced haze (Letchumanan, 2015; Sembiring and Trajano, 2014).

It could be argued that recent community-wide Chinese national initiatives have been designed to resolve the overlapping decision-making jurisdictions discussed immediately above. In this context brief reference has already been made to the RCEP. This has been initiated by the ten countries of ASEAN to establish a regional free trade agreement (FTA), including, for instance, Northeast Asian states like China, Japan and South Korea but extending beyond Southeast Asia to embrace also India as well as Australia and New Zealand by the end of this year. RCEP, if fully realized, would contain a total population of 3.5 billion with an aggregate Gross Domestic Product (GDP) of US$23 trillion, the latter representing one-third of the world's total. At the time of writing several rounds of negotiations have been conducted but as yet are hampered by sectoral interests within countries, witness Japan's sensitivity regarding agricultural goods, Australia's environmental and labour protection concerns and

India's high tariffs. Individual bilateral FTAs like that between China and South Korea could serve as templates, given divergent levels of development and areas of industrial specialization (Hu, 2015).

The second initiative by China was endorsed at the November 2014 APEC leaders' summit in Beijing. This called for the formation of the Free Trade Area of the Asia Pacific (FTAAP). Given, however, that the FTAAP concept was originally proposed by the Americans, the current Chinese initiative must be seen within the context of rivalry between the two powers in the Asia-Pacific. The Chinese seek to define the agenda in a trade grouping encompassing both China and the United States. Secondly, as a result the Chinese are in a prime position to draft new rules for a regional economic order from a position of equal standing with the United States. This stands in contrast with the proposed Trans-Pacific Partnership (TPP), from which China is currently excluded and where American rules are set to predominate. However, there are as yet limitations to China's regional leadership role; Chinese diplomacy may still be regarded as reactive, especially, for example, in agreeing to a Japanese proposal through RCEP to negotiate a trade agreement among the ASEAN countries in order to counter Japan's intended TPP accession, originally announced by Shinzo Abe in March 2013. While Japan's membership would give Japanese exporters easier access to foreign markets, the TPP itself goes beyond reduction of tariffs towards the implementation of stricter labour and environmental standards in addition to liberalization of the service sector. On these terms Abe's motive in Japan's membership is furthering structural reform in the wake of economic recession; such external pressure is intended to induce greater industrial competitiveness, thereby enhancing the country's role as a regional power. Certain exemptions, however, may be sought for the agricultural sector, notably, in the areas of beef, rice and wheat. Furthermore, membership will assist Japan's security strategy: it will serve to strengthen the United States-Japan alliance in the face of growing Chinese military power. The TPP will also help mitigate American fears of Chinese dominance in the Asia-Pacific (Robles, 2013; Solis, 2014).

CHINA'S ROLE IN PHYSICAL INFRASTRUCTURE

Increased Asian regional integration via the above mechanisms will nevertheless only be possible through enhanced and extended region-wide physical infrastructure and domestic national institutional reform. In their recent Silk Road and Asian Infrastructure Investment Bank (AIIB) initiatives, the Chinese leaders may be said to be addressing the concerns of other Asian governments regarding the funding of, for example, better regional transportation links. These concerns were earlier reflected in the Master Plan on ASEAN Connectivity (MPAC), adopted in 2010. This identified 15 priority projects for physical, institutional and people-to-people connectivity. While China's 21st Century Maritime Silk Road (MSR), proposed by President Xi Jinping during a visit to Indonesia in October 2013, and one element of its One Belt One Road (BRI) initiative, is a large-scale project similar to the MPAC, it has raised suspicions of Chinese motives, with security implications, given rival territorial claims over the Paracel and Spratly Islands in the South China Sea. In November 2014, at the 17th China-ASEAN Summit, the Chinese Premier, Li Keqiang, put forward a framework, implicitly linking MSR and MPAC, proposing priority areas, including maritime cooperation, finance, security, environmental protection and people-to-people exchanges. It is an open question, however, as to whether such linkage will allay regional anxiety regarding Chinese motives, even though the latter are nevertheless ostensibly related to furthering economic development via trade and investment, an advocacy not without precedent, given China's major commercial role in the region during the 17th and18th centuries (Chan, 2015; Li, 2015).

Likewise, the Silk Road Economic Belt Proposal, the Asia-Europe land bridge component of BRI, unveiled by President Xi Jinping in Kazakhstan in September 2013, has historical antecedents, although the proposed route is intended to extend beyond that explored by ancient Chinese merchants. It will link the middle kingdom with Central and Western Asia and part of the Mediterranean region, the current objective being to connect China with West European capitals (Fu, 2015; Li, 2015).

While Chinese leaders' public statements present the Silk Road Economic Belt initiative as designed to further development in, for example, Asian states through enhanced flows of trade, investment and capital via facilitated infrastructure projects, highlighting a benevolent global role for China, Xi Jinping and his cohorts also have a distinctly national domestic and foreign policy agenda. In fact, one observer has suggested that the BRI Initiative is unprecedented in the history of China's foreign relations, representing a move from a low profile to a more proactive stance. Perceiving a Chinese threat to United States supremacy in the Asia-Pacific, American policymakers have sought to strengthen their country's presence in the region through increased strategic deployment. Thus the Chinese leaders seek to bypass sea lanes subject to United States naval dominance and, in any case, China's rulers historically have given priority to land-based security rather than maritime expansion. Such security issues are also complicated by terrorist and separatist activity within China itself. Uighur separatists, with connections across China's central Asian borders, can capitalize on economic grievances and, in response to lagging development in the hinterland, Chinese policymakers have initiated the Go-West Policy, with priority given to infrastructure. Thus this Western strategy is likely to stimulate growth through cross-border trade and also forms an integral part of national economic restructuring, the latest stage in the evolution of China's open door policy. Because of rising costs Chinese enterprises face challenges, with the steel and construction sectors suffering from overproduction and overcapacity. The BRI could both open up foreign markets to Chinese companies and help move labour-intensive and low value-added production facilities overseas (Fu, 2014; Li, 2015; Rolland, 2015). Given the long-term cost of building infrastructure over an extended land mass and across the maritime route, the issue of financing is brought into focus.

Once again China's leaders have a political as well as an economic agenda. In November 2014 Xi Jinping committed US$40 billion to the BRI fund which was in December of that year officially established and opened to investors. The fund, however, is not exclusively state-financed, even though the first phase has seen US$10 billion in investment from the country's foreign exchange reserves. Thus the Silk Road Fund will in future operate like a private equity venture with mainly Chinese funding initially but also some foreign Asian investment which the Chinese are seeking. It will also be denominated in currencies other than the Chinese *yuan* (Dodillet, 2015).

While, however, the BRI is targeted at connectivity across a number of regions, there is demand for improved and extended infrastructure in the countries of South and Southeast Asia, if the MSR is to be realized. This is an objective of the AIIB, launched by the Chinese in November 2014. Thus the Chinese leaders have reaffirmed their country's credentials as a global economic power. This move may also be seen in the overall context of United States–China rivalry in the Asia-Pacific as, at the time of writing, the Obama Administration has voiced its opposition to the bank, seeking to dissuade its major allies, both in the Orient and the Western world from joining, although a number of ASEAN states including Indonesia and Singapore, together with India, signed a Memorandum of Understanding at the launching. Moreover, in early 2015 a host of European countries, including Britain, France, Germany, Luxembourg, Italy and Poland as well as Australia joined the AIIB (Armstrong, 2015; Stelzer, 2015; Yoná, 2015; Zhang and Ning, 2015b). In fact, in their creation of the AIIB the Chinese leaders have responded to the major concerns of the emerging economies. The leading decision-making positions at the International Monetary Fund (IMF), the World Bank (WB) and the Asian Development Bank (ADB) have been restricted to Europeans, Americans and Japanese (Drysdale, 2015). Moreover, the charge levelled against these existing banks is that they have been reluctant to lend money for investment in infrastructure, at the same time dictating the foci of development and cooperation. Specifically, it has been estimated that from now until 2020 Asia will need to spend US$8 trillion on infrastructure. For example, Indonesia alone will require US$230 billion, while the Greater Mekong region, designed to link the less developed areas of Vietnam, Laos, Cambodia and Thailand, is projected to need US$50 billion. In response to these needs the Chinese have asserted that the AIIB will target more effectively investment in areas like transportation, energy, telecommunications and other infrastructure. Undoubtedly, the Chinese, as prime movers, will set rules and regulations which, while stringent in banking best practice, will also serve their country's own interests. In addition, interested parties are concerned about tied aid; any tenders should not be the hunting ground of Chinese construction companies. The AIIB, nevertheless, is not designed to challenge or replace the functions of bodies like the WB and the ADB which are more focused on issues like poverty reduction.

The financing of the AIIB reflects the estimated future spending on Asian infrastructure. The Chinese state is to provide most of the initial capital of US$50 billion, with authorized capital, that is, the maximum amount that can be issued to shareholders, being US$100 billion. When the latter has been issued, in relative terms the AIIB will be two-thirds the size of the ADB and two-fifths of the World Bank's International Bank for Reconstruction and Development. In order to ensure investment in sectors like agriculture, energy, telecommunications and urban development, the bank will use diverse instruments, for example, loans and equity. Thus private capital is sought, offering opportunities for European as well as Asian investors (Bastin, 2014; Dodillet, 2014; Langhammer, 2015; Tay, 2014; Zhang and Ning, 2015a; Zhou and Zhao, 2015).

FROM PROTECTIONISM TO FREE TRADE

The foregoing has focused, from both regional and national perspectives, on the development of physical infrastructure to facilitate economic integration. Equally important prerequisites, however, are the enactment of legislation and the establishment of institutional mechanisms of compliance to regional directives at national level. To date, major impediments to cross-border trade include tariff and non-tariff barriers. There is reluctance to open protected service sectors to foreign interests in the Philippines and Indonesia. Another impediment, the banning of or a heavy restriction on foreign ownership of land, is evidenced in Thailand, Indonesia, the Philippines, Cambodia and Vietnam. In addition, special protection of privileged industries as well as complex systems of licences and permits will need to be overcome. Ultimately, however, as integration gains momentum, it is at community level that the harmonization of customs standards and the standardization of legal regimes should be effected (Desker, 2015a; Sheridan, 2012; Trajano, 2013).

THE ROLE OF MNCS

The above summary has provided the general background against which the themes discussed in the following chapters may be understood. Andreosso-O'Callaghan's chapter has a methodological focus, presenting a review of the main literature relating to strategies of both Western MNCs and those from emerging economies like China in an Asian context.

The chapter by Nicolas examines regional production networks in Asia, asserting that much East Asian trade is essentially intra-industry, resulting from processing of components and intermediate goods. Within this overall context the chapter's objective is to assess changes in trade and investment linkages between the Republic of Korea and China on one side and Japan and China on the other.

Zolin in her chapter concerning emerging Asia and the food industry offers a wider geographical focus. Increasing urbanization and greater discretionary incomes among a growing middle class are having an impact on food consumption, prompting investment in production capacity by such multinationals as the Kellogg Company and Nestlé, to satisfy the changing needs of consumers in countries like Singapore and Indonesia in addition to China.

In contrast, Zhao and Dzever in their study analyse how China's economic growth and changes in its trade structure are related to macroscopic transaction costs. They conclude that, in the mid- and long term, growth in China's macroscopic transaction costs stimulates exports while restraining domestic trade. This in turn leads to the accumulation of trade surpluses.

Yu and Mucchielli's concern is investment, specifically MNCs' Research and Development (R&D) clustering strategies in China, considering both the theoretical and empirical aspects. They identify American, European and Asian R&D localization strategies across 27 Chinese cities during the period from 1992 to 2011. Their study confirms differences in clustering among MNCs, with US firms stressing external linkages, European companies preferring internal links, while Asian businesses adopt market seeking rather than clustering strategies.

The internationalization of the renminbi (RMB) also comes into focus in the following chapter by Andreosso-O'Callaghan and Dathe which discusses the opportunities presented to Chinese outward investors in the wake of China's ongoing financial reform and the euro crisis which has unfolded since 2008. Thus Chinese outward investment trends in the EU are reviewed.

Feng and Jaussaud discuss the expatriation policies of Chinese MNCs. While existing literature has focused on MNCs from Western countries and Japan, their study is focused on Chinese companies and discusses the specificities involved in expatriation. It is concluded that training before expatriation is crucial and could be improved.

Uprasen studies the displacement effect emanating from export competition between ASEAN countries and the United States as they target the EU market, an issue especially relevant as the EU-US FTA may come into force in the near future. Empirical findings suggest that the displacement effect is detectable in two industries of three ASEAN countries.

Gupta and Subramanian examine how small and medium-sized enterprises (SMEs) in the Indian food processing industry manage innovation, given their resource constraints. Through a case study of an enterprise in Kerala, major factors affecting innovation performance, including technology, labour markets, financial resources, top management commitment, in addition to customer and supplier relationships, are identified.

Callinan's chapter discusses how the electronic giant, Samsung, benefited from favourable regulatory legislation in South Korea to attain a pivotal domestic market position which served as a springboard for rapid international expansion. By reference to evolutionary economic theory, the author concludes that the Samsung experience could be emulated by emerging economies to foster the growth of MNCs.

As regional economic integration gathers pace, investment by Asian MNCs will grow. This will demand mechanisms of labour mobility and deployment between countries, in addition to human resource strategies taking account of cultural differences. It is to projecting future developments in these areas that the epilogue to this volume is dedicated.

REFERENCES

Armstrong, S. (2015), 'The hole in the Asian doughnut', accessed 11 January 2015 at east_asia_forum@anu.edu.au.
Bastin, M. (2014), 'EU must grasp development opportunity', *China Daily European Weekly*, 31 October–6 November.
Chan, I. (2015), 'China's Maritime Silk Road: the politics of routes', accessed 12 March 2015 at www.rsis.ntu.edu.sg/publication/rsis051/2015.
Desker, B. (2015a), 'ASEAN integration remains an illusion', accessed 5 March 2015 at www.rsis.ntu.edu.sg/publication/rsis046/2015.

Desker, B. (2015b), 'Towards closer ASEAN-Latin American ties', accessed 19 March 2015 at www.rsis.ntu.edu.sg/publication/rsis059/2015.

Dodillet, L. (2014), 'China forms infrastructure bank despite U.S. Opposition', accessed 30 October 2014 at www.chinabusinessreview.com.

Dodillet, L. (2015), '$40 Billion Silk Road Fund kicks off China's "belt and road" initiatives', accessed 10 March 2015 at www.chinabusinessreview.com.

Drysdale, P. (2015), 'Banking on America's Asian choices', accessed 23 March 2015 at east_asia_forum@anu.edu.au.

Fu, J. (2014), 'Silk road idea given the blind eye treatment', *China Daily European Weekly*, 28 November–4 December.

Fu, J. (2015), 'Silk road initiative not simply about trade', *China Daily European Weekly*, 9–15 January.

Hu, Y.F. (2015), 'Pacts to reshape Asia-Pacific trade', *China Daily European Weekly*, 16–22 January.

Kesavapany, K. (2015), 'ASEAN integration: a work in progress, not an illusion', accessed 26 March 2015 at www.rsis.edu.sg/publications/rsis068/2015.

Langhammer, R.J. (2015), 'AIIB must avoid pitfalls to be effective', *China Daily European Weekly*, 3–9 April.

Letchumanan, R. (2015), 'What is the ASEAN Community 2015?', accessed 11 February 2015 at www.rsis.ntu.edu.sg/publications/rsis028/2015.

Li, M.J. (2015), 'China's "One Belt One Road" initiative: new round of opening up', accessed 12 March 2015 at www.rsis.ntu.edu.sg/publication/rsis050/2015.

Liu, C. (2014), 'Europe helps boost *yuan* use abroad', *China Daily European Weekly*, 26 September–2 October.

Luo, J.X. and Xue, H. (2013), 'The driving force behind Likonomics', *China Daily European Weekly*, 12–18 July.

Oh, E.S. (2015), 'More nuanced than just "hedging": Malaysia and the South China Sea disputes', accessed 16 January 2015 at www.rsis.ntu.edu.sg/publications/rsis014/2015.

Robles, T. (2013), 'Abe's TPP strategy: overcoming domestic division through reform?', accessed 9 April 2014 at www.rsis.ntu.edu.sg/publication/rsis058/2013.

Rolland, N. (2015), 'China's new silk road', accessed 13 February 2015 at www.nbr.org/research/activity.aspx?id=531.

Sembiring, M. and Trajano, J.C.I. (2014), 'Renewable energy in Southeast Asia: priorities and commitments needed', accessed 28 November 2014 at www.rsis.ntu.edu.sg/publications/rsis237/2014.

Sheridan, M. (2012), 'ASEAN Inc: tiger pack between India and China', *Sunday Times*, 15 July.

Solis, M. (2014), 'China flexes its muscles at APEC with the revival of FTAAP', accessed 23 November 2014 at east_asia_forum@anu.edu.au.

Stelzer, I. (2015), 'China rides off with the riches . . . until its coming crisis', *Sunday Times*, 26 April.

Tay, S. (2014), 'Asian bank will not just be China's domain', *China Daily European Weekly*, 31 October–6 November.

Trajano, J.C.I. (2013), 'Achieving the ASEAN Economic Community: are the Philippines and Indonesia ready for 2015?', accessed 30 April 2013 at www.rsis.ntu.edu.sg/publication/rsis080/2013.

Yoná, K. (2015), 'Assessing the APT Summits 2014 from the perspective of community building in East Asia', accessed 10 March 2015 at www.ceac.jp/e/index.html.

Zhang, C.Y. and Ning, H. (2015a), 'Bank will deal in more than just small change', *China Daily European Edition*, 3–9 April.
Zhang, C.Y. and Ning, H. (2015b), 'World banks on Asia's future', *China Daily European Edition*, 3–9 April.
Zhou, W. and Zhao, Y.N. (2015), 'European ties to bank to aid Asian integration', *China Daily European Weekly*, 20–26 March.

PART I

Overall overview

2. Emerging Asian economies and MNC strategies – a review of the literature

Bernadette Andreosso-O'Callaghan

1. INTRODUCTION

Although not new, the phenomenon of direct investment in advanced economies by developing countries – or what is commonly known today as emerging countries – has attracted much attention since the mid-2000s in academia, the business press as well as in policy-making circles. This is primarily because of the unprecedented size of the phenomenon, with the greater assertiveness on the foreign direct investment (FDI) scene of multinational corporations (MNCs) from two large protagonists, namely India, and above all, China. Recent figures show that developing Asia accounts now for nearly a quarter of all outward direct investment flows, whereas their share in total FDI inflows is 29 per cent, suggesting that, ceteris paribus, this group of countries should soon be a net direct investor (UNCTAD, 2015).

The phenomenon by itself is indeed already a relatively well-established phenomenon, as the experience of Japan and later on of Taiwan, South Korea and of other 'Asian tigers', as precursors of FDI from emerging economies in Europe and the USA after World War II (WWII), testifies. FDI from emerging countries such as today's BRICS (Brazil, Russia, India, China and South Africa) is commonly referred to as the 'third wave' of FDI from emerging countries (Gammeltoft, 2008), and it will be the focus of this chapter although other FDI waves will also be discussed.[1] Japan's economic miracle stemmed from a *dirigiste* catching-up strategy that can be traced back to the Meiji Restoration period, allowing the country to be termed as the 'lead goose' in Asia for several decades. This catching-up experience emulated others in the region with for example the South Korean economy experiencing its economic miracle after 1965, when growth rates jumped to 8.9 per cent in 1967, culminating at 16.9 per cent in 1973 (Sunoo, 1994).

15

What is different today is the scale of the phenomenon and the pace at which it has evolved in just ten years, since 2005. In particular, the surge of outward direct investment (ODI) from China, and the parallel increase in the number of studies relating to this phenomenon, correspond to the implementation of the 'go global strategy' launched in 2000 by the Chinese Government.

The objective of this chapter is therefore to propose a (non-exhaustive) review of the literature on ODI from East-Asian emerging economies, including whenever possible countries such as India as well as Southeast Asian countries; the selected literature will nevertheless suffice to allow us to identify the main recurrent themes in the recent ODI literature by the emerging countries (section 3). Before that, a discussion on the suitable theoretical background is proposed in section 2, where the old 'mainstream' theories are concisely and critically discussed in light of current insights drawn from the recent literature that could evolve eventually into a new or a substantially reformulated theory.

2.   THEORETICAL FRAMEWORK: OLD AND NEW THEORIES

Using as starting points Coase's view of the 'firm versus the market' (Coase, 1937) – an opposition arbitrated by transaction costs, Hymer-Kindleberger's monopolistic power hypothesis (Hymer, 1960/1976; Kindleberger, 1968),[2] as well as the concept of internalization, the theoretical FDI framework has evolved in both Western and Asian countries (starting with Japan) and has led to a typology of theories that can be labelled as falling into any of the three following levels: micro-, meso- or macro-economic level. All theories emphasize the firm with a scope of operation that goes beyond its national borders. The discussion in this chapter starts with the dominant or mainstream theories.

2.1   Mainstream Theories and their Limits

At the micro-economic level, Dunning's eclectic paradigm (or OLI model) developed in 1980 and modulated in a number of subsequent publications (Dunning, 1980, 1986, 1988) imposed itself as the mainstream theoretical framework explaining FDI. His ownership advantages (O) or firm-specific advantages, and internalization (I) or the allocation of resources by the firm itself rather than through the market, answer to the why and how a firm invests abroad, whereas location advantages (L), or country-specific advantages, explain where firms decide ultimately to invest. Borrowing from different strands of the economics literature, in particular from the work of Marshall (1899) and Weber (1909) on the locational aspects of industry activity, this industrial organization-based theoretical framework was successful enough in explaining US, EU as well as Japanese direct investment in less-developed countries after WWII.

From the outset, this micro-economic mainstream theory nevertheless failed to explain FDI from emerging economies into developed economies, given in particular the inability of firms originating from emerging countries to possess sufficient ownership advantages when investing in developed economies; this is the case for example of Korean MNCs' direct investment in the EU starting in the 1970s and gathering pace in the 1980s with companies such as Samsung investing in both Germany and the UK in 1976 (Cherry, 2001).

At the meso-economic level, Vernon's Product Life Cycle Model (PCM) also falls into the list of mainstream FDI theories (Vernon, 1966). Starting with the axiom that the USA is a high-income country characterized by high wages, plentiful capital and therefore a high demand for new products, the PCM shows how, in the take-off stage of the new product, the initial manufacturing takes place in the USA, where high unit production costs do not matter so much since the demand for innovations is price-inelastic in the early stages of manufacturing and marketing. While the product matures (standardization), the market widens, economies of scale set in, driving the price down and justifying exports (to Europe) up to a time when production costs (in particular labour costs) start becoming a major component of total cost, thereby shifting the production to lower labour-cost countries starting with Europe. FDI appears therefore with eventual exports from the US overseas subsidiaries back into the USA.

Limits and criticisms of the PCM include the fact that the model is not very explicit on why international production rather than licensing displaces exports from the innovating country. In testing the suitability of the PCM at the meso-economic level, Walker (1979) provides an illustration of one such industry which does not conform to the PCM, namely the motor car industry, whereas Baba (1987) illustrates the same point with the case of the Japanese colour television sector. The limited applicability of this model, again bearing in mind the case of South Korean investment in Europe in the 1980s led to the necessity to move towards other theoretical frameworks.

2.2 The Japanese School of FDI

What can be termed 'the Japanese school of FDI' is represented by a number of studies that have been less well known among Western economists for quite some time, studies that highlight the macro-economic dimension of FDI. As a starting point of the analysis, we will use Kaname Akamatsu's Flying Geese Model (FGM) developed in the 1930s, even though this model was conceived at the time to explain structural change in Japan through trade, rather than through FDI.

With the help of a statistical analysis of industrial development in pre-war Japan, Akamatsu (1935, 1937) observed two main production and export patterns as follows: (1) a basic pattern where a single industry grows through successive stages of import, production and export; and (2) a variant pattern showing how industries diversify and are being upgraded from consumer goods to capital goods and/or from standard to more sophisticated products. Akamatsu's 'flying geese' paradigm is therefore a model explaining the catching-up strategy of Asian countries, with Japan being the lead economy (or 'lead goose') in the region, and other Asian economies following as in a flying geese formation. Interestingly, the model was only popularized in Europe (Akamatsu, 1961, 1962) at a time when Rostow (1960) developed his 'stages approach of economic growth', leading subsequently to the Rostow-Balassa 'stages approach to comparative advantage' as one theoretical extension (Balassa, 1977).[3]

This model has attracted again some attention in academic circles at the turn of the third millennium (see for example Ozawa, 2009, 2011). On the Japanese side, the FGM has been reviewed and reformulated by Kojima (2000) and by Ozawa (2001).[4] Kojima (2000) combined aspects of the FGM with elements of neo-classical economic theory; for example, he introduced a theoretical model explaining how the accumulation of physical and human capital causes the economy to diversify into more capital-intensive key industries and then to adopt more efficient production methods (Kojima Model I). Questioning the pertinence of the industry-based FGM to explain Japan's low growth rates since the start of the 'lost decade', Ozawa (2001) argues that an institutional approach, particularly a financial dimension, ought to be introduced in the model to explain the woes of the once 'lead goose'.

Going one step further, the studies of both Edgington and Hayter (2000) and of Dowling and Cheang (2000) are two examples that test the applicability of the FGM to the case of FDI patterns in Asia. Using the case of Panasonic Corporation (formerly Matsushita Electric Industrial Co.) in the Asia Pacific region, Edgington and Hayter (2000) find some support for the pattern suggested by the FGM, whereas Dowling and Cheang (2000) examine the extent to which traditional FDI patterns of Asian economies can be explained by the FGM over the period 1970 to 1995. By using direct 'investment comparative advantage' indicators (developed in the same way as the revealed comparative advantage indicators), the authors find that, broadly, there is support for the FGM with economic development diffusing from Japan to the then newly industrialized economies such as South Korea, Taiwan and Singapore, as well as to Malaysia, Thailand and Indonesia.

Other work of the Japanese school on FDI brings to the fore the 'country specific' advantages of host countries and their sequential evolution over time. A first important breakthrough was suggested by Kojima (1973) in his 'macroeconomic approach to FDI'. This early work explains the overseas development of Japanese industry in terms of comparative advantages in factor endowments between nations. It highlights the impact of FDI on the industrial structure of both the host and home countries, and on the volume of trade between the two countries. Building on these challenging premises, Kojima and Ozawa (1985) criticize the OLI standard model for its neglect of the macro-global welfare considerations of overseas business operations. In their view, FDI alters the industrial structures of both the home and host countries while maximizing the benefits of specialization and exchange. Using the Rostow-Balassa 'stages approach to comparative advantage' (and cognizant also of the Akamatsu model), Ozawa (1992) summarizes the FDI development path in distinguishing three stages of FDI progression: 'factor driven', 'investment driven' and 'innovation driven'. A country going through the 'investment driven' stage attracts foreign investment of the market-seeking type in capital and intermediate goods industries from more developed countries. It generates outward investment towards less-developed countries in labour-intensive and resource-based industries. Typically, a Japanese MNC, as any other MNC in the world, transfers production abroad in industries where it is gradually losing its comparative advantage, due to rising wages. The process of FDI and that of industrial restructuring are thus interlinked.

An important feature of these models is that they all stress the endowments of the host countries and their comparative advantage, that is, the macro-economic dimension of economic phenomena, in stark opposition to the dominant OLI paradigm which emphasized the theory of the firm in quasi isolation from international trade theory. This is to say that the macro-economic conditions in which firms evolve have largely been ignored by mainstream (Western) FDI theorists, although later versions of the OLI paradigm do eventually take these dimensions into account in what became known as the 'investment development path' (Dunning and Narula, 1994). The more subtle stages-approach view (through export-imports and through in- and outward direct investment) suggests that the motives for investing abroad differ according to the epoch and to the country. It is therefore hard to conceive of a uniform path, as in the OLI paradigm.

2.3 Other Theoretical Avenues – the Key Role of Motives for FDI

Evolving partly from the OLI paradigm, from its limits and from its many reformulations, the more recent and contemporary business-economics literature on FDI tends to relegate elements such as the firm's specific advantages, which are so central to the OLI paradigm, to second place. This other strand of the literature stresses the importance of the *motives* for going abroad, that is again, by highlighting the external environment of the firm. In our increasingly globalized world, firms think and act globally as the impressive growth of FDI by emerging economies since the 2008 global financial crisis, as shown in Table 2A.1 in the appendix to this chapter, can attest. Demonstration effects explain why the presence of MNCs from emerging countries in diversified overseas markets is now a must, and how the choice of the host market depends ultimately on a specific motive.[5] To these motives we now turn.

Four main motives explain the strategy of direct investment by MNEs abroad, namely: resource-seeking, market-seeking, asset-seeking and efficiency-seeking (Richet, 2013). Resource-seeking implies the procurement and control of key natural or primary resources from specific locations and this motive explains traditional Western direct investment patterns in the Middle East, but it also increasingly explains Chinese involvement in Africa. Market-seeking explains a great deal of US investment in the EU post WWII, in line with the tariff jumping hypothesis (Jacobson and Andreosso, 1990). Asset-seeking behaviour implies investment by, say, Japanese firms in advanced European countries in the 1960s for the purpose of learning (Andreosso-O'Callaghan, 1999). As will be discussed later, the case of South Korean firms serves as an edifying example of asset-seeking behaviour. Finally, efficiency-seeking is a strategy dictated by cost differentials in different countries and can easily be connected with Vernon's model. In that vein, Andreff and Balcet (2013) turn the Heckscher-Ohlin (HO) theorem 'upside down' by suggesting that low labour costs in a home market are actually an advantage for India's and China's FDI abroad.

This typology into four main motives has also helped with the delineation of other international business-based models such as the LLL model (Linkage, Leverage, Learning) by Mathews (2002) in his explanation of the new 'dragon MNEs', and the 'fresh capability-based model' of Singal and Jain (2012). In particular, the LLL model shows how the co-operation (or linkage) with firms positioned on the high value added spectrum on a contractual basis (for example through joint ventures in Asia or indeed through partial acquisitions in Europe) has been allowing Asian firms to benefit from a leverage effect. This in turn allows them to acquire new capabilities through learning. Singal and Jain (2012) argue that Indian firms develop a strategic capability at home before contemplating the penetration of the global market through strategic alliances and technology acquisition. This view converges with the findings of Andreff and Balcet (2013).

Despite the continuous fine-tuning of the FDI theory based on the neoclassical and more modern theories of the firm – such as the managerial theory and the transaction cost theory – as well as on the OLI paradigm, it seems that neither the revised versions of OLI nor the product life cycle (PCM) model, or more recent approaches such as LLL, can satisfactorily explain FDI by Asian countries today. Indeed, a recent literature review of 62 articles published in mostly management-based journals between 1986 and 2012 on Chinese ODI states that the majority of these articles conclude in the inability of mainstream theories to explain satisfactorily ODI by China (Berning and Holtbrugge, 2012). The main limitation of these theories is, again, that they view the firm in isolation from its home environment, and in particular from its political institutional framework, the latter being a crucial dimension when studying the 'Asian firm'. This leads logically to a novel stream of further investigation, which looks at the firm as being part of a *network* of business and non-business activities.

2.4 The Firm and the Network Approach to FDI

This sub-section explores the need to focus on the theory of the (Asian) firm in its home context by focusing on its relationships with economic *as well as* non-economic actors.

Before it does so, it is worth recalling the abundant literature on the topic of the firm as being part of a network of economic and non-economic activities. Since space is a core element in the understanding of the firm in its network, a large strand of this economics literature falls under the double heading of industrial economics and regional economics. From an industrial economics and/or strategic management angle, contributions on the network approach of the firm since the 1980s have highlighted the benefits accruing to the firm in its network relationships primarily with its sub-suppliers, through for example knowledge sharing and transaction cost minimization, locally as in the case of early studies (Belussi, 1992; Hakansson and Johanson, 1988), but also globally in more recent work (Andreosso-O'Callaghan and Lenihan, 2008). Another strand of this literature looks at the connections between the firm and a number of socio-economic actors or institutions in a specific territory or, more recently, further afield. These connections involving non-economic actors have indeed been thoroughly studied by the abundant industrial districts literature flourishing in post-WWII Italy. Authors such as Capecchi (1990) and Garofoli (1991) explain how a homogenous system of values, a great degree of social cohesion, and a strong sense of belonging to the local community – all amplified by the role of the family, the Church and/or of political parties – were all important ingredients in supporting capital accumulation and the emergence of firms in post-WWII Northern Italy; lately these firms have been able to enlarge their space of action by connecting for example to markets in China (Bellandi and Caloffi, 2006).

This is to say that when appraising the Asian globalized firm in the context of its network activities with economic and non-economic actors, the economic analyst does not start from a *tabula rasa*. The network approach to the global firm is even more compelling in the Asian case given the specific type of firms in Asia, the role of the state, and the firm-state connection in most Asian countries, and particularly in China. In terms of the specific type of firm prevailing in Asia, explaining ODI by business groups or by complex entities such as Japanese keiretsu firms and networks, Korean *chaebols* or indeed Chinese state-owned enterprises (SOEs), leads naturally to the network approach of FDI. The firms at the centre of the business group or of the network are normally large and highly diversified conglomerates (such as the Korean LG) and the advantages of being large are quite well known; these encompass, but are not limited to, cross-subsidization. In particular, the very strong firm-state connection in these countries is such that a government-led drive for change, such as in the case of the emergence of the software industry in South Korea or of the 'go global strategy' in China, delivers prompt and impressive results. Yang's book on China's offshore investment was one of the first comprehensive analyses that used the network approach to explain ODI by Chinese firms (Yang, 2005). Filling an important void in the FDI literature on the new emerging economies, the author's network approach is based on price and hierarchy, as the most pertinent institutional form explaining the organization of economic activity by Chinese firms beyond their national boundaries. By restoring some equilibrium between the supply and demand sides (an equilibrium absent from the OLI paradigm), Yang's network approach uses simple mathematical expressions to derive the mathematical conditions that justify networking activity. This cost-based model – combining governance as well as transaction costs – concludes with six possible choices for the organization of economic activity. Interestingly, the concept of network is also used to explain the organization of production both during Maoist times – with the SOEs at the centre of the system – and since the beginning of the economic reforms in the late 1970s. In particular, it is shown how, with the establishment of a number of special economic zones (SEZs), networks started extending over several regions and provinces.

In the particular case of China, state-firm relations are so crucial and so strong that even though the Chinese MNC or global SOE is relatively economically weak, state ownership becomes *de facto* and ultimately a firm specific advantage, therefore giving some credit (admittedly by twisting it slightly) to the 'ownership advantage' concept. This strength should be appreciated in the context of large financial assets accumulated by the Chinese state and by Chinese state-owned companies over the course of the country's export-led growth policy. This view is therefore close to the 'fresh capability-based model' mentioned above and it is also compatible with the arguments of Andreff and Balcet (2013).

It follows that recent attempts at explaining Chinese ODI from a theoretical viewpoint have tended to either stumble on or to converge towards the inescapable nature of the institutional (in particular political) dimension. Chinese ODI ought to be appraised from the viewpoint of the firm through its many connections with actors lying outside of its purely business space, in short, from the viewpoint of network relations. After having dealt with the theory, the remainder of the chapter will review recently published articles and books by organizing them according to a number of main recurring themes.

3. RECURRENT THEMES IN THE 'THIRD WAVE' ASIAN ODI LITERATURE

3.1 Motives Behind ODI by Asian Emerging Countries

The question of motives is one such recurrent theme, although most of the articles and books reviewed do not attempt at placing this theme in a theoretical framework.

Starting from the categorization of motives into four main types (namely resource-seeking, market-seeking, asset-seeking and efficiency-seeking), the motivation of asset-seeking had already been identified as a major motivation during the first and second waves of ODI from developing/emerging countries. During the first wave (1980s), Japanese firms kept acquiring highly-sophisticated technology from developed countries by setting up laboratories in key European countries (Andreosso-O'Callaghan, 1999). Miotti and Sachwald (2001) and Hoesel (1999) show how South Korean firms used outward investment in developed countries in the 1990s as a strategy to come closer to the technological frontier in their quest to catch up in a number of high-tech sectors and industries. In some cases, the strategy followed by these South Korean firms in the

1990s was to buy into US and European firms or to establish co-operative networks with domestic firms, a new pattern in their entry mode. One example of the latter strategy is represented by the case of Samsung establishing a television set manufacturing plant in the UK in 1995. This was done through a co-operation agreement with the German manufacturer Braun to benefit from the supply of low-cost components to Samsung from plants located in former East Germany. Of crucial importance in this 'second' wave of ODI by South Korean firms has been the institutional framework in which South Korean firms have been able to evolve, going back to August 1969 when President Park's policy started giving more weight to industrialization and to outward FDI (Sunoo, 1994). The setting up of Free Trade Zones (starting with Masan in 1970), combined with inward Japanese investors attracted by a myriad of fiscal and other incentives (including institutional support), led to an important industrial and technology shift. The emergence of the Korean software industry during the 1980s was strongly stimulated by the Korean Government and its direct involvement in the large *chaebols*. These large conglomerates were first movers in terms of ODI from South Korea, although the importance of small and medium-sized enterprises (SMEs) increased over time. Taiwan provides another example of early ODI from emerging countries during the 'second wave'. From the 1970s, institutional support and appropriate policies all helped develop an export-led growth strategy coupled with the development of high-tech industries investing abroad (Hsu and Chiang, 2001).

Being less technology-oriented than its Japanese or South Korean counterpart, Malaysia is also an Asian country that has succeeded in exporting capital abroad; recent United Nations Conference on Trade and Development (UNCTAD) statistics show however that outflows of FDI from Malaysia now surpass FDI inflows (UNCTAD, 2015). This is an unusual pattern in the Southeast Asian region, as this is more due to a decrease in the country's attractiveness in the eyes of foreign investors, in particular with regard to its human capital offer, rather than in the country's ability to export more capital (Athukorala and Waglé, 2011). Goh and Wong (2011) show how the motive of market-seeking has been a primary motive for Malaysian firms investing abroad. Hattari and Rajan (2010) discuss how Indian ODI tends to be more market- and resource-seeking compared with ODI from other countries. In the case of China, Chinese firms have been catching up with their South Korean and Taiwanese counterparts during the 'third wave' as they have 'used' and are still 'using' advanced countries to close the technology gap (Richet, 2013; Yang, 2005). The statistical analysis conducted by Yang (2005) at the beginning of the 'go global strategy' shows how the main motives for Chinese outward

FDI were both the wide technology gap and also the shortages of natural resources leading these firms to use Australia – a resource-rich advanced economy – as a stepping stone in their globalization strategy (Ferguson and Hendrischke, 2014). Kolstad and Wiig's econometric analysis of Chinese ODI shows that the size of the market (in OECD countries) as well as large natural resources (in the case of non-OECD countries) were the major motivations for Chinese ODI over the period 2003–2006 (Kolstad and Wiig, 2012). Zhang (2012) highlights the changing path of Chinese ODI and its changing motives over time, with the resource-seeking motive gradually being superseded by the technology-seeking motive as well as by strategic moves in the financial sector.

All examples in this sub-section show how emerging Asian global firms investing abroad at different epochs are the result of a 'picking-the-winner' strategy from a highly involved state.

3.2 Positive Impact of Direct Investment

This sub-section will briefly highlight the beneficial impact of direct investment as seen in the recent literature; this impact ranges from economic growth effects to the financial implications effects.

3.2.1 The 'FDI-growth nexus'
This nexus is probably best epitomized by the China-Africa connection. As noted by Weisbrod and Whalley (2011), the relatively high growth rates in sub-Saharan African countries during the three years preceding the 2008 financial crisis coincided with unprecedented Chinese ODI flows into these economies. Their growth accounting method-based calculations show that a significant share (in some cases) and that a non-negligible share (in other cases) of this growth can be attributed to Chinese inward direct investment in these countries. Ayodele and Sotola (2014) highlight the overall positive impact of Chinese FDI when engaging in infrastructural projects upon which African countries' economic growth has been able to flourish. The more nuanced view by Renard (2011) discusses both opportunities and challenges in terms of Chinese ODI and growth in African countries. On the positive side, the author notes how Chinese direct investment has contributed to build local capacity, to transfer technology and to raise exports levels in several African countries. An interesting angle to the FDI-growth nexus is to look at the impact of ODI on home economic growth. In this vein, Wong (2013) shows that the intensity of growth-led outward FDI in the case of Malaysia very much depends on the institutional set-up in that country, in particular on the ability of the government to prepare the private business sector for globalization through direct investment.

3.2.2 The 'FDI-trade nexus'

The FDI-trade nexus (an expression coined by Urata, 2001) has multifaceted dimensions. Chow (2012) shows that outward Taiwanese direct investment has a complementarity effect on Taiwan's exports; this is highlighted by the Taiwan-China economic relationship, particularly since the 1990s. Goh *et al.* (2013) use a gravity model in the case of Malaysia and conclude that there is complementarity between outward/inward FDI and trade in that country, although FDI from Malaysia and trade linkages are found to be non-significant. In the case of ODI by Indian firms since the 1991 reforms, Kumar (2007) finds that the firms that were already exporting were also more likely to invest abroad.

3.2.3 Financial implications

Far less research has been expanded on the connection existing between FDI from emerging countries and capital markets. This calls for more studies to be done along these lines, in response to the trends towards financialization, a phenomenon that is spreading rapidly to China. The study by Chiou *et al.* (2013) is one of the rare recent studies that looks at Taiwanese direct investment in emerging markets and at its impact on bondholders' yield spread. The authors find that the negative relationship between FDI and yield spread is stronger in the case of Taiwanese firms investing in China than in the case of firms investing in developed countries.

3.3 Negative Impact of FDI

FDI leads both to job creation (mostly, but not solely, in the host country) as well as to job destruction (mostly, but not only, in the home country). The case of de-industrialization (*kudoka*) in post-bubble Japan and the concomitant phenomenon of outward Japanese direct investment in Asia (Guelle, 2001) is a typical example of outward investment destroying jobs in a mature economy. Turning to the case of Asian emerging economies as recipient countries of FDI, inward investment in these countries normally results in positive employment and growth effects, since FDI adds to the capital stock and leads to an upgrading of skills. However, although the effect is positive in the main, there is also evidence of crowding-out effects in these host economies (Andreosso-O'Callaghan and Hu, 2010). Going one step further, Driffield and Chiang (2009) find some strong evidence that Taiwan's FDI in China has contributed to raising the unemployment rate in the home country – that is, Taiwan – in some specific industries. The authors also show that through supply-chain effects, Taiwanese direct investment in China has also led to a reduction in employment in upstream stages of production. In their analysis of patterns of FDI in Malaysia in a comparative analysis, Athukorala and Waglé (2011) do not find evidence that an increasing flow of FDI into China crowds-out FDI in Malaysia, or indeed in any other neighbouring country. In their view, Malaysia can benefit from a complementary FDI relationship with China, given that the two countries are situated on different levels of the global production networks.

All these effects are in line with what is suggested by the stages approach of FDI as seen earlier. A further line of enquiry would be whether the constitution of Chinese global production networks leads to diminished local outsourcing; this is reminiscent of the old keiretsu effect.

3.4 Other Themes: Role of the Diaspora, Culture and Perception

The role of the diaspora, as a form of social capital, in attracting FDI 'back home' is another recurrent theme in the literature on emerging countries' ODI, given the large communities of Chinese, Indian and other Asian nationalities living abroad. Anwar and Mughal (2013) use a quantitative methodology over the period 1999–2008 to investigate the role of Indian migrants in attracting direct investment in their respective host countries. They find an important positive effect of the Indian diaspora in attracting Indian direct investment in some countries, in particular into the Asia-Pacific region although the results for European countries are less clear-cut. Of crucial importance at this juncture is the cultural (including the institutional) distance, particularly in the case of large Asian countries such as India and China. Drogendijk and Martin (2015) show how both the cultural and historical distances are important in explaining Chinese ODI.

When the distance is too great, antagonism can ensue. Chinese direct investment has particularly been under the scrutiny of policy-makers in the more advanced countries such as the EU and Australia. The fact that China does not abide by the principles of democracy, that it has a lenient attitude *vis-à-vis* the rule of law and above all *vis-à-vis* its enforcement, in spite of it being a member of the World Trade Organization (WTO), has stirred some debate. For example, the antagonism derived from some Chinese direct investment in Australia has been noted (Lowy Institute, 2014).

4.   CONCLUSION

FDI from emerging countries is a fairly well-established and -investigated phenomenon, since today's involvement of China and, to a lesser extent of India, as the main protagonists on the emerging countries' ODI scene constitutes what has been termed the 'third wave' of FDI from emerging countries. The magnitude and growth of FDI outflows from these new investing countries in less than two decades is however unprecedented, given the scale of the two economies involved.

First, this chapter has highlighted the increasing inability of firm-centred or micro-economic-based theories to explain the Asian ODI case in general and the Chinese investment case in particular. Limits to the mainstream theories (PLC, OLI, variations of OLI) had already been highlighted by Japanese scholars such as Kojima (1973) who developed his macro-economic approach to FDI. These mainstream FDI theories tend to look at the firm in isolation from its home environment particularly from its network of business activities and from its political institutional environment. Consequently, the network approach to FDI is a more satisfactory theoretical framework to explain the different waves of ODI from emerging countries, given inter alia, the prominent role of the Asian state. Contemporary FDI theory cannot therefore dispense itself from placing the international firm in its institutional dimension, and from highlighting the role of the state and, particularly in the Chinese case, from highlighting the political system dimension.

Second, the literature reviewed in this chapter has been organized according to the main recurrent themes such as for example the motives (thereby shifting the focus on firms' strategies) behind emerging countries' FDI. It has been shown for example that Chinese and Indian firms today are motivated by asset-seeking (more precisely by technology sourcing) when investing in advanced economies, thereby replicating the exact same pattern as Taiwanese and South Korean firms during the 'second wave'. Indeed, Korean FDI from the 1980s was motivated by the search of complementary resources in the USA and in the EU. The themes of FDI-trade and FDI-growth connections from the viewpoints of both China and India as investing countries are also prominent in the literature whereas more research should be expanded on the implications of emerging countries' direct investment in financial markets, particularly given the global trend towards financialization. Finally, some of the literature investigates the cultural proximity (role of the diaspora), or conversely the cultural distance (antagonism) in explaining FDI.

Of specific and crucial note is the role of the (strong) state in these countries in their quest to catch up with Western economies; by following this train of thought, it can be argued that of particular relevance are the true motivations behind China's 2001 'go global strategy'. Can this strategy be explained solely by economic motivations, or is the strategy also explained by political motivations? To what extent is the government-state nexus far more important in the Chinese case today than it was in the past for example under Park Chung Hee's rule in the 1970s when appropriate policies were being implemented to prepare South Korean MNCs such as Daewoo and Samsung to venture into Western markets? All these questions would need to be fully explored before a new and more adequate FDI theory explaining today's direct investment from countries such as China can be proposed.

ACKNOWLEDGEMENTS

The author would like to thank Magdalena Stolz and Qin Tang, Ruhr Universität Bochum, for excellent research support.

NOTES

1. On early waves of FDI from developing countries, see Lall (1983) and Kumar and McLeod (1981). The literature on FDI from developing countries identified a new type of MNC, with different ownership advantages, motives and geographical location (Dunning *et al.*, 1996). The 'first wave' corresponds to MNCs from developing/emerging countries in the 1980s (mostly from South America). In the 1990s, an important shift in both the type and motives of FDI from some newly industrialized countries (mostly from Asia and in particular from South Korea and Taiwan) is referred to as the 'second wave'.
2. This hypothesis states that relatively large and high-tech oriented MNCs take advantage of their 'firm-specific' assets, such as for example their technological superiority.
3. Interestingly, Rostow's approach (and later Balassa's extension) follows the same sequential logic as in the 'flying geese' pattern of industrial development (the latter being coined by Akamatsu).
4. Note that Kojima and Ozawa put forward major criticisms of internalization theory.
5. This shift of theoretical attention from the firm per se to its motives underlying its global strategy is comparable to the shift in the industrial economics literature from the structure of the market to the firm's conduct (or strategy) in the well-established SCP (structure-conduct-performance) paradigm.

REFERENCES

Akamatsu, Kaname (1935), 'Waga kuni yomo kogyohin no susei' [Trend of Japan's woollen products industry], *Shogyo Keizai Ronso*, **13**, 129–212.
Akamatsu, Kaname (1937), 'Waga kuni keizai hatten no sogo benshoho' [Synthetic dialectics of industrial development in Japan], *Shogyo Keizai Ronso*, **15**, 179–210.
Akamatsu, Kaname (1961), 'A theory of unbalanced growth in the world economy', *Welwirtschaftliches Archiv*, **86** (2), 192–215.
Akamatsu, Kaname (1962), 'A historical pattern of economic growth in developing countries', *Developing Economies*, **1** (1), 1–23.
Andreff, Wladimir and Giovanni Balcet (2013), 'Emerging countries' multinational

companies investing in developed countries: at odds with the HOS paradigm?', *The European Journal of Comparative Economics*, **10** (1), 3–26.

Andreosso-O'Callaghan, B. (1999), 'Japanese manufacturing investment in France in an EU comparative framework. Theory and practice', in F.P. Cerase, F. Mazzei and C. Molteni (eds), *Japan and the Mediterranean World*, Proceedings of the International Conference, Naples, October 1997, pp. 145–77.

Andreosso-O'Callaghan, B. and Ju Hu (2010), 'Is the strategy of technology acquisition in China an indisputable success? On the impact of FDI on Chinese domestic enterprises' technology improvement', in B. Andreosso-O'Callaghan and Bruna Zolin (eds), *Asia and Europe – Connections and Contrasts*, Venice: Libreria Editrice Cafoscarina, pp. 257–74.

Andreosso-O'Callaghan, B. and H. Lenihan (2008), 'Networking: a question of firm characteristics? The case of the Shannon region in Ireland', *Entrepreneurship and Regional Development*, **20** (6), 561–80.

Anwar, Amar and Mazhar Mughal (2013), 'The role of diaspora in attracting Indian outward FDI', *International Journal of Social Economics*, **40** (11), 944–55.

Athukorala, Prema-chandra and Swarnim Waglé (2011), 'Foreign direct investment in Southeast Asia – is Malaysia falling behind?', *ASEAN Economic Bulletin*, **28** (2), 115–33.

Ayodele, Thompson and Olusegun Sotola (2014), 'China in Africa: an evaluation of Chinese investment', IPPA Working Paper Series 2014, Initiative for Public Policy Analysis, Lagos.

Baba, Y. (1987), 'Internationalisation and technical change in Japanese electronics firms, or why the product cycle does not work', paper presented at the EIASM Meeting on Internationalisation and Competition, Brussels, June.

Balassa, B. (1977), 'A stages approach to comparative advantage', *World Bank Staff Working Papers*, No. 256.

Bellandi, Marco and Annalisa Caloffi (2006), 'Distretti industriali italiani e internazionalizzazione fra gli anni novanta e la prima metà del nuovo decennio', in *Rapporto ICE 2005–2006, L'Italia nell'Economia Internazionale*, Roma: Agenzia ICE, Italian Trade Agency, pp. 466–82.

Belussi, F. (1992), 'Benetton Italy: beyond Fordism and flexible specialization: the evolution of the network firm model', in Mitter Swasti (ed.), *Computer-Aided Manufacturing and Women's Employment: The Clothing Industry in Four EC Countries*, London: Springer Verlag, pp. 73–91.

Berning, Sue C. and Dirk Holtbrugge (2012), 'Chinese outward foreign direct investment – a challenge for internationalization theories?', *Journal für Betriebswirtschaft*, December, **62** (3–4), 169–224.

Capecchi, Vittorio (1990), 'A history of flexible specialisation and industrial districts in Emiglia-Romagna', in F. Pyke, G. Becattini and W. Sengenberger (eds), *Industrial Districts and Inter-Firm Co-operation in Italy*, Geneva: International Institute for Labour Studies, pp. 20–36.

Cherry, Judith (2001), *Korean Multinationals in Europe*, Richmond, Surrey: Curzon Press.

Chiou, Chyi-Lun, Mao-Wei Hung and Pei-Gi Shu (2013), 'Foreign direct investment in emerging markets: bondholders' perspective', *Emerging Markets Finance and Trade*, **49** (Supplement 4), 5–16.

Chow, Peter (2012), 'The effect of outward foreign direct investment on home country's exports: a case study on Taiwan', *Journal of Economic Trade and Development*, **21** (5), 725–54.

Coase, R.H. (1937), 'The nature of the firm', *Economica*, **4** (November), 386–405. Reprinted as Chapter 2 in Coase, R.H. (1988), *The Firm, the Market and the Law*, Chicago: University of Chicago Press.

Dowling, Malcolm and Cheang Chia Tien (2000), 'Shifting comparative advantage in Asia: new tests of the "flying geese" model', *Journal of Asian Economics*, **11** (4), 443–63.

Driffield, Nigel and P.C. (Michelle) Chiang (2009), 'The effects of offshoring to China: reallocation, employment and productivity in Taiwan', *International Journal of the Economics of Business*, **16** (1), 19–38.

Drogendiijk, Rian and Oscar M. Martin (2015), 'Relevant dimensions and contextual weights of distance in international business decisions: evidence from Spanish and Chinese outward FDI', *International Business Review*, **24** (1) February, 133–47.

Dunning, J.H. (1980), 'Toward an eclectic theory of international production: some empirical tests', *Journal of International Business Studies*, **11** (1), 9–31.

Dunning, J.H. (1986), 'The investment development cycle revisited', *Weltwirtschaftliches Archiv*, **122** (4), 667–77.

Dunning, J.H. (1988), 'The eclectic paradigm of international production: a restatement and some possible extensions', *Journal of International Business Studies*, **19** (1), 1–31.

Dunning, J.H. and R. Narula (1994), 'Transpacific foreign direct investment and the investment development path: the record assessed', *Essays in International Business No. 10*, South Carolina: The University of South Carolina.

Dunning, J.H., Roger van Hoesel and Rajneesh Narula (1996), 'Explaining the "new" wave of outward FDI from developing countries: the case of Taiwan and Korea', Research Papers in Economics, MERIT, Maastricht Economic Research Institute on Innovation and Technology.

Edgington, David W. and Roger Hayter (2000), 'Foreign direct investment and the flying geese model: Japanese electronics firms in Asia-Pacific', *Environment and Planning*, **32** (2), 281–304.

Ferguson, D. and H. Hendrischke (2014), 'Demystifying Chinese investment in Australia: Chinese investors in Australia survey', KPMG, accessed 1 June 2015 at http://demystifyingchina.com.au/reports/Demystifying-Chinese-Investment-Survey.pdf.

Gammeltoft, Peter (2008), 'Emerging multinationals: outward FDI from the BRICS countries', *International Journal of Technology and Globalisation*, **4** (1), 26–34.

Garofoli, Gioacchino (1991), 'Industrial districts: structure and transformation', in G. Garofoli (ed.), *Endogenous Development and Southern Europe*, Aldershot: Avebury, pp. 49–60.

Goh, Soo Khoon and Koi Nyen Wong (2011), 'Malaysia's outward FDI: the effects of market size and government policy', *Journal of Policy Modeling*, **33** (3), 497–510.

Goh, Soo Khoon, Koi Nyen Wong and Siew Yean Tham (2013), 'Trade linkages of inward and outward FDI: evidence from Malaysia', *Economic Modeling*, **35**, 224–30.

Guelle, Françoise (2001), 'The links between Japanese investment in Asia and de-industrialization in Japan', in Bernadette Andreosso-O'Callaghan, Jean-Pascal Bassino and Jacques Jaussaud (eds), *The Changing Economic Environment in Asia – Firms' Strategies in the Region*, London: Macmillan, pp. 52–61.

Hakansson, H. and J. Johanson (1988), 'Formal and informal cooperation strategies in international industrial networks', in F.J. Contractor and P. Lorange (eds), *Cooperative Strategies in International Business*, Lanham, MD: Lexington Books, pp. 369–79.

Hattari, R. and R.S. Rajan (2010), 'India as a source of outward foreign direct investment', *Oxford Development Studies*, **38** (4), 497–518.

Hoesel, Roger van (1999), *New Multinational Enterprises from Korea and Taiwan*, London, New York: Routledge.

Hsu, C.-W. and H.C. Chiang (2001), 'The government strategy for the upgrading of industrial technology', *Technovation*, **21** (2), 123–31.

Hymer, S. ([1960] 1976), *The International Operations of National Firms: A Study of Direct Foreign Investment* (reprint of 1960 dissertation), Cambridge, MA: MIT Press.

Jacobson, David and Bernadette Andreosso (1990), 'Ireland as a location for multinational investment', in Anthony Foley and Mulreany (eds), *The Single European Market and the Irish Economy*, Dublin: IPA, pp. 307–34.

Kindleberger, C.P. (1968), *American Business Abroad*, New Haven, CT: Yale University Press.

Kojima, Kiyoshi (1973), 'A macroeconomic approach to foreign direct investment', *Hitotsubashi Journal of Economics*, **14** (1), 1–21.

Kojima, Kiyoshi (2000), 'The "flying geese" model of Asian economic development: origin, theoretical extensions and regional policy implications', *Journal of Asian Economics*, **11** (4), 375–401.

Kojima, Kiyoshi and Terutomo Ozawa (1985), 'Toward a theory of industrial restructuring and dynamic comparative advantage', *Hitotsubashi Journal of Economics*, **26** (2), 135–45.

Kolstad, Ivar and Arne Wiig (2012), 'What determines Chinese outward FDI?', *Journal of World Business*, **47** (1), 26–34.

Kumar, K. and G. McLeod (eds) (1981), *Multinationals from Developing Countries*, Lanham, MD: Lexington Books.

Kumar, Nagesh (2007), 'Emerging TNCs: trends, patterns and determinants of outward FDI by Indian enterprises', *Transnational Corporations*, **16** (1), 1–26.

Lall, S. (ed.) (1983), *Third World Multinationals*, Chichester: John Wiley & Sons.

Lowy Institute (2014), *Chinese Direct Investment in Australia, A PwC and Lowy Institute Roundtable*, accessed 5 June 2015 at http://www.pwc.com.au/deals/assets/Australia-Open-For-Business-Mar14.pdf.

Marshall, Alfred (1899), *The Economics of Industry*, 3rd edition, London: Macmillan.

Mathews, J.A. (2002), *Dragon Multinationals. A New Model for Global Growth*, Oxford: Oxford University Press.

Miotti, L. and F. Sachwald (2001), 'Korean multinationals' strategies and international learning', in F. Sachwald (ed.), *Going Multinational. The Korean Experience of Direct Investment*, London and New York: Routledge, pp. 127–65.

Ozawa, Terumoto (1992), 'Foreign direct investment and economic development', *Transnational Corporations*, **1** (1), 27–54.

Ozawa, Terumoto (2001), 'The "hidden" side of the "flying geese "catch-up" model: Japan's dirigiste institutional setup and a deepening financial morass', *Journal of Asian Economics*, **12** (4), 471–91.

Ozawa, Terumoto (2009), *The Rise of Asia: The 'Flying Geese' Theory of Tandem*

Growth and Regional Agglomeration, Cheltenham, UK and Northampton, MA, USA: Edward Elgar.

Ozawa, Terumoto (2011), 'The (Japan-born) "flying geese" theory of economic development revisited', *Global Policy*, **2** (3), 272–85.

Renard, Mary Françoise (2011), *China's Trade and DFI in Africa*, African Development Bank Group, Working Papers Series No. 126, April.

Richet, Xavier (2013), 'L'internationalisation des firmes chinoises: croissance, motivations, stratégies', Fondation Maison des Sciences de l'Homme, Paris, Working Papers Series No. 02, Février.

Rostow, W.W. (1960), *The Stages of Economic Growth*, Cambridge: Cambridge University Press.

Singal, Ajay and Arun Kumar Jain (2012), 'Outward FDI trends from India: emerging MNCs and strategic issues', *International Journal of Emerging Markets*, **7** (4), 443–56.

Sunoo, Harold Hakwon (1994), *Twentieth Century Korea*, Seoul: NANAM Publishing House.

UNCTAD (2015), World Investment Report 2015, Reforming International Investment Governance, 25 June 2015, New York and Geneva.

Urata, S. (2001), 'Emergence of an FDI-trade nexus and economic growth in East Asia', in J.E. Stiglitz and S. Yusuf (eds), *Rethinking the East Asian Miracle*, New York: Oxford University Press, pp. 409–59.

Vernon, R. (1966), 'International investment and international trade in the product cycle', *Quarterly Journal of Economics*, **80** (2), 190–207.

Walker, W. (1979), *Industrial Innovation and International Trading Performance*, Greenwich, CT: JAI Press.

Weber, Alfred (1909), *Über den Standort der Industrien: Reine Theorie des Standorts*, Tübingen: Tübingen Verlag.

Weisbrod, Aaron and John Whalley (2011), 'The contribution of Chinese FDI to Africa's pre-crisis growth surge', NBER Working Paper Series No. 17544, accessed 15 June 2015 at http://www.nber.org/papers/w17544.

Wong, Koi-Nyen (2013), 'Outward FDI and economic growth in Malaysia: an empirical study', *International Journal of Business & Society*, **14** (1), 163–72.

Yang, Dexin (2005), *China's Offshore Investments – A Network Approach*, Cheltenham, UK and Northampton, MA, USA: Edward Elgar.

Zhang, Yansheng (2012), 'The accession to the World Trade Organization and China's overseas investment' (加入世界贸易组织与中国企业对外投资), in L. Wang (ed.), *China: Ten Years after WTO Accession* (王洛林主编《加入WTO十年后的中国》), Beijing: China Development Press, pp. 318–36.

APPENDIX

Table 2A.1   FDI flows by major region, 2012–14 (bn. USD and %)

Region	FDI inflows			FDI outflows		
	2012	2013	2014	2012	2013	2014
World	*1403*	*1467*	*1228*	*1284*	*1306*	*1354*
Developed economies	679	697	499	873	834	823
Europe	401	326	289	376	317	316
North America	209	301	146	365	379	390
Developing economies	639	671	681	357	381	468
Africa	56	54	54	12	16	13
Asia	401	428	465	299	335	432
East and Southeast Asia	321	348	381	266	292	383
South Asia	32	36	41	10	2	11
West Asia	48	45	43	23	41	38
Latin America and the Caribbean	178	186	159	44	28	23
Oceania	4	3	3	2	1	0
Transition economies	85	100	48	54	91	63
Structurally weak, vulnerable and small economies[a]	*58*	*51*	*52*	*10*	*13*	*10*
LDCs	24	22	23	5	7	3
LLDCs	34	30	29	2	4	6
SIDS	7	6	7	2	1	1
Memorandum: percentage share in world FDI flows						
Developed economies	48.4	47.5	40.6	68.0	63.8	60.8
Europe	28.6	22.2	23.5	29.3	24.3	23.3
North America	14.9	20.5	11.9	28.5	29.0	28.8
Developing economies	45.6	45.7	55.5	27.8	29.2	34.6
Africa	4.0	3.7	4.4	1.0	1.2	1.0
Asia	28.6	29.2	37.9	23.3	25.7	31.9
East and Southeast Asia	22.9	23.7	31.0	20.7	22.4	28.3
South Asia	2.3	2.3	3.4	0.8	0.2	0.8
West Asia	3.4	3.0	3.5	1.8	3.1	2.8
Latin America and the Caribbean	12.7	12.7	13.0	3.4	2.2	1.7
Oceania	0.3	0.2	0.2	0.1	0.1	0.0
Transition economies	6.1	6.8	3.9	4.2	7.0	4.7

Table 2A.1   (continued)

Region	FDI inflows			FDI outflows		
	2012	2013	2014	2012	2013	2014
Structurally weak, vulnerable and small economies[a]	*4.1*	*3.5*	*4.3*	*0.7*	*1.0*	*0.8*
LDCs	1.7	1.5	1.9	0.4	0.6	0.2
LLDCs	2.5	2.0	2.4	0.2	0.3	0.4
SIDS	0.5	0.4	0.6	0.2	0.1	0.1

Notes:
[a] Without double counting countries that are part of multiple groups.
LDCs = least developed countries, LLDCs = landlocked developing countries, SIDS = small island developing states.

Source: UNCTAD, FDI/MNE database (www.unctad.org/fdistatistics).

3. Regional production networks in East Asia – a focus on China, Japan and Korea

Françoise Nicolas

1. INTRODUCTION

The expansion of intra-East-Asian trade over the past decades is now well documented. Two salient features have often been underlined in the recent literature to explain these developments; firstly, the central contribution of China as a result of its economic rise, and secondly, the crucial role played by trade in parts and components and the emergence of regional production networks. To be more specific, it is a well-known fact that parts, components and intermediate goods account for the bulk of China's imports from East Asia (especially from Japan, South Korea – hereafter Korea – and Taiwan), and that intra-East-Asian trade is essentially intra-industry trade resulting from processing activities. Over the past few years, however, a number of developments have occurred which may bring about major changes in the way the countries are connected. Shifts in China's economic policy in response to the global economic crisis constitute such changes.

The objective of this chapter is to examine the changing nature and structure of the Korea-China and Japan-China trade and investment linkages, as well as the rationale for these changes and to highlight the implications for the definition of the countries' economic policies and for their performances.

Based on a descriptive statistical analysis, the chapter starts by providing a comprehensive assessment of trade and investment interlinkages between China, Japan and Korea and of recently observed changes. The chapter concludes by examining the implications this may have on the countries' respective policy options, with a focus on their free trade agreement (FTA) strategies.

2. OVERALL TRADE DYNAMICS: CONTRASTED TRAJECTORIES

For a long time Japan has been one of China's largest trading partners. In the early 1980s Japan accounted for over one-quarter of Chinese total imports. As can be seen in Figure 3.1, China's accession to the World Trade Organization (WTO) in 2001 ushered in a new phase, with an acceleration of imports from Japan. However, other countries also benefited from China opening up and the role of Japan as a source of imports has been consistently declining ever since the early 1990s (as shown in Figure 3.2). Today, Japan accounts for a mere 8.4 percent of China's imports. The last few years have been particularly negative for Japan.

Japan's total trade with China dropped 6.5 percent to US$312 billion in 2013, a decrease for the second consecutive year. Japan's exports to China witnessed a double-digit decline for the second straight year, while imports from China fell 3.7 percent to US$182 billion, making it the first drop since 2009.

The year 2011 appears to be a high watermark of China–Japan economic integration with potentially important implications. Although it should not be overblown, the deterioration of a formerly well-developed relationship may be a source of concern. Certainly, a high level of

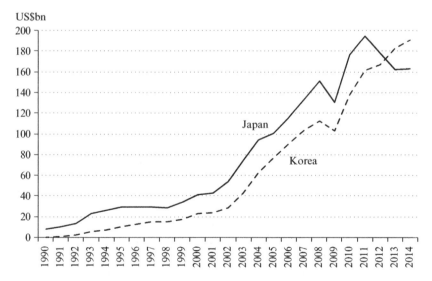

Source: IMF, Direction of Trade Statistics.

Figure 3.1   China's imports from Japan and Korea

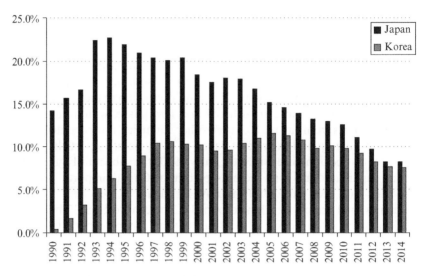

Source: IMF, Direction of Trade Statistics.

Figure 3.2   Shares of Japan and Korea in China's imports

economic integration should not be seen as a strong bulwark against potential tension and conflict. However, as the dynamics of trade probably matter more than its absolute level, deteriorating trade relations are likely to pave the way to a rise in potential conflict.

Similarly, Korea looms large among the beneficiaries of China's opening up. Following the normalization of economic relations between the two countries,[1] China's imports from (and exports to) Korea have been steadily expanding. As can be seen in Figure 3.1 again, the trend in Sino-Korean trade changed in the early 2000s, with a sharp acceleration in the rate of growth. Bilateral trade dropped sharply in the wake of the global economic crisis, but since 2009 China's imports from Korea have soared. Trade between the two countries surpassed US$210 billion in 2013, an increase of 7 percent year on year, equaling Korea's trade volume with the United States and Japan combined. China is now Korea's number one trading partner and its largest export destination[2] and import source. It is also the number one destination of Korean overseas investment.

More surprisingly, given its relatively modest economic size, in 2013 Korea was China's fourth largest export destination and second largest source of imports (accounting for close to 10 percent of China's total imports),[3] and its fifth largest source of foreign direct investment (FDI).

Comparing Japan and Korea, a sharp reduction in the gap (in value terms)

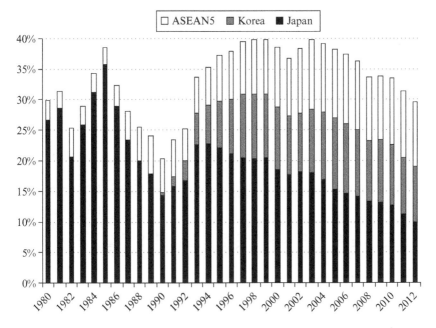

Source: IMF, Direction of Trade Statistics.

Figure 3.3   China's imports by country of origin

between their respective exports to China can be observed. To be more specific, the most recent years suggest that Korea's exports have been more resilient. While Japanese exports to China started to decline in 2011 (probably as a result of a combination of factors, namely the great East Japan earthquake of 11 March and the deterioration in political relations between Japan and China following the Senkaku/Diaoyu dispute and repeated visits of Japanese officials to the Yasukuni Shrine), Korean exports kept momentum, allowing Korea to overtake Japan for the first time in 2013.

As a result of these developments, the relative role of Japan in China has been declining over time, while Korea has managed to maintain its overall share in China's imports, next to the ASEAN5 countries (Association of Southeast Asian Nations) (Figure 3.3). It is worth noting that the rise in Korea's importance as a source of imports for China is not in line with the role of Korea in global trade. China tends to have a strong bias in favor of Korea (Figure 3.4). The bias reached a peak in 1998 before declining gradually, but it is still stronger than that for Japan.

Interestingly, the two countries also exhibit different trade balances trends

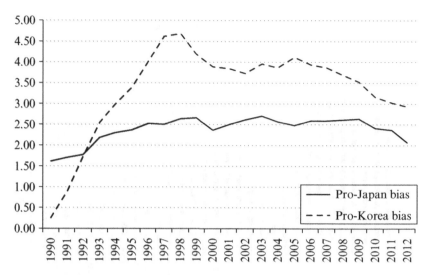

Source: IMF, Direction of Trade Statistics.

Figure 3.4   China's import bias

vis-à-vis China. China has a large and growing deficit with Korea, while its deficit *vis-à-vis* Japan has tended to decline over the past two years.[4]

Another major difference between the two countries lies in the degree of concentration observed in their exports to China. Based on the Herfindahl-Hirschman index,[5] Korean exports to China used to be highly concentrated, in the mid-1990s (0.49), while Japanese exports were far more diversified (0.28). Over time however the degree of concentration of the former has dropped and become much closer to that of the latter (0.29 and 0.23 respectively).

Lastly, it is worth noting that the tightening of Sino-Korean trade relations is mirrored by a decline in bilateral trade between Japan and Korea. From Korea's perspective, Japan has been gradually replaced by China as a source of imports and as an outlet for exports.

3.   COMPOSITION OF BILATERAL TRADE FLOWS

Trade in Intermediate Products: The Rising Importance of Korea

It is a well-known fact that intense cross-border business activities between China and East-Asian economies have led to the formation of a deep and extensive production-sharing network in East Asia. As explained by Thorbecke (2014), starting in 2001, there was a surge in intermediate goods flowing into China. Many have argued that, after it became clear in 2001 that China would join the WTO, investors gained confidence that China would follow the rule of law. This contributed to a surge of FDI and of parts and components flowing to China.

Among China's East-Asian partners, Taiwan plays a specific role. Beginning in 2001, there was a marked surge of intermediate goods going from Taiwan to China. Of course, this was driven not only by China's WTO accession but also by the fact that the government of Taiwan deregulated outgoing FDI by laptop PC makers into China in 2001. Taiwanese original design manufacturers (ODMs) established a value chain centered in the Yangtze River Valley. Soon the lion's share of the world's laptop computers was made in this location. More generally, the Greater China region (Hong Kong, Macau and Taiwan) used to be mainland China's main source of imported intermediate goods (Fung et al., 2013).

However, Greater China's importance to China, as regards to both imports and exports, has diminished substantially over time. China's trade in parts and components is no longer just a mainland China-Hong Kong-Macau-Taiwan production network. Instead it is now a pan-East and Southeast Asian network, including Japan, Korea, and increasingly ASEAN countries.[6] As stressed by Fung et al. (2013), amid the continuous expansion of the Chinese parts and components trade with the region and the world, the past decade has witnessed a pronounced increase in parts and components trade between China and Korea in particular (see Figure 3.5).

The interesting feature of the study shows that Korea seems to be gradually replacing Japan as a source of intermediate goods for China. Although their combined shares have declined from 37 percent of China's total imports in 1995, the balance between the two countries has clearly shifted in favor of Korea.

According to data from UN Comtrade, in 2012 Korea accounted for 15.4 percent of China's imports of intermediate goods.[7] As such, Korea became the single largest exporter of intermediate goods to China in 2012, ahead of Japan (with less than 14 percent), as well as ahead of China's traditional partners such as Hong Kong and Taiwan (see Figure 3.6).

The rise in China's imports of intermediate goods from Korea is also examined by Lee, Park and Wang (2011) and found to be larger than expected. Using a gravity equation, they show that when imports of final products and parts and components are estimated separately, China imports more parts and components from the ASEAN6 countries, Japan, and Korea than expected. Interestingly, among these three East-Asian partners, Korea yields the largest coefficient.[8]

US$ bn

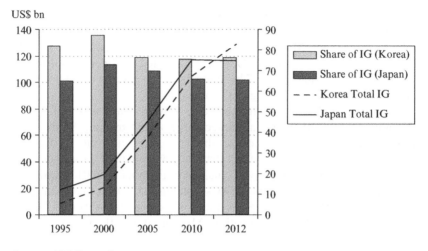

Source: UN Comtrade.

Figure 3.5   China's imports of intermediate goods from Japan and Korea

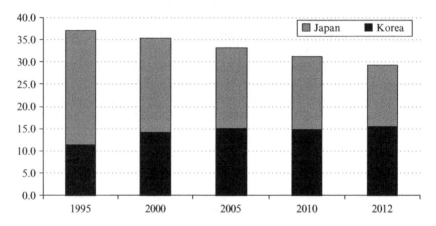

Source: UN Comtrade.

*Figure 3.6   China's imports of intermediate goods from Japan and Korea,
          as share of total imports*

Seen from Japan's and Korea's perspective, while intermediate products traditionally account for a substantial share (at least 70 percent) of China's imports from both Japan and Korea, this share has been declining over the past decade or so. In the case of Korea, an initial drop in the share of

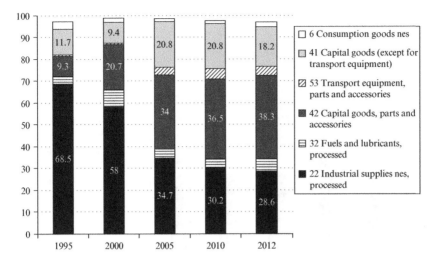

Source: UN Comtrade.

Figure 3.7 China's imports from Korea by category

intermediate goods starting in the early 2000s can be observed, followed by a period of stabilization[9] (dropping from more than 85 percent in 2000 to 78.1 percent in 2013). In the case of Japan, the share of intermediate goods has dropped more systematically from a maximum of 73 percent in 2000 to 65.8 percent in 2013, and the trend seems to be ongoing (see Figures 3.7 and 3.8). As already suggested by observations at the aggregate level, there was a turning point in Sino-Japan trade in 2011 when the political situation started getting strained between the two countries, but other factors also may have been at play as explained below.

Another feature worth noting is the strong link between trade and FDI flows. As shown by Thorbecke (2014), East-Asian countries export increasing quantities of parts and components and capital goods to foreign-owned enterprises located in mainland China and producing for the local market.

Composition of Intermediate Goods Exports: Japan's and Korea's Diverging Paths

In order to better understand what may be at play behind the aforementioned changes, breaking down intermediate goods imports into subcategories proves to be necessary.

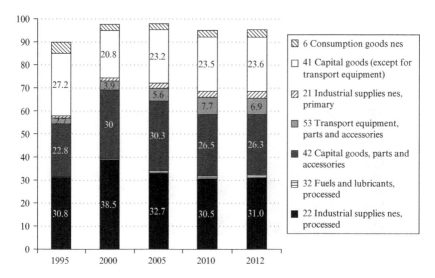

Source: UN Comtrade.

Figure 3.8 China's imports from Japan by category

In the case of Korea, category 42 goods (parts and components of capital goods – excluding transport equipment) account for a substantial and rising share of these intermediate goods (up from less than 10 percent in 1995 to 38.3 percent in 2013). As a result, Korean exports of category 42 goods are now ahead of Japan in absolute terms (US$64 billion vs US$47 billion). By contrast, the share of processed industrial supplies (category 22) dropped sharply from 69 percent to 29 percent over the same period of time. This shift among intermediate goods is a clear indication of the existence of cross-border production-sharing systems based on the fragmentation of production processes in sectors which are particularly amenable to a modularization of the production process (namely electronics).

Of particular note in the case of Korea is also the rise in the share of parts and components of capital goods for transport equipment (category 53). As explained by Shim (2011), Korean automakers have increased their production capacity in China and their exports of related materials and components. By contrast, Korea has changed its strategy in the information and communications technology (ICT) sector and increased its imports of products manufactured in China, especially medium- and low-level technology products while manufacturing high value-added products in Korea. These opposite changes in two of the most important sectors of Sino-Korean trade are indicative of different industrial strategies. While

Korean ICT producers may be losing ground in the Chinese market, Korean automakers are apparently becoming increasingly active in China. This trend is confirmed by the relative decline in Korean outward direct investment (ODI) in China in the ICT industry (see below).

In the case of Japan, the shares of categories 22 and 42 have been either stagnating or declining over the past decade and a half, while the share of category 53 has been rising slightly (from about 4 percent to close to 7 percent). Moreover, the drop in intermediate goods has been compensated for by a rise in the share of final goods, in particular, capital goods (category 41). The latter development clearly sets Japan apart from Korea.

Using the correspondence table between the broad economic categories (BEC) and the harmonized system (HS) classification, Korea appears to be a major exporter of goods in category 8542 (electronic integrated circuits and micro-assemblies). Category 8542 alone accounts for 23.5 percent of China's total imports from Korea (and 61.4 percent of China's imports of category 42 goods). The heavy concentration in the case of Korea may be a source of vulnerability.

This category also looms large in the case of Japan, but while China's imports from Japan exceeded imports from Korea until the early 2000s for this category of goods, things started to change by the mid-2000s and imports from Korea are today almost three times as great as those coming from Japan.

Overall, the pattern of Japanese exports is better balanced than that of Korean exports. The degree of concentration of Japanese exports to China is also substantially lower than that of Korea. Category 8542 for instance accounts for merely 8.2 percent of China's total imports from Japan and 32.3 percent of China's imports of category 42 originating in Japan.

Although the changes in the trade patterns between China and its two East-Asian partners are not dramatic, they tend to be more pronounced for Japan than for Korea, with a rise in the case of the former in the relative importance of capital goods and consumption goods exported to China. This suggests that China may be increasingly perceived by Japanese firms as a market in its own right, rather than exclusively as a production base.

Ordinary vs Processed Trade

The role of China in regional production networks can also be analyzed by making use of China's customs statistics which traditionally differentiate between various customs régimes, in particular between ordinary and non-ordinary trade. Ordinary trade refers primarily to imports intended for China's domestic market, and exports that are mostly based on local Chinese input. Ordinary trade involves primary goods, capital goods and consumption goods. As explained by Thorbecke (2014), the latter still account for only a marginal share, suggesting that the rebalancing of the Chinese economy is still at a very early stage.

Non-ordinary trade, by contrast, refers to other forms of trade, namely, processing trade with imported inputs or process and assembly trade (in both cases, imports of goods are intended to be assembled or transformed in China and subsequently re-exported, but the difference lies in the way imported inputs are purchased and taxed).[10]

At the aggregate level, China runs a trade deficit in ordinary trade. Focusing on China's trade with the rest of the East-Asian region, China runs trade deficits with advanced East Asia (Japan, Korea, Taiwan), small surpluses with ASEAN and a substantial surplus with Hong Kong in ordinary trade (Thorbecke, 2014). The surplus with ASEAN reflects the fact, noted by Gaulier et al. (2011), that Chinese ordinary exports are less sophisticated, lower-priced goods that are especially likely to penetrate markets in the south. China's trade balance with industrial countries is also in surplus.

The situation is quite different for non-ordinary trade which is dominated by processing trade. At the aggregate level, China runs a trade surplus in processing trade which more than compensates for the deficit in ordinary trade, hence China's overall trade surplus. It is worth noting, however, that although processing trade remains the source of China's overall trade surplus, its relative importance has been shrinking consistently since 2007 (Lemoine et al., 2015).[11]

The percentage of Chinese imports for processing coming from Korea, Taiwan, Japan, and ASEAN is large. In 2010, 55 percent of imports for processing came from East Asia and only 5 percent from the EU and the United States respectively (Thorbecke, 2014). These figures are, however, probably understated, as part of Chinese imports for processing come from China itself. Altogether, more than 75 percent of Chinese imports for processing are sourced in East Asia. Recent research further confirms that processing firms operating in China primarily come from Hong Kong, Japan and Korea (Yu and Tian, 2012).

Over the last decade (and in particular since the global economic crisis), Korea has improved its position *vis-à-vis* China as a supplier of goods for processing. Interestingly, imports for processing from Korea have soared since 2009, while those coming from Taiwan, ASEAN4 countries,[12] and Japan have stagnated.

Korea has thus become the leading source of imports for processing. In 2012, with almost US$85 billion imports, Korea's share in China's total imports for processing amounted to 17.5 percent (compared to 11.8 percent in 2002 and 15.2 percent in 2007).[13]

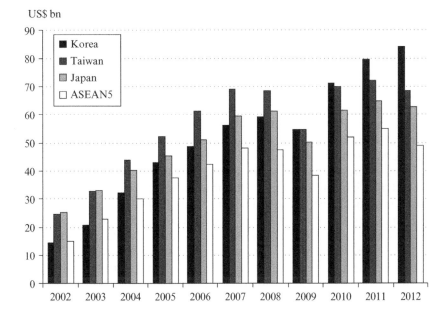

US$ bn

Source: China Customs Statistics.

Figure 3.9 *China's imports for processing by country of origin*

Taiwan is the second leading provider of imports for processing, exporting US$69 billion to China in 2012.

Japan is the third leading supplier, sending China US$63 billion of these goods. China's imports for processing originating in Japan have lost momentum over the past decade, dropping from 20.4 percent in 2002 to 16.1 percent in 2007 and 13 percent in 2012 (see Figure 3.9).

Seen from Korea's perspective, while imports for processing accounted for 62 percent of China's total imports from Korea in 2001, their share had risen to 69 percent in 2011 (Yang et al., 2013). This surge reflects the growth of the Korean electronics industry after 2009. After a sharp drop in 2009 (as a result of the economic crisis), Korea has managed to maintain a constant flow of exports of parts and components (for processing) to China. This is in contrast to both Japan and Taiwan.

Sino-Korean processing trade is dominated by the electric and electronics industry, but chemicals and general machinery also loom relatively large. In the case of the textile and automobile industries, the size of the processing trade has been decreasing while ordinary trade has been increasing. The dramatic rise in ordinary trade in the automobile industry can be accounted for by the explosive surge in domestic demand in China.

Korea is the only country where China's imports for processing have risen in parallel to Chinese processed exports, but with the former in excess of the latter, China runs a trade deficit with Korea. In the case of Taiwan, the slight rise in China's processed exports cannot offset imports for processing, thus leading to a deficit for China. Lastly in the case of Japan, the large rise in processed exports in the absence of a parallel rise in imports for processing leads to a surplus for China and suggests that more value-added is now produced in China (Thorbecke, 2014).

Interestingly, Korea now ranks among the top suppliers to China both for ordinary imports and imports for processing (Thorbecke, 2014). China runs a trade deficit with Korea in both ordinary trade and processing trade.

Japan's position *vis-à-vis* China is significantly different. First of all, China's trade with Japan is dominated by ordinary trade; in particular, ordinary imports account for 58 percent of China's imports from Japan. Secondly, China records a deficit in ordinary trade and a surplus in processing trade with Japan. Interestingly, Japan's deficit in processing trade with China is nothing new and results from high levels of both imports and exports. This suggests that Japan and China are part of the same regional production networks but that China exports final goods back to Japan. These are final goods such as computers produced using parts and components (imports for processing) that are imported duty free. Japan is, in this respect, in the same position as the EU and the United States.

It is worth noting, however, that the amount of imports for processing coming from Japan has been stagnant since 2007 while those originating in Korea have risen sharply over the same period of time. Overall, China imports about the same amount of processing goods from Japan, Taiwan and Korea (about US$70 billion) but the latter two countries together only received US$62 billion of processed exports.[14] Because of these trading patterns, Korea and Taiwan together ran surpluses with China of more than US$90 billion in processing trade.

Summing up, the ways in which Korea and Japan relate to China have become increasingly divergent. Korea is apparently more closely integrated in China-centered regional production networks, while Japan's trade pattern with China is better balanced with ordinary trade playing a more important role.

Overall, China's processed exports and imports for processing have been going in different directions since 2007.[15] For instance, imports for processing from Japan did not increase over this period while processed exports did. This suggests that more of the value-added of processed exports is now produced in China. This may result from the Chinese government's efforts to direct Chinese industries into higher value-added activities as well as from Chinese firms' ability to produce more intermediate goods (Thorbecke, 2014). Logically, a further evolution in this direction can be expected in the years to come, potentially posing a direct threat to Korean firms.

4. JAPAN'S AND KOREA'S DIRECT INVESTMENT IN CHINA

Overall Dynamics

Next to trade, both countries are also active investors in the mainland, but, again, contrasted developments can be observed in the two sets of bilateral relations.

Although the exact origin of FDI flows into China is not easily determined, the key involvement of East-Asian investors is widely recognized. They are usually thought to account for at least 60 percent of China's total inward inflows. Of course, this contribution may be vastly overstated as a substantial share of these flows is the result of "round-tripping" investment between Hong Kong and the mainland, but the role of East-Asian investors in China remains a reality.

According to the Chinese MOFCOM, in 2013 the top ten nations and regions with investment in China (as per the actual input of foreign capital) were as follows: Hong Kong (US$78.302 billion), Singapore (US$7.327 billion), Japan (US$7.064 billion), Taiwan Province (US$5.246 billion), United States (US$3.353 billion), Korea (US$3.059 billion), Germany (US$2.095 billion), Netherlands (US$1.281 billion), United Kingdom (US$1.039 billion) and France (US$762 million), the sum of which accounted for 93.15 percent of total actual foreign investment in the country.

The exemption of imported inputs for further processing and re-exporting from import duties undoubtedly encourages local firms to engage in processing trade, and induces overseas companies to offshore production to China (Manova and Yu, 2014). Under these circumstances the link between trade and investment flows is particularly tight.

Japanese ODI in China

From Japan's perspective, China looms large as a destination for direct investment abroad: China ranks number two after the United States, and the number one investment destination for Japanese manufacturers, accounting in 2012 for 11 percent of Japan's total ODI and 40 percent of its ODI to Asia. As was the case with trade flows, China's accession to the WTO has clearly boosted Japan's direct investment in China.[16]

However, in the past few years, China seems to have fallen out of favor with Japan-based companies. Japanese investment in China fell 4.3 percent to US$7.06 billion in 2013, an amount representing about 6 percent of China's overall FDI inflows (MOFCOM data). In 2012 it had surged 16.3 percent to US$7.38 billion, a pace much faster than FDI from the United States and the EU.

According to a JETRO survey (2013), set against the backdrop of rising risk in relation to China as an investment location, investment in ASEAN countries by Japanese companies picked up speed at the beginning of 2013 while investment in China did not keep up, leading to a widening gap between the value of investment in ASEAN and China. According to the same source, since 2006, Japanese ODI in China had been either on a par with or lagging behind ODI in ASEAN[17] but it dropped particularly sharply in 2013. This is a marked shift from 2011 and 2012 when Japanese direct investment in China totaled US$13 billion a year. A survey by Japan Bank of International Cooperation (2013) further confirms that Japanese firms no longer see China as the most promising location for outward direct investment. As a result, Japan and China may be said to be increasingly delinking. The slowdown in Japanese direct investment in China is also in line with Japan's decreasing involvement in China-centered regional production networks.

As explained by Nicolas and Thomsen (1999) however, FDI is not a zero-sum game with investors choosing one country at the expense of all others. This assertion certainly holds true in the case of Japanese firms. The rise in labor costs and the associated shift in China's economic strategy have not necessarily led foreign manufacturers to leave the country, but it has certainly induced them to contemplate other solutions. In order to avoid an excessive concentration of investment in China, Japanese firms, for instance, have been seeking to diversify away from China, and other ASEAN economies (such as Indonesia, Vietnam, or Myanmar) are increasingly perceived as alternative production locations. Following a China+1 strategy, Japanese firms in particular are investing in ASEAN so as to restrict their vulnerability to fluctuations in China's economic conditions.

The rise of ASEAN as an increasingly attractive market has also lured foreign (primarily Japanese but also Taiwanese and Chinese) manufacturers and may also account for their more active involvement in the region. In some sectors such as the automotive industry, several production centers are likely to emerge in ASEAN.

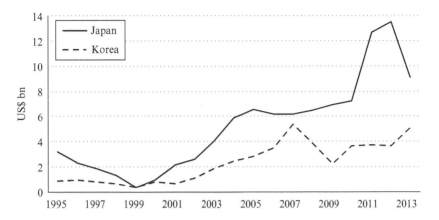

Source: JETRO and Korea Exim Bank.

Figure 3.10   Japanese and Korean direct investment in China (1995–2013)

Korean ODI in China

After reaching a peak in 2007, Korean investment in China sharply declined in the following years, shrinking by almost half in 2009. Since then, however, there have been signs of a recovery and Korean investment had returned to its 2006 level by 2010 and stayed at about this level over the two following years. Korean investment in China soared in 2013 to reach US$5.1 billion only to fall back to its 2010 level in 2014 (Korea Exim Bank).

Despite the recent upturn, Korean investment still lags behind Japanese investment in China in absolute terms. According to the Korea International Trade Association (KITA) (April 2014), while Japanese direct investment in China totaled about US$53 billion between 2004 and 2013, that of Korean firms amounted merely to US$36 billion over the same period of time (see Figure 3.10). However, this is easily explained by the differences in size between the two economies.

Like their Japanese counterparts, Korean firms are following a China+1 strategy, exemplified by Samsung's simultaneous investments in Vietnam and in Xian (Shaanxi Province), for instance.

Interestingly, Korea's investment pattern in China has diversified from its initial focus on low-tech, labor-intensive industries like textiles, toys, etc., to medium-to-high-tech capital-intensive industries like electronics, automobiles and shipbuilding. This sectoral pattern suggests that in the case of Korea the link between trade and investment is particularly tight.

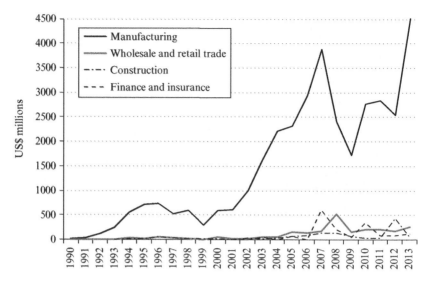

Source: Korea Exim Bank.

Figure 3.11   Korean direct investment in China

Lastly, although manufacturing still accounts for about 90 percent of total Korean FDI to China, investment in the less capital-intensive wholesale/retail sector has been on an upward trend since 2009 (see Figure 3.11).

On the latter point, however, Korean firms are lagging behind Japanese firms which increasingly target the distribution and service segments. Japan's investment in the latter two sectors accounted for 26 percent of the total, comparable to a mere 10.8 percent for Korea.

This distribution by sector is in line with Japanese and Korean firms' declared objectives. Increasingly, Japanese firms tend to view China primarily as a market rather than as a production base.[18] As already shown by Nakamura (2004), the growth pattern of Japanese-affiliated manufacturers in China has been transitioning to one characterized by increasing supply to the domestic Japanese and Chinese markets, from one led by promotion of third-country exports.

By contrast, Korean companies still primarily invest in China in order to take advantage of its cheap labor force so as to cut back on costs of production. This has raised concerns in Korea that Korean companies run the risk of being edged out by their Japanese rivals in the Chinese consumer market, hence the recent move to expand in distribution activities.

5. ASSESSMENT AND POLICY IMPLICATIONS

Korea has overtaken Japan as a source of imports for China, and its role is particularly big in the electronics sector. Unlike Japan, it has a surplus with China in both ordinary and processed trade. China and Korea's ordinary trade, however, is not as important in volume terms as processed trade, while the reverse is true between China and Japan. China's surplus in processed trade with Japan may be accounted for to some extent by the size of the Japanese market for processed exports but it is also the result of diverging strategies on the part of Japanese and Korean companies.

Over time, the composition of exports to China (or imports by China) has further widened, with Korea still very much involved in intermediate products and in processing exports, while Japan seems to be, to some extent, delinking from China.

As a result, there is a rising risk for Korean firms if they merely keep exporting communication equipment devices, electronic parts and computer hardware and technology. Efforts on China's side to move up the value chain and avoid staying trapped in low value-added manufacturing activities does not bode well for Korean firms operating in China. By contrast, Japan seems to be in a better position to take advantage of this change.

Recent data suggest that China indeed has been moving in the direction of more domestic value-added activities and fewer processing activities. While processing trade has traditionally been the main engine of growth in China, this is no longer the case (Lemoine et al., 2015). Korea is, in this respect, more at risk than Japan.

Trade policy has undoubtedly played a role in the way China has been connected to its two neighboring economies. After it joined the WTO in 2001, China sharply reduced its import tariffs on a wide range of goods but it maintained relatively high tariffs on consumption goods. China's tariff rates on intermediate goods and capital goods hover around 6 to 8 percent while those on consumption goods are about 14 percent and may reach 25 percent in the case of passenger cars for instance. As can be seen in Table 3.1, there are only marginal differences between the tariffs applied to Japanese and Korean goods.

Overall, China's trade policy so far has clearly facilitated the imports of intermediate goods, while it has discriminated against that of consumption goods. Moreover, industries involved in processing activities have benefited from preferential treatment. In the case of China, imported inputs are exempt from tariffs or may benefit from a duty drawback mechanism (Kuroiwa and Ozeki, 2010). Furthermore, more liberal policies are applied to the electronics sector. In particular, the WTO Information Technology Agreement (ITA) has reduced trade barriers and significantly facilitated

Table 3.1 Tariff rates effectively applied by China on different categories of goods*

	Japan	Korea
Semi-finished industrial products (22)		
1995	31.46 (n.a.)	33.42 (n.a.)
2000	14.23 (n.a.)	14.61 (n.a.)
2005	8.12 (8.25)	8.13 (8.24)
2010	7.91 (8.24)	7.69 (8.23)
2012	7.82 (8.16)	7.55 (8.13)
Capital goods (excluding transport equipment) (41)		
2000	14.73 (n.a.)	14.75 (n.a.)
2005	8.17 (8.22)	8.17 (8.30)
2010	8.06 (8.23)	7.81 (8.25)
2012	7.99 (8.21)	7.70 (8.22)
Parts and accessories of capital goods (excluding transport equipment) (42)		
1995	18.08 (n.a.)	18.28 (n.a.)
2000	9.99 (n.a.)	10.01 (n.a.)
2005	6.28 (6.31)	6.27 (6.33)
2010	6.04 (6.48)	5.79 (6.46)
2012	5.89 (6.30)	5.58 (6.22)
Passenger cars (51)		
2000	81.25 (n.a.)	88.57 (n.a.)
2005	29.38 (25.00)	29.38 (25.00)
2009	25.00 (25.00)	22.86 (25.00)
2012	25.00 (25.00)	22.50 (25.00)
Consumption goods (6)		
1995	60.77 (n.a.)	n.a. (n.a.)
2000	23.47 (n.a.)	23.50 (n.a.)
2005	14.27 (14.31)	13.31 (14.15)
2010	14.21 (14.72)	12.60 (14.71)
2012	14.00 (14.60)	12.24 (14.45)
Parts and accessories of transport equipment (53)		
2000	19.61 (n.a.)	21.07 (n.a.)
2005	10.81 (10.12)	11.58 (10.86)
2010	10.24 (10.60)	10.44 (11.18)
2012	10.32 (10.70)	9.79 (10.60)

Note: * The given values are average tariff rates for product categories in the BEC classification. Bound tariff rates are indicated between brackets.

Source: TRAINS database, UNCTAD, accessed on 13 June 2015.

trade in intermediate parts and components as well as final products. This explains the importance of such goods in China's trade patterns.

In this context the implementation of the recently signed China-Korea FTA is of great importance as it is likely to broaden the scope of bilateral trade and, in particular, to boost ordinary trade between the two countries (and, in particular, Korean ordinary exports to China). The snag is that a large number of products are excluded from the agreement as it is; in particular: steel, cars and auto parts. Expanding the coverage of tariff liberalization would be a positive development for Korea.

As for Japan, given the nature and pattern of its bilateral trade with China, the case for a bilateral FTA seems to be less compelling. However, from a strategic viewpoint, Japan cannot risk being sidelined by not participating in the general FTA frenzy which has been spreading throughout East Asia over the past few years. Moreover, it is worth emphasizing that FTAs are also usually instrumental in removing non-tariff barriers, further contributing to potentially expanding trade opportunities. As a result, the negotiation of a trilateral China-Japan-Korea FTA should still rank high on the priority list of the Japanese government despite the persistent tensions associated with territorial and historical issues.

The organization of regional production networks is very much in flux in East Asia as a result of China's changing economic strategy. The challenge for neighboring economies is to take the appropriate steps to adapt to these changes and make the best of them. Japan and Korea have apparently chosen different options and only time will tell which strategy was best.

ACKNOWLEDGMENTS

The author would like to thank Laure Vigneron, French Institute of International Relations (Ifri) Paris, for excellent research assistance.

NOTES

1. The Republic of Korea and China established diplomatic relations on 24 August 1992.
2. In 2013, China accounted for 26 percent of Korea's $560 billion in total exports, while the US share stood at 11 percent (down from around 40 percent in the 1980s), and Japan's share at 6.2 percent (down from a maximum of 26 percent in the late 1980s).
3. Based on IMF, *Direction of Trade Statistics*.
4. Depending on the data used, Japan has a surplus or a deficit with China. According to JETRO, Japan is in deficit and according to China's customs administration, it is in surplus.
5. The index is calculated as the sum of the squares of the product shares.

6. The decline in Greater China's importance to China is confirmed by Nicolas (2014).
7. According to Fung et al. (2013), this is just under the trade share of Greater China (Hong Kong, Macau and Taiwan), which accounted for 16.5 percent.
8. At the same time China does not import more final products from Hong Kong than expected.
9. The breakdown of exports to China by product category uses the Broad Economic Categories (BEC) classification. Following Gaulier et al. (2005) commodities are aggregated by stages of production and a distinction is made between: (1) *primary goods* [food and beverages, primary mainly for industry (111), primary industrial supplies (21), primary fuels and lubricants (31)]; (2) *intermediate goods* [processed industrial supplies (22), processed fuels and lubricants (32), parts and components of capital goods excluding transport equipment (42) and of transport equipment (53)]; and (3) *final goods* [capital goods (41), and consumption goods: food and beverages (112 and 122), passenger motor cars (51), consumer goods (61, 62, 63)].
10. With import-and-assembly processing trade (also referred to as processing with imported materials), the processing firm sources and pays for imported inputs, while in the case of pure-assembly processing trade (also known as processing with foreign client-supplied materials), the processing firm receives foreign inputs for free.
11. While ordinary imports accounted for 47 percent of China's total manufactured imports in 2007, their share rose to 60 percent in 2014 (Lemoine et al., 2015).
12. ASEAN4 refers to the four most advanced economies in the association, namely Indonesia, Malaysia, the Philippines and Thailand. ASEAN5 includes ASEAN4 + Singapore.
13. These imports account for close to 31 percent of China's total imports from East Asia in 2012, up from less than 17 percent in 2002.
14. Hong Kong, the United States and the EU are the top destinations of China's processed exports and run trade deficits with China.
15. This finding is confirmed by Lemoine et al. (2015).
16. As stressed by Thorbecke and Salike (2013), China's WTO accession increased investors' confidence that China would provide fair enforcement of the relevant laws and regulations and thus increased their willingness to invest in China.
17. With the exception of 2012 when Japan's FDI in China surpassed the value in ASEAN (US$10.7 billion), due primarily to the plunge in Japanese investment in Thailand, as the country was hit by massive flooding that caused severe disruption to its supply chains starting in the fall of 2011.
18. This was already the case in the late 1990s, when surveys of Japanese firms suggested that they invested in China primarily to supply goods or services to the local market (Nicolas and Thomsen, 1999, p. 23).

BIBLIOGRAPHY

Ando, Mitsuyo (2013), 'Development and Restructuring of Regional Production/ Distribution Networks in East Asia', *ERIA Discussion Paper Series*, 2013–33, November.

Ando, Mitsuyo and Fukunari Kimura (2008), 'Fragmentation in East Asia: Further Evidence', *mimeo*, January.

Athukorala, P.-C. (2008), 'China's Integration into Global Production Networks and its Implications for Export-led Growth Strategy in Other Countries in the Region', *Working Papers on Trade and Development*, 2008, Australian National University, April.

Chae, Wook and Pyeong-Seob Yang (2012), 'China, World Economy, and

China-Korea Economic Cooperation', Policy Analysis, No. 12-01, KIEP, December.

Chung, C. and H.J. Hyun (2009), 'Korea's Investment and Trade Outlook', *mimeo*, KIET.

Chung, Whan-Woo (2011), 'The Decrease in South Korea's Investment in China after the Global Financial Crisis', *POSRI Chindia Quarterly*, Summer, pp. 63–69.

Dean, Judith, K.C. Fung and Zhi Wang (2008), 'How Vertically-specialized is Chinese Trade', *BOFIT Discussion Papers*, Bank of Finland Institute for Economies in Transition, No. 31, December.

Fung, K.C., Hsiang-Chih Hwang, Francis Ng and Jesús Seade (2013), 'International Trade and Production Networks: Comparisons of China and Greater China versus India and South Asia', *Bofit Online*, No. 1, Bank of Finland.

Gaulier, Guillaume, Françoise Lemoine and Deniz Ünal-Kesenci (2005), 'China's Integration in East Asia: Production Sharing, FDI and High-Tech Trade', *CEPII Working Papers*, 2005-09, June.

Gaulier, Guillaume, Françoise Lemoine and Deniz Ünal-Kesenci (2011), 'China's Foreign Trade in the Perspective of a More Balanced Economic Growth', *CEPII Working Papers*, 2011-03, March.

Japan Bank of International Cooperation (JBIC) (2013), *Survey Report on Overseas Business Operations by Japanese Manufacturing Companies – Results of the JBIC FY2013 Survey*, November.

JETRO (2013), *JETRO Global Trade and Investment Report 2013 – Revitalizing Japan Through Global Business*, JETRO, Tokyo.

Kim, J.K., Y. Kim and C.H. Lee (2005), 'Trade, Investment and Economic Integration Between South Korea and China: A Step Toward East Asian Regionalism', *mimeo*.

Kimura, Fukunari et al. (2005), 'Fragmentation and Parts and Components Trade: A Comparison Between East Asia and Europe', *mimeo*, July.

Kuroiwa, Ikuo (2014), 'Value-added Trade and Structure of High Technology Exports in China', *IDE Discussion Papers*, No. 449, IDE-JETRO, March.

Kuroiwa, Ikuo and Hiromichi Ozeki (2010), 'Intra-regional Trade Between China, Japan and Korea: Before and After the Financial Crisis', *IDE Discussion Papers*, No. 237, IDE-JETRO, May.

Lee, Hyun-Hoon, Donghyun Park and Jing Wang (2011), 'The Role of the People's Republic of China in International Fragmentation and Production Networks: An Empirical Investigation', *ADB Working Paper Series on Regional Economic Integration*, No. 87, September.

Lemoine, Françoise et al. (2015), 'L'usine du monde au ralenti ou la mutation du commerce extérieur chinois', *Document de travail du CEPII*, March.

Li, Y., Q.L. Dai and Q.-B. Huang (2015), 'Analysis of the Influential Factors of Manufactured Products Intra-Industry Trade between China-South Korea and China Policy', *Theoretical Economics Letters*, **5**, 114–124. Available at: http://dx.doi.org/10.4236/tel.2015.51016.

Manova, Kalina and Zhihong Yu (2014), 'Firms and Credit Constraints Along the Global Value Chain: Processing Trade in China', *unpublished mimeo*, NBER.

Nakamura, Yoichi (2004), 'Decreasing Dependence of Japanese-affiliated Manufacturers in China on Third Countries', *JCER Researcher Report*, No. 47, November.

Nicolas, Françoise (2008), 'The Political Economy of Regional Integration in East Asia', *Economic Change and Restructuring*, **41** (4), 345–367.

Nicolas, Françoise (2014), 'Regional Integration within Greater China – State of Play and Future Prospects', in B. Andreosso-O'Callaghan, J. Jaussaud and B. Zolin (eds.), *Economic Integration in Asia – Towards the Delineation of a Sustainable Path*, Basingstoke: Palgrave Macmillan.

Nicolas, Françoise and Stephen Thomsen (1999), *Foreign Direct Investment and Recovery in Southeast Asia*, Paris: OECD.

Okubo, Toshihiro, Fukunari Kimura and Nozomu Teshima (2013), 'Asian Fragmentation in the Global Financial Crisis', *ERIA Discussion Paper Series*, 2013–38, December.

Rhee, Tae-Wan (2013), 'Reassessing Korea-China-Japan Trade Structure', *Korea Economic Trends*, SERI, October.

Shim, Sang-Hyung (2011), 'Rapidly Changing Division of Labor in East Asia', *POSRI Chindia Quarterly*, Autumn, pp. 17–23.

Song, Yoocheul (2008), 'The Structure of Trade between China and Korea', in David Daokui Li and Youngrok Cheong (eds.), *China and Korea in the World Economy: Common Opportunities and Challenges*, Seoul: KIEP.

Thorbecke, Willem (2014), 'Rebalancing Trade within East Asian Supply Chains', *RIETI Discussion Papers*, 14-E-002, January.

Thorbecke, Willem and Nimesh Salike (2013), 'Foreign Direct Investment in East Asia', *RIETI Policy Discussion Papers*, 13-P-003, March.

Wang, Zheng and Zhihong Yu (2012), 'Trading Partners, Traded Products, and Firm Performances of China's Exporters and Importers: Does Processing Trade Make a Difference?', *The World Economy*, 35 (12), 1795–1824.

Yang, Pyeong Seob et al. (2013), 'The Economic Integration of China, Taiwan and Hong Kong – Implications for Korea's Trade Policy', *World Economy*, 3 (39), KIEP.

Yu, Miaojie and Wei Tian (2012), 'China's Processing Trade: A Firm-level Analysis', in Huw McMay and Ligang Song (eds.), *Rebalancing and Sustaining Growth in China*, Canberra: Australian National University E-press, pp. 111–148.

Zhang, Jian (2010), 'Vigorous Waves of East Asia Economic Integration and the Sino-South Korea Trade Relationship', *mimeo*, Brookings Center for Northeast Asia Policy Studies, January.

4. Selected Asian countries and the food supply chain (between food security and food safety)

M. Bruna Zolin

1. INTRODUCTION

The world's population is suffering from a huge paradox: the coexistence of obesity and malnutrition. According to the World Health Organization (WHO, 2014), 39 per cent of adults aged 18+ were overweight (BMI[1] $\geq$25 kg/m^2) (39 per cent of men and 40 per cent of women) and 13 per cent were obese (BMI $\geq$30 kg/m^2) (11 per cent of men and 15 per cent of women) in 2014. Thus, nearly two billion adults worldwide are overweight and, of these, more than half a billion are obese. The prevalence of overweight and obese people was highest in the regions of the Americas (61 per cent overweight in both sexes, and 27 per cent obese) and lowest in the Southeast Asia region (22 per cent overweight in both sexes and 5 per cent obese). In the American, European and eastern Mediterranean regions over 50 per cent of women were overweight. In all three of these regions, roughly half of overweight women were obese (25 per cent in Europe, 24 per cent in the eastern Mediterranean and 30 per cent in the Americas). In the African, eastern Mediterranean and Southeast Asian regions, women had roughly double the obesity prevalence of men. On the other hand, about 805 million people (11.3 per cent of the world's population) were estimated to be chronically undernourished in 2012 (FAO, 2014b) with marked differences across regions. Sub-Saharan Africa has the highest prevalence of undernourishment, with only modest progress in recent years in alleviating this. Around one in four people in the region remains undernourished. Asia, the most populous region in the world, still has the highest number of undernourished people.

The issue of emerging Asia, where there has been a gradual increase in income per capita and in population, especially in those countries where rice is the most important food, food security and food safety can become an impediment to growth. With increasing urbanization, the need for processed foods has accentuated the importance of the food industry that is not always sufficiently widespread and efficiently managed. Against this background, the aim of this chapter is to describe the field of food and beverages in the selected Asian countries, comparing it, where appropriate, with the European field, and highlighting future trends. The chapter is divided into several sections. Starting with a brief description of the food supply chain in section 2, it goes on to analyse the dynamics of food supply in kilocalories per capita terms and describes the strong duality that exists within the sector in section 3. Section 4 describes in more detail the food sector in the selected Asian countries. Some synthetic considerations conclude the chapter.

2.   FOOD SUPPLY CHAIN: OVERVIEW

Many factors have influenced and are influencing the food supply chain in the world economy, but the food supply chain is a complex issue because it is composed of a diverse range of companies operating in different markets and selling varied food products to meet the tastes and demands of different customers. The food supply chain connects three economically important sectors: the agricultural sector, the food processing industry and the distribution sector (wholesale and retail). The food supply chain plays a substantial role in all countries of the world because it must satisfy the basic need of the population. Food needs and diets evolve over time, being influenced by many factors and complex interactions. Income levels and income distribution, prices, individual preferences, cultural traditions, as well as geographical, environmental, social and economic factors all interact in a complex manner to shape dietary consumption patterns. If food security[2] is the requirement to provide the amount of food needed to satisfy the food needs of the world population, food safety encompasses actions aimed at ensuring that all food is as safe as possible. Food safety policies and actions need to cover the entire food chain, from production to consumption. Thus, the sector can offer great opportunities to the food industry in terms of food value-added and differentiation, real or perceived, by consumers. Since the early 1990s, mainly population growth but also income growth and urbanization have driven the growth in demand for food in developing countries, but in parallel, a demand for products with higher quality at reasonable prices has been created. According to the UN Food and Agriculture Organization (FAO), with income growth, food demand has gradually shifted from a vegetable diet to a higher content of animal protein diet (FAO, 2012, 2015). Agribusiness companies, in this

Table 4.1   Per capita food supply

Country	Quantity (kcal/capita/day)			
	1996	2001	2006	2011
China	2703	2819	2883	3074
India	2343	2331	2331	2459
Indonesia	2548	2484	2484	2713
Japan	2963	2890	2777	2719
Malaysia	2924	2822	2816	2855
Philippines	2364	2374	2516	2608
Singapore	n.a.	n.a.	n.a.	n.a.
South Korea	3060	3080	3121	3329
Thailand	2563	2578	2795	2757
Vietnam	2018	2298	2482	2703
EU of which				
Germany	3297	3363	3463	3539
France	3519	3640	3513	3524
Italy	3558	3674	3610	3539
Spain	3360	3366	3278	3183

Source: FAO (2014a).

way, gained more power, increasing the value-added of processed food. Exporting companies in developing countries have also benefited from a global demand for exotic products from developed countries, which constitute a niche market with a rather inelastic demand curve, in respect of prices. The introduction of standardization for food products is growing in importance, changing the way the world trades, and is driven by consumers, more and more alert and aware, willing to buy, even at higher prices, products with specific properties or obtained with sustainable production processes. It is very difficult to assess the value generated by the food supply chain because food or drink may be considered at the same time as a commodity and as an ingredient (such as meal), and its value should be calculated at each stage of production and processing. However, some information is available to better understand the size and the relevance of the sector. As far as food quantity is concerned, the most widely used data on food supply and consumption is published by the FAO (FAO, 2014a). Food supply expressed in kilocalories (kcal) per capita per day is a key variable used for measuring the evolution of the global and regional food situation. Table 4.1 shows that food supply has been almost constant in European countries while it has been rising rapidly in some Asian countries.

From an economic and social point of view, according to the International Labour Organization of the United Nations (ILO, 2012), in 2008 the food and beverage (F&B) industry employed 22 million people in the world. Women represent 40 per cent of the total. In some sub-sectors such as fish processing and the processing of fruits and vegetables, women make up the majority of the workforce. The world food and beverage sector, which comprises farming, food production, distribution, retail and catering, has surpassed US$5.7 trillion since 2009. According to the Food and Beverage Industry Global Report (IMAP, 2010), Europe accounts for the largest share in the global F&B industry and Asia-Pacific is emerging as a major contributor of raw materials. China, Russia and India have increased their production capacities. During 2003–2007 China increased its wheat production capacity by 26 per cent, while Russia raised its capacity by 45 per cent. Over the same period, wheat production in the United States decreased by 12.5 per cent. In 2009, roughly 58 per cent of produced food was consumed by developing countries (the majority of the increase in global population from 6.6 billion in 2008 to 9 billion in 2050 is expected to come from developing countries) and it is expected the ratio will climb to 72 per cent by 2050 based on current population projections. Approximately 37 per cent of the world's population lives in China and India in 2015. Packaged food forms the majority of total food consumed, with developed countries (namely the United States, Japan and the EU) accounting for more than half of global sales of packaged products, while raw products, which need to be processed before becoming edible, account for a large proportion of retail sales in developing countries. However, with rising income levels, consumption in developing countries is also shifting towards packaged food products. The United States, Italy, Peru, Germany, Australia and India are some of the top countries exporting processed food and beverages. The United States, Germany, France, Australia and Switzerland are some of the leading exporters of food processing equipment. Saudi Arabia, Asia, Africa, Russia, China and South America are some of the leading countries and regions that import processed food and beverages. Moreover, in the EU in 2012, the food and beverage sector is, in terms of employment and turnover, the most important contributor to the manufacturing sector (European Commission, 2015).[3] Even in the United States, the industry is a crucial sector for the economy as it employs a large number of workers, about 1.5 million people (USDA, 2013). Lastly, the number of large retail stores, both in developed and in developing countries, has grown exponentially. With their global spread, they can promote products differentiated by their nature, origin and processes. Small to medium retail stores in local areas coexist with large companies, and, generally, offer local food based on seasonal production.

3. DUALISM IN THE F&B INDUSTRIAL SECTOR

A strong dualism characterizes the F&B sector. On the one hand, a few very large multinational companies, widely distributed in the world and with a strong bargaining power, are able to meet a significant percentage of the world's food needs. On the other hand, many small businesses operate locally with a geographically limited range of action. Oxfam's 'Behind the Brands' report estimated that worldwide in the food and drink sector, there are about 1.5 billion producers, of which no more than 500 companies control 70 per cent of food choices, satisfying the needs of about 7 billion people (Oxfam, 2013). Within these, a very small group plays an oligopolistic role. According to Oxfam the ten top F&B multinational companies are:

1. Associated British Food (ABF), a British multinational food processing and retailing company whose headquarters are in London. It is the world's second-largest producer of both sugar and baker's yeast and a major producer of other ingredients (emulsifiers, enzymes and lactose). The grocery division is a major manufacturer of both branded and private label grocery products. The key brands are Askeys, Billington's, Blue Dragon, Crusha, Jacksons of Piccadilly, Jordans, La Tisaniere and Patak's. In the future, it is going to expand sugar operations in Africa, bio-ethanol production in the United Kingdom and yeast/yeast extract production in China.
2. The Coca-Cola Company is one of the largest manufacturers and distributors of soft drinks and concentrate syrups worldwide, better known by the name of its original product, Coca-Cola. The headquarters is located in Atlanta (Georgia). The key brands are Powerade, Minute Maid, Coca-Cola, Fanta and Sprite. Future plans are to cater to the growing non-alcoholic, ready-to-drink and water markets.
3. Danone is a France-based food company that primarily produces fresh milk products, baby foods, biscuits, cereal products and medical nutrition products. It also co-produces bottled water (Evian). The key brands are Activia, Danette, Nutricia and Evian. Future plans are linked to concentration on the promotion of health through food products to as many people as possible.

4. General Mills is an American multinational manufacturer and marketer of branded consumer foods sold through retail stores. Its headquarters is in Minneapolis. The company markets many well-known North American brands. The main products sold are: bread, cereals, fruit snacks and ice cream. The key brands are Flavor Wave, Fruit Brute, General Mills, Frosted Cheerios, Cheddar Classics, Bake Shop and Better for Bread. Future plans are for the introduction of new products and extending existing brands to new markets.
5. Kellogg's is an American multinational food manufacturing company headquartered in Michigan. Kellogg's produces cereal and convenience foods, including cookies, crackers, toaster pastries, cereal bars, fruit-flavoured snacks, frozen waffles and vegetarian foods. Key brands are Kellogg's, Crunch, Murray, Honey Smacks, Fruit Harvest and Froot Loops. The future strategy is entry into the natural foods segment.
6. Mars is a US family-owned company in the chocolate and confectionery space. The headquarters is located in Virginia. It is known primarily for confectionery products, and its key brands include M&M's, Snickers, Orbit, Extra, Uncle Bens, Flavia, Galaxy, Milky Way and Twix.
7. Mondelez International (previously Kraft Foods) is a US multinational company operating in the food sector. The company is the brand owner of food and snacks which previously fell under the brand Kraft Foods (the corporation decided to keep the brand Kraft Foods for North America only). The key brands are: Easy Cheese, Pepito, Toasted Chips, Toblerone, Twist, Splendid, Jacob's and Honey Maid. The future strategy is to boost higher-quality organic revenue growth.
8. Nestlé, based in Switzerland, is a large multinational company operating in the nutrition, health and wellness sectors. Nine categories divide products: prepared dishes and cooking aids, beverages, confectionery, ice cream, water, pet care, milk products, nutrition and pharmaceuticals. The key brands are Nescafé, Maggi, Milo, Kit Kat, Gloria, Nestlé and Power Bar. For the future, it intends to increase its presence in the out-of-home market by doubling Nestlé Professional's sales over the next ten years and focusing on developing and emerging markets.
9. PepsiCo Incorporated (in short, Pepsi Company) is a US multinational active in the production, marketing and sale of a wide variety of drinks, both carbonated and non-carbonated, but also of food, such as snacks. The key brands are Pepsi, Diet Pepsi, Mirinda, Mountain Dew and Chips & Chunks. The future programmes are to expand businesses in key emerging markets.

10. Unilever is a British–Dutch multinational consumer goods company co-headquartered in the Netherlands and the United Kingdom. Products include food and beverages, cleaning agents and personal care products. Key brands are Lipton and Knorr. The future strategy is improved market development in developing and emerging markets.

Expanding the range of analysis to the top 50 companies in the food and beverage sector, according to IMAP (IMAP, 2010), businesses located in the United States and in Canada are the most numerous, followed by those in Europe and South America (Table 4.2). The Asian continent is in fourth place, achieved thanks to the high number of Japanese companies. In terms of market share, the Americas account for almost 50 per cent of the world total (Table 4.3).

In addition, the sector is involved in a large number of mergers and acquisitions. In terms of continents, first place, according to rankings compiled in 2009, is occupied (according to the number of transactions) by Europe and, in terms of value, by Asia. If the analysis is made comparing countries, the most active are the United States (in terms of number and value), followed by Brazil and Australia. Among the Asian countries, the Philippines occupies fourth place (Table 4.4).

Table 4.2   Top 50 global food and beverage companies per region (2010)

	Europe	US and Canada	South America	Asia	
				Total	Japan
Number	15	20	8	7	6
% of total	30	40	16	14	86*

Note: * Per cent of Asian total.

Source: IMAP (2010).

Table 4.3   Top 50 global food and beverages companies: market shares (per cent of total) (2010)

Europe	Americas	Canada	Asia	Oceania	Africa
22.2	46.7	5.5	19.4	2.4	3.9

Source: Author's elaboration on IMAP (2010).

Table 4.4   Transactions in the F&B sector in the top five countries and continents by value (2009)

Top 5 countries	Number of transactions	Value (USD mn)
United States	174	7475
Brazil	15	7089
Australia	29	6079
Philippines	6	4230
Belgium	13	3558
Top 5 continents	Number of transactions	Value (USD mn)
Asia	183	11127
Europe	520	9182
North America	197	8027
South America	34	7785
Oceania	44	6145

Source: Author's elaboration on IMAP (2010).

Table 4.5   Top ten grocery markets by value

2010			2014*		
Rank	Country	€ (billions)	Rank	Country	€ (billions)
1	US	638	1	China	761
2	China	529	2	US	745
3	Japan	345	3	India	448
4	India	279	4	Japan	360
5	France	205	5	Russia	322
6	Russia	186	6	Brazil	284
7	Brazil	185	7	France	228
8	UK	170	8	UK	198
9	Germany	160	9	Germany	168
10	Italy	130	10	Indonesia	167

Note: * 2014 is calculated using fixed exchange rates based on the average rates of 2009 from www.oanda.com.

Source: Author's elaboration on IMAP (2010).

In 2010, according to the classification of the top ten grocery markets by value (Table 4.5), China, Japan and India are respectively second, third and fourth. In 2014, China exceeded the United States and was ranked first. It is worth pointing out, again in 2014, the exit of Italy and the entry of Indonesia among the top ten grocery markets.

3.1 The EU

The prevalence of small businesses from agriculture to retail characterizes the European supply chain. The agricultural sector of the EU28, in 2010, is composed of about 12.2 million farms, involving a surface area of 174.1 million hectares[4] (approximately 40 per cent of the total EU). The average size of each agricultural holding (farm) is 14.2 hectares. There are substantial farm size differences across member states, regions and types of farming. A large number (6 million and half of all holdings) consists of very small farms (less than two hectares in size) that occupy a small proportion (2.5 per cent) of the total land area and a small number of holdings (2.7 per cent) of very large farms (more than 100 hectares) covers almost half (50.2 per cent) of the arable land in the EU28. Of the 12.2 million agricultural holdings in the EU28 in 2010, 5.5 million holdings (44.6 per cent) have a standard output less than EUR2000 per annum and contribute to forming only 1.4 per cent of total agricultural economic output. By contrast, the 1.9 per cent of holdings with an output higher than EUR250 000 accounted for almost one half (47.8 per cent) of all agricultural economic output (European Commission, 2013a). The sector is highly supported – the Common Agricultural Policy (CAP) is one of the oldest policies of the EU. The CAP has been modified on many occasions. The reforms gradually moved from a production-oriented policy to a market-oriented vision. In particular, the 2003 reform introduced the Single Payment Scheme (SPS) or the Single Farm Payment (SFP). The new scheme was introduced to change the way the EU supported its farming sector by removing the link between subsidies and production. This reform focused on consumers and taxpayers, while giving farmers the freedom to produce what the market wanted[5] (European Commission, 2013b). The food and drink industry sector is one of the largest and most important manufacturing sectors in Europe. In 2011 Europe's food market was made up of about 287 000 companies and 4.25 million employees (15 per cent of direct employment in the EU manufacturing sector). France, Italy, Spain and the United Kingdom accounted for 70 per cent of the turnover for the EU27, whereas the twelve new member states accounted for only 8.7 per cent. A large part of the food and drink companies are small and medium-sized enterprises (SMEs) (accounting for 49.3 per cent of the food and drink turnover and

Table 4.6   Number of SMEs and large companies by sub-sector (2011)

	SMEs (%)	Large companies (%)
Food and drink industry	99.1	0.9
Bakery and farinaceous products	99.6	0.4
Oils and fats	99.5	0.4
Grain mill and starch products	99.0	1.0
Beverages	98.8	1.2
Animal feeds	98.7	1.3
Meat products	98.6	1.4
Various food products	98.2	1.8
Processed fruit and vegetables	98.0	2.0
Fish products	97.9	2.1
Dairy products	97.7	2.3

Source: FoodDrinkEurope (2014).

63.4 per cent of food and drink employment). In the food and drink sector, SMEs and micro-enterprises comprise 99.1 per cent of European food and drink businesses (Table 4.6). These companies generate 48.1 per cent of food and drink turnover, and employ 61.6 per cent of the food and drink workforce. In contrast, large companies account for just 0.9 per cent of all food and drink enterprises in Europe but provide 51.6 per cent of the turnover and 53.5 per cent of the value-added and contribute 38.4 per cent of the employment (FoodDrinkEurope, 2014). Small-scale enterprises by their size prevent the acquisition of economies of scale and make them impermeable to the introduction of innovations and of new products. There are few European multinational companies competing worldwide with a wide variety of products. In total, research and innovation expenditure is only 0.53 per cent of food and drink industry turnover.

During 2005–2015 the European F&B industry has had relatively limited but stable growth in production and has maintained the characteristics of a non-cyclical and robust sector despite the economic crisis: production increased with 2.6 per cent growth between 2008 and 2011, compared to a 4.2 per cent decrease in the whole European manufacturing sector. However, labour productivity in the European food and drink industry is lower than in most other industries due to the high number of employees per company, the higher percentage of part-time employees and a generally lower percentage of employees with high-level skills (FoodDrinkEurope, 2014).

3.2   Asia

According to the Asian Development Bank (ADB, 2009), the agricultural sector is important for all Asian countries: on average, more than 60 per cent of the working population depends on agricultural activities. If the incidence of agriculture in GDP decreases, this affects a significant part of the population who live in rural areas and, therefore, depend directly or indirectly (for employment or income) on the agricultural sector. Poverty is concentrated in rural areas, the disparity between rural and urban areas is widespread and the importance of agriculture varies from region to region. In some areas, agriculture and rural development are not means for economic development, but their importance is in terms of food security. Over the years in Central Asia and East Asia the incidence of agriculture in gross domestic product (GDP) has decreased, even if a large percentage of workers are still employed in it. The main problem of the eastern Asian countries is land scarcity that drives some countries to land procurement (purchases or rentals) in other parts of the world. Also in Southeast Asia, the importance of the agricultural sector is shrinking, but to meet additional food requirements natural resources (land and water) have been hyper-exploited. As in Central and East Asia, agriculture in Southeast Asia is important as a source of employment. In this region, however, the share in the GDP contribution of the agricultural sector decreases more slowly. Generally speaking, agriculture is important for Asia to achieve food security and maintain employment. The systems of production and innovation and types of crops cultivated, however, vary from region to region, as well as the public support systems. The impact of climate change, finally, could in future erode productivity and, as a consequence, the ability to achieve food security. This vulnerability is especially feared in respect of rice and wheat, which are staple foodstuffs for the population (FAO, 2015). With a growing population, an increasingly accentuated price volatility of agricultural commodities and the unpredictable effects of climate change, the Asian continent has to face a number of challenges. In the 1970s, many Asian countries, thanks to the green revolution, became self-sufficient, but recent agricultural investments have tended to decrease or remain constant (Carrasco and Mukhopadhyay, 2012). By contrast, Asia is also the continent where biotech crops are very common (ADB, 2013) and this contributes to the global emissions from agriculture of 37 per cent of total global emissions (including 18 per cent of the total emissions from China).

4. FOOD SECTOR IN SELECTED ASIAN COUNTRIES

Asia is an immense continent with a population of more than four billion people (2011) and a surface area of 32 million km^2 incorporating conditions varying from moist tropical to arid and semi-arid desert. As would be expected by this geography, the human and social dimensions of the Asian continent are equally diverse (World Bank, 2015). As regard to agriculture, as shown in Table 4.7, agricultural land is 53.7 per cent and arable land 16.3 per cent of the total area.[6] The Asian continent has a shortage, compared to population, in available land (values always lower than the world average figure) and water resources. In some of the selected Asian countries, namely Singapore, Taiwan, Korea, India and Japan, this particular deficiency is pronounced, while a better situation characterizes, in relative terms, Malaysia, Indonesia and China. A dramatic shortage is noted in water resources (Table 4.7) and this is a common denominator in all the selected Asian countries.

Permanent crops per capita are higher than the world average in Malaysia and, if permanent crops are calculated as a percentage of agricultural land, Malaysia is followed by the Philippines, Indonesia and Vietnam. Values per capita in respect of meadows and pastures are generally very low, except for China. The other selected countries are far below the Asian and the world averages (Table 4.8).

With regard to the industrial and retail F&B sector, the situation is extremely diversified and varies from country to country. Regional growth projections principally reflect the evolution of demand. According to the International Monetary Fund (IMF, 2015) in 2013, China is the second largest economy in the world. The same source forecasts that by 2018 China will be the world's largest economy measured in GDP. The population is increasing at a lower rate compared to the last two decades, with a fertility rate of 1.8 per female, which is lower than the replacement rate. China is facing increased urbanization; about 51.3 per cent of the population lives in urban areas and according to expectations by 2030 more than 70 per cent will be urbanized. According to Euromonitor International (2014a), in 2030 the population of China will reach 1.4 billion, an increase of 4.7 per cent from 2012. Falling birth rates and increasing life expectancy mean that the population is ageing rapidly. In 2030, the median age will be 47.1 years and China will have the largest number of people over 65 years in the world. Imbalances between the sexes will continue, with men aged 0–20 years accounting for 55.0 per cent of all 0–20 year olds in 2030, compared to 54.8 per cent in 2012. The demographic trend will have strong consequences on food needs and socio-economic aspects of life. To improve the

Table 4.7   Land use in Asia and in some selected Asian countries

	Land area/1000 population km² (2011)	Water surface/1000 population km² (2011)	Agricultural land/1000 population km² (2007)	Agricultural land (percentage of land area) (2007)	Arable land/1000 population km² (2007)	Arable land (percentage of land area) (2007)	Arable land (percentage of agricultural land) (2007)
Asia	7.4	0.2	4.0	53.7	1.2	16.3	30.4
China	7.0	0.2	4.1	59.3	1.1	15.1	25.4
India	2.8	0.3	1.5	60.5	1.3	53.4	88.2
Indonesia	7.4	0.4	2.0	26.8	0.9	12.1	45.5
Japan	2.9	0.1	0.4	12.8	0.3	11.9	93.0
Malaysia	11.4	0.0	2.7	24.0	0.6	5.5	22.9
Philippines	2.9	0.0	1.1	38.6	0.5	17.1	44.3
Singapore	0.1	0.0	0.0	1.1	0.0	0.9	75.0
Korea	2.0	0.1	0.4	19.0	0.3	16.5	86.8
Taiwan	1.4	0.2	0.4	27.2	0.3	24.1	79.6
Thailand	7.7	0.0	3.0	38.7	2.3	29.8	77.0
Vietnam	3.4	0.2	1.1	20.5	0.7	20.5	63.0
World	18.8	0.9	7.1	37.9	2.0	10.9	28.6

Source: Worldstat (2015).

Table 4.8 *Permanent crops and permanent meadows and pastures in Asia and selected Asian countries (2007)*

	Permanent crops/1000 population km²	Permanent crops (percentage of agricultural land)	Permanent meadows and pastures/1000 population km²	Permanent meadows and pastures (percentage of agricultural land)
Asia	0.2	4.1	2.6	65.5
China	0.1	2.2	3.0	72.4
India	0.1	6.0	0.1	5.8
Indonesia	0.6	32.0	0.4	22.7
Japan	0.0	7.0	0.0	0.0
Malaysia	2.0	73.5	0.1	3.6
Philippines	0.5	42.6	0.1	13.3
Singapore	0.0	25.0	0.0	0.0
Korea	0.0	10.1	0.0	3.2
Taiwan	0.0	3.6	0.1	5.1
Thailand	0.6	19.0	0.1	4.1
Vietnam	0.3	30.6	0.1	6.4
World	0.2	2.9	4.9	68.5

Source: Worldstat (2015).

quality of life, the demand for food will increase and this will be met by increasing imports. In this way, China attracts an increasing number of foreign businesses and to this end a number of bilateral agreements with neighbouring countries have been signed. The competition for the conquest of the Chinese market occurs mainly in two directions: commodity-type products (such as frozen meat, poultry meat, fish, fresh fruit) and Western-style niche products (olive oil, pasta, tomato sauce, wine). Export competition takes place among the Pacific countries (including New Zealand and Australia) for commodity-type products. For Western-style foods, the competition is more global. The trend of food consumption, however, is differentiated according to geographical location. In eastern China the demand is for healthy products and is very close to the Western style (in Shanghai, especially). Mid-China is more conservative and shows little interest in imported products. In the Chinese north and northeast, consumers demand high-quality products and proper packaging and food is perceived as wellness (products containing information on ingredients, expiration date, origin of raw materials and so on are preferred). The southwest is influenced by its geographical location, close to the sea, and consumers demand packaged dry or fresh fish and ice cream. Internet retailing is expanding from books to food and from electronics to cosmetics. Even conventional retailers are acquiring online shopping tools and the industry is expecting increased demand. The consumption of food outside the home is growing, thereby increasing demand for food with high value-added. Food consumption patterns are becoming more flexible and informal primarily among young and high-income urban consumers. For many Chinese, dinner outside the home has become a way of establishing and strengthening relationships both professional and personal. Restaurants offering imported products of high quality, a friendly environment and fast service are particularly attractive. Multinational companies operating in China have changed the flavour of food by introducing Chinese and Asian flavours and menus aimed at meeting the diverse local demands. The Chinese food industry showed significant changes in 2011–2012. Even though the food industry had achieved record sales, at the end of 2012 a slowdown occurred. In addition, the increasingly frequent incidents of adulteration have undermined consumer confidence. From 2012, the reduction in the growth rate is the result of the combined action of several factors: higher cost of ingredients, increased labour costs and production costs, higher costs of entry for new businesses, and financial problems for small companies. In response to these trends, many food companies have adopted new strategies such as product innovations inspired by Western styles, processes and business organization innovations.

The Indian population in 2013 was about 1252 billion (World Bank, 2014). India has one of the youngest populations globally, with the country's average age being just under 29 years in 2014. A growing number of these young Indians have higher disposable incomes compared to their older counterparts. They also have a lower propensity to save (Euromonitor International, 2014b). Unlike China, the Indian fertility rate is higher than that of the replacement rate. As an emerging country, India is a very interesting place in terms of food consumption. Whilst staples such as dairy, baked goods, and oils and fats account for the largest proportion of packaged food sales in India, the bulk of the growth is set to come from impulse/indulgence products such as confectionery, ice cream, and sweet and savoury snacks. These products are growing very quickly in India. To protect domestic production, the Indian government has placed high tariffs and bans on imported products. However, rising incomes, increased urbanization and the availability of cheap credit presage a market in continuous and rapid expansion. India is a major producer of agricultural products and a net exporter of food. India is one of the world's largest producers of fruits, vegetables, cereals and milk. Domestic production takes advantage of low labour costs, ease of access to raw materials and the high level of protection provided by tariffs and duties imposed on imported products. Multinational companies have opted for investment and production in India rather than export to India. As a result, a significant number of international companies develop products in India and these are marketed as Indian products. The restaurant sector in India is not yet fully developed. Young Indians tend more frequently to have meals outside the home, going against the prejudice of adult classes against foreign and international food. The Indian food industry continues to expand in response to demographic changes. It is, however, a small expansion in percentage terms. Only a small portion of agricultural products is processed. The problem relates to Indian food losses due to lack of infrastructure such as storage facilities and transport.

Indonesia, a food importing country, is the fourth most populous country in the world with 249.9 million inhabitants in 2014, according to the World Bank (2015). The population is ageing rapidly and the number of those aged 50+ will increase by 84 per cent between 2012–2030, according to Euromonitor estimates (Euromonitor International, 2013a), while the number of children aged 0–9 years will decline by 14.6 per cent. In 2030, Jakarta, the capital, will continue to dominate the urban landscape with a population of 13.7 million. According to forecasts, by 2030 the middle classes will be 80 per cent of the population (Euromonitor International, 2013a). Indonesia is the most stable democracy in Southeast Asia. Despite the extremely positive trend of the Indonesian economy, a significant part of the population is low-income, infrastructure is poorly developed and imports are subject to complex rules. This means that any foreign company needs a local agent. Labels, written in Indonesian, must be attached to products before entering the Indonesian market. The prices of imported products are generally higher than those domestically produced. Hypermarkets, supermarkets and minimarkets are growing and are in direct competition with local sellers for price, cleanliness, comfort and health standards. The Western style is common in large cities, but variety is limited. Restaurants which offer noodles, pizza and Japanese food, as well as bakeries and cafes, are the main outlet of the Western-style food supply and depend on imports. Indonesian ties with Europe are strong and they influence domestic consumer preferences.

Japan will be in the midst of a demographic crisis between 2012–2030 as it is experiencing depopulation and ageing. According to Euromonitor International (2013b), in 2030 nearly one-third of the population will be aged 65+ and the median age of the population will continue to be the highest in the world. Net migration, although positive, will not be able to mitigate the effects of ageing or depopulation. The (albeit weak) GDP growth in real terms of the Japanese economy in recent years has been driven by consumption, especially public expenditure. Investments, by contrast, have played a marginal role and energy concerns accentuated after the disaster of Fukushima led to a slowdown in the growth rate. The population is decreasing and the average age is higher compared with that recorded by other Asian countries. Japan is a net importer of agricultural products and food, due to limited arable land (Table 4.7). The demand for products with high value-added is growing and this makes the market attractive to multinationals. Generally, the Japanese consumer is willing to pay a higher price for a higher-quality product, but the reducing rate of growth has brought greater attention to prices, compared to the past. As previously mentioned, the Japanese market is a saturated market and thus some supermarkets have closed and, to face the new challenge based on pricing, the distribution system has been focusing on controlling costs and improving efficiency. An important part of food expenditure is for meals away from home. Dinners outside the home are part of Japanese culture: one food category which continues to post growth rates is meals sold in retail stores. Young and old single professionals influence the trend of meals away from home. While older people buy ready-to-eat meals in the local 'conbini' (local convenience store), young professionals, by contrast, prefer Western-style restaurants. The key drivers of the food processing sector are more women in the workforce, an ageing population and health conscious consumers (OECD, 2001). Thus, the Japanese food processing industry remains a vibrant market. The food processing industry is rather concentrated in Japan. A total of 15 companies have a market share of around 50 per cent of sales. The United States is the largest exporter of agricultural products to Japan. The greatest agricultural competitor to the United States is China, whose exports are growing.

According to Euromonitor International (2014c), the population of Malaysia will reach 36.0 million in 2030, an increase of 22.6 per cent from 2012. Population growth has been slowing since the 1980s and this trend will continue between 2012–2030 due to a fall in fertility rates and in lower flows of net immigration. Despite the rapid growth of the 60+ age group between 2012–2030, the population will remain relatively young with three-quarters of the population aged under 50 by 2030. Malaysia is a politically and economically stable country, open to trade and with good transport and communications systems. Infrastructure is generally modern and efficient. In Southeast Asia it is the most developed country, with 61 per cent of the population falling into the medium-high income category. Even if Malaysia is a net importer of food, the food supply sector is well developed and sophisticated, thanks to domestic production and imports. Even with high productivity, Malaysia still only produces 80 per cent of what it needs to support itself and thus must import the rest, while food demand continues to grow due to improved incomes. China is the largest exporter of food to Malaysia, followed by India and New Zealand. A total of 60 per cent of the population are Muslims, therefore only halal meat can enter the country. Further, before being sold, imported products must be approved by the Malaysian Islamic Development Department. The Islamic food certification involves meat and other products, such as snacks, confectionery, dairy foods, bakery products, and so on. The government of Malaysia has identified the processed food sector as one of the strategic sectors. Despite being an importing country there are approximately 3200 Malaysian companies operating in the food industry, with a turnover of about 10 per cent for manufacturing as a whole. The main exported products (to more than 200 countries) are cocoa and processed cocoa, vegetable margarines and vegetable preparations. Operating in Malaysia are not only local companies but also large multinationals such as Nestlé, Unilever and Campbell's. Hypermarkets are the retail formula most prevalent in urban areas, while the traditional markets are losing ground; however, small shops selling fresh fruit and vegetables are still widespread.

By 2030, the population of the Philippines will reach nearly 128 million, an increase of 32.1 per cent from 2012. Population growth will be driven by increases in all age groups with a particularly fast growth in the 60+ age groups. However, according to forecasts (Euromonitor International, 2013c) the Philippines will remain an overwhelmingly young country by 2030, with 71.4 per cent of the population aged 40 years or under. The urban population will overtake the rural population for the first time in 2016 and will comprise, by 2030, 56.3 per cent of the population. The economy of the Philippines is growing as a result of domestic demand and the efforts of rebuilding after Typhoon Haiyan in 2013. The United States is the largest exporter of agricultural products, especially processed food. Recently, other actors such as New Zealand, Australia, the EU, Canada and ASEAN countries have entered the market. It should be noted that China has obtained through aggressive marketing significant segments of the import market, especially for fresh fruit and dry goods. There are approximately 11 000 businesses operating in the food sector, with an extremely varied range of products. These companies depend on imported ingredients from abroad. Despite the prevalence, in the sector, of multinational companies, local businesses are family owned and hold a significant portion of the market. The processed food sector is the largest sector of the economy of the Philippines with a turnover of about 40 per cent of the total manufacturing sector and a contribution to GDP of around 20 per cent. The retail sector, dominated by multinationals, is undergoing modernization and expansion.

By 2030 the population of Singapore is expected to reach 6.9 million, an increase of 30.8 per cent from 2012: net migration will account for over three-quarters of this growth. The number of live births will increase because of rising fertility, while the number of deaths will rise due to increases in older population groups. Singapore is a city-state and had the fourth highest population density in the world in 2012 at 7589 persons per square kilometre (Euromonitor International, 2013d). Singapore is one of the most open and competitive markets in the world. The economy depends on exports especially in the services sector. Its high per capita income places Singapore as Asia's richest nation. Its geographical position ensures its central distribution role (by sea, land and air) of products for the major regions of Southeast Asia and the Indian sub-continent. It is a food importing country and the demand for food must meet both the local population's and the foreign population's (generally tourism) food needs. The food industry of Singapore is extremely limited, because the country does not produce agricultural raw materials and all ingredients have to be imported. According to the statistics of the government of Singapore (Department of Statistics of Singapore, 2015) there are about 300 companies operating in the agro-food sector, all of which range from small to medium in size. Imported food origins vary from product to product: dairy products come mainly from Australia, cereals from China, and fruit and fruit processing from the United States.

South Korea is known for its population density, which is more than ten times the global average. Due to rapid migration from rural areas as a result of the quick economic expansion since the 1970s, South Korea is now Asia's fourth largest economy. The population is now being shaped by international immigration. This trend of net entry reverses over 40 years of emigration (World Population Review, 2015). The population of Korea is gradually ageing and one-child families are increasing. To limit concerns on public expenditure to support the retirement of older people, the entry of women into the working world is being facilitated. Korean food consumption patterns reflect its demographic changes, its increasing urbanization and the adoption of new technologies (namely online shopping). Korea is a food importing country and the government protects local food industries and farmers by imposing constraints on food imports such as high tariffs, quotas and high phytosanitary standards. But, in order to reduce barriers to imports to ensure food security, many regional free trade agreements have been signed (Zolin and Andreosso-O'Callaghan, 2013). Large-scale stores dominate small retail stores. Some social initiatives are pressing the government to introduce limits to the expansion of large-scale stores in order to protect jobs and enable small businesses to survive.

Taiwan's population of about 23 million in 2014 (World Bank, 2015) is showing a fast and progressive ageing trend reflecting low fertility rates. Despite being an economic power, domestic agricultural production is limited. As a result, imports of food and agricultural products increase annually. The globalization of markets and the growing consumer demand for new and different varieties makes Taiwan extremely attractive for food and raw materials' exporters of agricultural origin. Food is sold mainly in convenience stores (Taiwan has the highest density of convenience stores in the world), although hypermarkets and supermarkets count for a good share of the consumer market. Western foodstuffs are popular; in particular, Italian foodstuffs. Increased tourism has driven the growth of restaurants and hotels. Processed food increases can also be attributed to rises in average per capita income, women's entry into the workplace, small families (single child), and the development of online shopping. The food processing industry has benefited from the market opening up. At the same time, imported finished food products have been taking an increased market share from domestically produced products and this trend is expected to continue.

The Thai food processing industry has benefited from the opening up of food markets, but import duties are very high even for products that are not competitive with domestic products. Many multinational companies prefer to produce locally, or in neighbouring countries with which Thailand has signed free trade agreements rather than import. The problem with the Thai economy is the shortage of labour, which is resolved by immigration of workers from Burma. If these workers should ever return to Burma, the problem of labour non-availability would significantly affect the industry. The demand for packaged food is growing and Thailand is, from this point of view, the most interesting market in the Asia-Pacific region. This growth has attracted foreign investors, especially Europeans. The food service sector is driven by tourism. Sidewalk restaurants are gradually being replaced by food centres and food courts, which are more hygienic and convenient. The food processing industry is one of the most developed in Southeast Asia and Thailand is one of the largest manufacturers of a wide variety of agricultural commodities such as rice, rubber, cassava, sugar, seafood, processed fruits and vegetables. Company sizes range from small to medium to large. SMEs are oriented to the domestic market, while the medium-sized enterprises also produce, generally, high-value-added products destined for both the domestic market and export. About 50 per cent of domestic production is exported.

A young population, growing middle-class incomes and high labour participation by women drive the trend of consumption in Vietnam. Despite positive demographic trends, the fertility rate is decreasing and has fallen to a level below replacement level and below the Asian average. There is also a movement of population from rural to urban areas. These factors help to shape the demand for food, especially ready-to-eat meals. The packaged food sector has experienced and is experiencing high growth rates. Even if traditional fresh food markets and small independent shops catering to high-frequency food purchases dominate the retail market, hypermarkets and supermarkets are widespread in urban areas. Local importers continue to play a decisive role in the introduction and marketing of imported food products. The food service sector is affected not only by the dynamics of income and population growth, but also by tourist flows, with the diffusion of Western consumption patterns. Competition among local companies has intensified with the entry of multinationals and some local operators are diversifying their production by following a strategy of Westernization. With regulations that are more transparent, the Vietnamese government has managed to attract foreign investment and to intensify internal investments. The government also protects local production by imposing higher customs rates on imports the greater the competition between imports and domestic products.

5. CONCLUDING REMARKS

What emerges from the analysis is that in the long term an impressive number of factors will affect Asian food supply and demand. In Asian countries, food demand is generally expected to increase, with the exception of some developed countries (Japan), because of demographic changes. The increasing population pushing up food requirements in some regions could aggravate the risks of food shortages. Economic growth, rising incomes and urbanization may also contribute to the expected surge in food demand, not least via rapid changes in diets in favour of more grain-intensive foods such as meat, and in particular red meat. In respect of population forecasts, a variety of factors, including enhanced family planning and reduction of poverty, could lead to lower demographic growth, and thus to a lower increase in food demand. However, for a given level of national income, a more uneven income distribution among the population might also weaken food demand. This could be the case of China where, in 2012, for the first time, China's urban population surpassed that of rural areas (World Bank, 2015). Moreover, the evolution of consumer tastes and diets may gain in importance at the expense of the traditional determinants of demand. For instance, growing safety and ecological concerns may lead to a sustained demand for products with certain organic attributes ('semi-organic' produce). In the developed countries, like in European countries, or Japan, on the other hand, per capita food demand could gradually level off, and consumption is likely to change much more in composition and quality than in volume over the next two decades. On the supply side, the availability of land, water and other natural resources emerges as a matter of major concern. Water resources, which have been affected by intensive use of fertilizers and pesticides and by excessive pumping, are becoming scarce in many parts of the world, inhibiting the development of irrigation. In relation to land, it is generally acknowledged that the net expansion of cultivated areas will be modest in the future, not least due to urbanization and the need to preserve forests. Climate change effects emphasize that the risk of land losses due to erosion, salinization, water logging or contamination may actually outweigh new lands brought into cultivation. Another major source of uncertainty is the evolution of productivity that still offers the potential for major improvements in food production, most notably in developing Asian countries. It is generally agreed that food supply will be highly responsive to price signals in the two next decades. An increase in world prices would trigger intensification in production and the use of reserves of land, but local imbalances cannot be excluded. For some less developed Asian countries and transition economies, the necessary market infrastructure (transport, processing, marketing and storage) is still poorly developed. Constraints on natural resources could limit the agricultural capacity of specific countries where demand is expected to surge, thus increasing their net imports. Some analysts, for instance, underline the risk of agricultural supply in China being handicapped by substantial land losses due, in particular, to urbanization, and a weakening of productivity gains linked to insufficient investment in agricultural research. The Asian continent is facing some pressure on resources in respect of its food needs, and the main challenges are related to:

1. ensuring the matching of supply and demand for food without compromising resources for future generations;
2. reducing poverty and vulnerability of the poorer part of the population, protecting against price fluctuations and providing adequate social security;
3. improving the food chain, aiming at providing sufficient and safe food;
4. creating a system and tools of risk management in terms of food safety and food reserve stocks for emergencies including natural and technological disasters.

According to the Asian Development Bank (2013), the Asian continent, in relation to food security and food safety, has two faces. Economic growth continues to influence the demand for more protein-rich food and better nutrition. Calories per capita per day on average have increased, but a significant share of the population lives in poverty and suffers from undernourishment.

NOTES

1. BMI (Body Mass Index) is the calculation of the ratio between weight and height, usually used as a simple tool to estimate fatness.
2. The World Food Summit of 1996 defined food security as existing 'when all people at all times have access to sufficient, safe, nutritious food to maintain a healthy and active life'. Commonly, the concept of food security includes both physical and economic access to food that meets people's dietary needs as well as their food preferences. In many countries, health problems related to dietary excess are an ever increasing threat. In fact, malnutrition and food-borne diarrhoea are becoming double burdens. Food security is built on three pillars: food availability – sufficient quantities of food available on a consistent basis; food access – having sufficient resources to obtain appropriate foods for a nutritious diet; and food use – appropriate use based on knowledge of basic nutrition and care, as well as adequate water and sanitation (FAO, 1996, p. 4).
3. With more than four million persons employed and an annual turnover in excess of EUR 900 billion.
4. In terms of utilized agricultural area.
5. In the reforms made in 2013 for the period 2014 to 2020, each country can choose if the payment is established at the farm level or at the regional level. Farmers receiving the SFP have the flexibility to produce any commodity on their land except fruit, vegetables and table potatoes, but they have to keep their land in good agricultural and environmental condition (cross-compliance). If farmers do not respect these standards, their payment will be reduced.
6. The FAOSTAT glossary defines agricultural land or agricultural area as the total of: arable land (describing land producing crops requiring annual replanting or fallow land or pasture used for such crops within any five-year period), permanent cropland (land producing crops which do not require annual replanting) and permanent pasture (natural or artificial grassland able to be used for grazing livestock). Permanent cropland includes forested plantations used to harvest coffee, rubber or fruit but not tree farms or proper forests used for wood or timber (FAOSTAT, 2014).

REFERENCES

Asian Development Bank (ADB) (2013), 'Food Security in Asia and the Pacific', Manila: Asian Development Bank.

Asian Development Bank–International Food Policy Research Institute (2009), 'Building Climate Resilience in the Agriculture Sector in Asia and the Pacific', Manila: Asian Development Bank.

Carrasco, B. and Mukhopadhyay, H. (2012), 'Food Price Escalation in South Asia: A Serious and Growing Concern', ADB Working Paper Series No. 10, February.

Department of Statistics of Singapore (2015), 'Latest Key Indicators', available at http://www.singstat.gov.sg/.

Euromonitor International (2013a), 'Indonesia in 2030: The Future Demographic', available at http://www.euromonitor.com/indonesia-in-2030-the-future-demographic/report.

Euromonitor International (2013b), 'Japan in 2030: The Future Demographic', available at http://www.euromonitor.com/japan-in-2030-the-future-demographic/report.

Euromonitor International (2013c), 'Philippines in 2030: The Future Demographic', available at http://www.euromonitor.com/philippines-in-2030-the-future-demographic/report.

Euromonitor International (2013d), 'Singapore in 2030: The Future Demographic', available at http://www.euromonitor.com/singapore-in-2030-the-future-demo graphic/report.

Euromonitor International (2014a), 'China in 2030: The Future Demographic', available at http://www.euromonitor.com/china-in-2030-the-future-demographic/ report.

Euromonitor International (2014b), 'Food Trends in India: What Makes the Indian Market so Different?', October, available at http://www.euromonitor. com/food-trends-in-india-what-makes-the-indian-market-so-different-/report.

Euromonitor International (2014c), 'Malaysia in 2030: The Future Demographic', available at http://www.euromonitor.com/malaysia-in-2030-the-future-demo graphic/report.

European Commission (2013a), 'Structure and Dynamics of EU Farms: Changes, Trends and Policy Relevance', EU Agricultural Economics Briefs, No. 9, October.

European Commission, Directorate General for Agriculture and Rural Development (2013b), 'Agriculture in the European Union: Statistical and Economic Information', available at http://ec.europa.eu/agriculture/statistics/ agricultural/2013/index_en.htm.

European Commission, Enterprise and Industry (2015), 'Raising the Bar for Europe's Food Industry', available at http://ec.europa.eu/growth/sectors/food/.

FAO (1996), 'World Food Summit', 13–17 November 1996, Rome, available at http://www.fao.org/docrep/003/w3613e/w3613e00.htm.

FAO (2012), 'The State of Food Insecurity in the World', Food and Agriculture Organization of the United Nations, Rome, available at http://www.fao.org/ docrep/016/i3027e/i3027e.pdf.

FAO (2014a), 'Country Profile', available at http://www.fao.org/countryprofiles/ en/.

FAO (2014b), 'The State of Food Insecurity in the World', Food and Agriculture Organization of the United Nations, Rome, available at http://www.fao.org/3/a-- i4030e.pdf.

FAO (2015), 'The State of Food Insecurity in the World', Food and Agriculture Organization of the United Nations, Rome, available at http://www.fao.org/3/ a4ef2d16-70a7-460a-a9ac-2a65a533269a/i4646e.pdf.

FAOSTAT (2014), available at http://faostat.fao.org/site/375/default.aspx.

FoodDrinkEurope (2014), 'Data & Trends of the European Food and Drink Industry 2013–2014', Brussels, available at http://www.fooddrinkeurope.eu/S=0/ publication/data-trends-of-the-european-food-and-drink-industry-2013-2014/ http://www.fooddrinkeurope.eu/uploads/publications_documents/Data__ Trends_%28interactive%29.pdf.

ILO (2012), 'Food, Drink and Tobacco Industry Driving Rural Employment and Development', available at http://www.ilo.org/wcmsp5/groups/public/---ed_ dialogue/---sector/documents/publication/wcms_160872.pdf.

IMAP (2010), 'Food and Beverage Industry Global Report', available at http:// www.imap.com/imap/media/resources/IMAP_Food__Beverage_Report_WEB_ AD6498A02CAF4.pdf.

IMF (2015), 'World Economic Outlook – Uneven Growth: Short- and Long-Term Factors', April, Washington DC, available at http://www.imf.org/external/pubs/ ft/weo/2015/01/pdf/text.pdf.

OECD (2001), 'Working Party on National Environmental Policy. Sustainable

Consumption, Sector Case Study Series – Household Food Consumption Trends, Environmental Impacts and Policy Responses', Environment Directorate, 14 December, available at http://www.oecd.org/officialdocuments/publicdisplaydocumentpdf/?cote=ENV/EPOC/WPNEP%282001%2913/FINAL&docLanguage=En.

Oxfam (2013), 'Behind the Brands – Food Justice and the "Big 10" Food and Beverage Companies', 26 February, Oxfam Briefing Paper No. 166, available at http://www.oxfam.de/sites/www.oxfam.de/files/studie_behind_the_brands_260213.pdf.

USDA (2013), 'Chart: Food Manufacturing Accounts for 14 Percent of all U.S. Manufacturing Employees', United States Department of Agriculture, Economic Research Service using data from US Census Bureau Annual Survey of Manufactures 2013, available at http://ers.usda.gov/data-products/chart-gallery/detail.aspx?chartId=40045&ref=collection&embed=True&widgetId=39734.

WHO (2014), 'Global and Regional Food Consumption Patterns and Trends', available at http://www.who.int/nutrition/topics/3_foodconsumption/en/index3.html.

World Bank (2014), 'India Development Update: Towards a Higher Growth Path', India development update, Washington DC, World Bank Group, available at http://www-wds.worldbank.org/external/default/WDSContentServer/WDSP/IB/2015/04/27/090224b082e11f0f/1_0/Rendered/PDF/India0developm0a0higher0growth0path.pdf.

World Bank (2015), 'Database', available at http://data.worldbank.org/indicator.

World Population Review (2015), 'Country Populations 2015', available at http://worldpopulationreview.com/countries/.

WorldStat (2015), 'WorldStat Info', available at http://www.wboxi.com/site/worldstat.info.

Zolin, M.B. and Andreosso-O'Callaghan, B. (2013), 'The Korea-EU FTA: New Prospects for and Patterns of Agricultural and Agrifood Trade?', *Journal of Global Policy and Governance*, **1** (2), 129–142.

PART II

China and Chinese MNCs

5. A correlation of China's economic growth and trade structure induced by transaction costs

Zhao Guoqin and Sam Dzever

1. INTRODUCTION[1]

The term "transaction costs" is generally regarded as the theoretical foundation of the New Institutional Economics (NIE) and the question of how to measure it has attracted considerable interest among researchers in recent years. In order to settle the numerous difficulties in measuring transaction costs, Lu Xianxiang and Zhu Qiaoling (2006) have proposed that transaction costs can be defined at two levels: macroscopic and microscopic transaction costs. The researchers maintain that the rise in total transaction costs coexists with the decline in the single transaction cost. Using the existing literature as a point of departure our research analyzes the nature of the quantitative relationship that exists between China's transaction costs, economic growth, and trade structure seen from a macroscopic perspective.

China's dependency on foreign trade is increasing rapidly and the disequilibrium in its international balance of payments has enlarged significantly during the past several years. As a result there is an increasing call internationally for the country to rapidly appreciate its currency, the Renminbi (RMB). This notwithstanding, some researchers (Xu Jianwei and Yao Yang, 2010) maintain that the RMB exchange rate accounts for a mere 2% of China's trade surplus with the U.S., for example, suggesting that there may be other, more serious, mechanisms at the heart of the problem. The research of Wang Zetian and Yao Yang (2008) suggests that the present RMB evaluation is consistent with international standards and that the current exchange rate of the RMB should not be taken as the cause of China's rapidly increasing trade surplus. The question therefore that immediately comes to mind is if the RMB exchange rate is not the root cause of China's trade surplus what then are the possible factors at the heart of this problem? In order to gain some insight into this issue our research analyzes the dynamic effect that macroscopic transaction costs have on both domestic and foreign trade output of China.

2.   REVIEW OF THE LITERATURE[2]

As mentioned earlier, research addressing the issue of transaction costs can be seen from the perspectives of both macroscopic and microscopic transaction costs. In terms of measuring macroscopic transaction costs, Wallis and North (1986) have made a pioneering contribution in which the authors divide the national economic system into two main categories which they have identified as *transaction* sector and *transformation* sector. Seen from this perspective transaction cost measurement can be carried out by way of calculating the number and wages of employees in transaction occupations in the transformation sector as well as the overall value-added derived in the transaction sector. Although this has generally been the most authoritative method for measuring transaction costs, when it comes to the Chinese economy two main approaches have so far commonly been used. One is based on employees in transaction occupations which has been proposed by Liao Renbin and Chen Zhi'ang (2002) while the other uses the value-added of a transaction sector to calculate transaction costs. For instance, the measurement of the average transaction costs of all Chinese provinces by Lu Xianxiang and Li Xiaoping (2008) is based on the second approach while Huang Yue-se (2008) has taken the first approach to measure the transaction cost level of Guangdong Province. In terms of measuring microscopic transaction costs, Benham and Benham (2001) have proposed the concept of *costs of exchange* in which transaction costs can be measured through contrasting opportunity costs of some microscopic transaction behaviors such as the property rights transfer of real estate, company establishment, and so on. Taking China's provincial capitals for example, Jin Yuguo and Zhang Juan (2009) have studied the measurement of non-market related transaction costs, the meaning of which is very close to that of microscopic transaction costs.

The measurement of transaction costs has preoccupied research addressing these issues for quite some time although to date there appears to be far greater emphasis attached to measuring the nature of relationship and interaction between transaction costs and the macro-economy. North (1986) posits that the decline of transaction costs is the source of economic growth and the purpose of institutional changes is to save transaction costs. According to Williamson (1985) the main purpose and effect of economic institutions lie in saving transaction costs. Using time series data, Jin Yuguo and Zhang Wei (2005) have extensively analyzed the relationship between transaction costs and economic growth in China. And using the vector autoregression (VAR) model Jin Yuguo and Zhang Juan (2009) have carried out a detailed analysis of the variations in transaction costs within the Chinese economy.

3. SAMPLE DATA AND METHODOLOGY

The merit of a measurement method which is based on employees in transaction occupations is in the fact that transaction costs of the transformation sector can be absorbed into a unified measurement and consequently the effect of the internal transaction costs can be taken into account. As a result, considering the restrictions of the present accounting system in China's economy and the wider coverage of the measurement method based on value-added, it will be more accurate to use the value-added method to study the dynamic relationship between transaction costs and the macroscopic variables. Table 5.1 provides a summary of the relationship between different measurement methods of transaction costs.

In order to reflect as correctly as possible the changes in China's macro-economy and transaction costs in recent years, the present research has taken the sample interval to be 1978 to 2008. The construction method of variables is as follows.

3.1   Transaction Costs

Using the measurement method proposed by Jin Yuguo and Zhang Wei (2005) and Lu Xianxiang and Zhu Qiaoling (2006) as a point of departure, the present research investigates industry attributes and restricts the measurement range of transaction costs to the transaction sector in the tertiary industry within the Chinese economy. Data for this research is derived primarily from *China Statistical Yearbook 2009*.

It is important to note that the yearbook only dates back to 1991. It provides data in relation to both value-added activities by sector as well as valued-added of the tertiary industry from 1991. However, the industry classification of these data is comparatively detailed and corresponds to the generally used classification of the transaction sector (see Table 5.2). *China Statistical Yearbook* after 2007 provides the value-added data of the tertiary industry which dates back to 1978 but the industry classification of these data is relatively rough: only data for transport, storage and postal services, wholesale and retail trade, accommodation and catering services, finance, real estate, and another six categories are provided. Table 5.3 shows the statistical caliber of *China Statistical Yearbook* (different years).

Table 5.1   An overview of measurement methods of transaction costs

Macroscopic transaction costs		Microscopic transaction costs
External transaction costs	External and internal transaction costs	Method — *For example*: The time spent in establishing enterprises The cost of installing the telephone The property rights transfer of real estate
Method — Value-added of the transaction sector (the tertiary industry)	The wages of (the private and public) employees in transaction occupations in the transaction sector + the wages of employees in transaction occupations in the transformation sector	
	The sum of value-added of the transaction sector in three industries	

90

Table 5.2   Classification of the tertiary industry

Industry	Industry attribute	Industry	Industry attribute
Transport, storage and postal services	Non-transaction sector	Public management and social organization	Transaction sector
Accommodation and catering services	Non-transaction sector	Wholesale and retail trade	Transaction sector
Scientific research, technical service and geologic prospecting	Non-transaction sector	Finance	Transaction sector
Management of water conservancy, environment and public facilities	Non-transaction sector	Real estate	Transaction sector
Information transmission, computer services and software	Non-transaction sector	Leasing and business services	Transaction sector
Health, social securities and social welfare	Non-transaction sector	Services to households and other services	Transaction sector
Culture, sports and entertainment	Transaction sector	Education	Transaction sector

It can be seen from Table 5.3 that data related to detailed industry classification is closer to that of transaction sector classification. The statistical caliber of the valued-added activities of the tertiary industry from 1978 to 2000 (*China Statistical Yearbook 2009*) is consistent and the sample size of these data is relatively robust which is more useful for an econometric analysis. In order to overcome the problem of "approximate" classification of industries and, at the same time, take sufficient account of sectors which have not been classified in the *Yearbook* the following equation has been developed as the basis for measuring transaction costs:

1. Absolute transaction costs = 0.5 × value-added activities of transport, storage and postal services + value-added activities of wholesale and retail trade + value-added activities of finance and insurance + value-added activities of real estate + 0.65 × the other categories.[3]
2. Relative transaction costs = absolute transaction costs/GDP.

Table 5.3   Comparison of the statistical caliber (selected years)

Yearbook	Nature of data	Number of industries	Data name	Number of industry
2009	2005–2007 value-added of three industries	17	1978–2008 value-added of the tertiary industry	6
2008	2004–2006 value-added of three industries	17	1978–2007 value-added of the tertiary industry	6
2006	2004 value-added of three industries	17		
2005	1997–2003 value-added of the tertiary industry	12		
2003	1996–2001 value-added of the tertiary industry	12		
1999	1991–1997 value-added of the tertiary industry	12		

3.2   Trade Structure

Variables investigated in trade structure relate to both domestic and foreign trade. Our research adopts total retail sales of consumer goods as the data for domestic trade while data for foreign trade encompasses gross export volume, export volume of primary products, export volume of manufactured goods, export volume of general trade, and export volume of processing trade.

3.3   Economic Growth

This is represented by growth in the GDP.

Table 5.4[4] provides a detailed outline of the above-mentioned items. Data for GDP and transaction costs are the actual values used in 1978 as the base year, while data for domestic and foreign trade represents the actual values of the RMB after price adjustment of the consumer price index (CPI)[5].

As can be seen in Table 5.4 there is a strong correlation between transaction costs, actual GDP, and different trade data. The classic method of researching this kind of problem is to put forward the basic structure of

Table 5.4   Data for China's trade and transaction costs (100 million Yuan)

Year	Relative transaction cost	Absolute transaction cost	GDP	Total retail sales of consumer goods	Gross export volume	Export volume of primary products	Export volume of manufactured goods	Export volume of general trade	Export volume of processing trade
1978	0.1776	647.54	3645.20	1558.60	167.60				
1981	0.1857	826.40	4450.44	2122.85	332.10	174.74	200.50	354.66	19.28
1983	0.1958	1053.44	5380.27	2488.56	382.80	183.75	240.79	385.08	37.13
1985	0.2241	1575.76	7031.25	3283.75	617.00	342.89	335.30	588.42	82.23
1987	0.2422	2068.28	8539.75	3885.18	981.30	363.93	720.82	815.35	247.39
1989	0.2440	2412.97	9889.22	3857.62	931.40	299.26	743.49	626.23	392.68
1991	0.2355	2640.34	11211.44	4207.15	1710.10	425.12	1466.59	1003.74	853.92
1994	0.2239	3696.16	16505.92	5493.48	3074.30	554.67	2850.96	1732.56	1603.66
1999	0.2211	5648.08	25547.54	8248.01	3739.00	422.82	3710.37	1677.93	2351.07
2001	0.2265	6794.76	30000.84	9852.49	5039.90	552.23	5027.08	2345.82	3091.25
2002	0.2281	7464.73	32725.54	11104.01	6216.40	603.23	6278.70	2878.51	3803.03
2004	0.2236	8864.76	39637.66	13054.19	10773.00	815.11	11111.83	4896.93	6592.81
2006	0.2267	11081.25	48871.20	16222.93	16474.40	991.50	17162.74	7798.04	9562.15
2008	0.2346	14123.14	60189.54	20755.25	19207.00	1146.64	19896.96	9749.83	9930.03

Sources: Data in the third and fourth columns is calculated and arranged according to *China Statistical Yearbook 2009*; data in the fifth column is arranged according to *China Statistical Yearbook 2009*, *China Statistical Yearbook 1996*, and *China Statistical Yearbook 1991*; data in the last five columns is calculated according to *China Statistical Yearbook 2009* and *China Statistical Yearbook 1999*.

the model according to economic theories and then estimate all the parameters of the variables by using econometric methods. Using a structural econometric model the complicated relationship between endogenous and exogenous variables can be meticulously analyzed. However, this approach needs to meet two requirements: (1) economic theory must provide strict definitions for the relationship between variables; (2) the endogeneity and exogeneity of the variables must be strictly defined and distinguished. As far as transaction costs, economic growth, and trade structure are concerned there presently does not exist a universally accepted theoretical model. With regard to the endogeneity of transaction costs, economic growth, and trade structure it is generally acknowledged that these are not strictly exogenous variables and consequently it is impossible to construct a recognizable structural equation model. Moreover, all of the variables used in the present research contain secular trends but the classical modeling methods require the stability of data otherwise the spurious regression phenomenon will very easily occur. However, stabilizing data inevitably means that the long-term information between variables, which is none other than what people care about, will be lost. In view of these contradictions the objective of our research is to analyze the long-term equilibrium relationship and short-term adjustment mechanism in China's transaction costs, economic growth, and trade structure using VAR and vector error correction (VEC) models.

4.   RESULTS OF THE ECONOMETRIC ANALYSIS

In order to resolve the heteroskedasticity problem and enable a more clear display of their secular trend our research starts by logarithmizing the eight groups of time series data which are:

- Absolute transaction costs
- Actual GDP
- Total retail sales of consumer goods
- Gross export volume
- Export volume of primary products
- Export volume of manufactured goods
- Export volume of general trade
- Export volume of processing trade.

The above is respectively labeled JY, GDP, XF, CK, CJ, GY, YB, and JG.

Table 5.5   ADF test result

Variable	JY	GDP	XF	CK	CJ	GY	YB	JG
ADF statistics	−2.767	−3.672	−3.30	−5.639	−5.894	−5.397	−5.807	−11.934
p-value	0.0755	0.011	0.0242	0.0001	0	0.0002	0.0001	0
Conclusion	I(1)	I(1)	I(1)	I(1)	I(1)	I(1)	I(1)	I(1)

4.1   Stationary Test

Whether in VAR model or VEC model, fixing the series' order of integration is the premise of analysis since the precondition of conducting the Johansen test on co-integration vectors and then constructing the VEC mechanism is to require all the series to integrate in the order of one. As for VAR model, if there exists any unit root in the data it will mean that the model estimated is unstable which effectively means that the original data must be stabilized through the *difference method* or *filtering process*.

Our research has respectively conducted the Augmented Dickey-Fuller (ADF) test to the eight variables: JY, GDP, XF, CK, CJ, GY, YB, and JG and the result shows that at the significance level of 10% they all represent an integration of order one while at the significance level of 5% only JY is not remarkable.

Table 5.5 shows the ADF test result of the first difference of the above-mentioned eight variables.

4.2   VAR Model and Granger Non-Causality Test

Since the original data is integration of order one, it is necessary to stabilize the data before constructing the VAR model. The usual practice of doing this is to directly obtain the first difference of the original data. The merit of the first difference method lies in the fact that it can reflect the explicit economic connotation and indicate the growth rate of variables while it has the defect of easily covering up the relationship between short-term fluctuation and secular trends. In order to overcome this problem the present research has applied Hodrick-Prescott filter (H-P filter) to stabilize the data.

4.2.1   Variable selection

Because the number of the analyzed variables of foreign trade is relatively large it is impossible to absorb all into one model. Consequently we have firstly conducted Granger non-causality test to the filtered data and then selected the variables with obvious causal relationship to construct the

Table 5.6   Remarkable variable pairs in Granger non-causality test

Causality	F-statistics	p-value	Causality	F-statistics	p-value
HPGDP does not Granger-cause HPCJ	5.4074***	0.007	HPJG does not Granger-cause HPGDP	0.4356	0.781
HPCJ does not Granger-cause HPGDP	2.5184*	0.085	HPGDP does not Granger-cause HPJG	5.0562***	0.009
HPGDP does not Granger-cause HPCK	6.6042***	0.002	HPYB does not Granger-cause HPGDP	0.6013	0.668
HPCK does not Granger-cause HPGDP	0.2606	0.899	HPGDP does not Granger-cause HPYB	8.0163***	0.001
HPGY does not Granger-cause HPGDP	0.1035	0.980	HPJG does not Granger-cause HPJY	3.6099**	0.030
HPGDP does not Granger-cause HPGY	4.9315***	0.010	HPJY does not Granger-cause HPJG	3.6304**	0.029
HPJY does not Granger-cause HPGDP	2.2737	0.101	HPXF does not Granger-cause HPJY	3.2430**	0.036
HPGDP does not Granger-cause HPJY	3.05250**	0.044	HPJY does not Granger-cause HPXF	4.8936***	0.008

Note: HP represents the data adjusted by H-P filter; in the test, lag order= 4; *, **, and *** respectively indicate that the data are remarkable at the significance level of 10%, 5%, and 1%.

VAR model in order to carry out a short-term analysis. Table 5.6 represents the result of the test.

The result of the Granger test shows that through H-P filter among actual GDP, absolute transaction costs, export volume of processing trade, and the total retail sales of consumer goods, there exists a relationship with transaction costs as the core. As shown in Figure 5.1, transaction costs have bidirectional causal relationships with the total retail sales of consumer goods and export volume of processing trade; actual GDP, Granger causes of absolute transaction costs, and export volume of processing trade. There is no causal relationship between other trade variables and transaction costs.

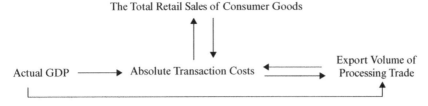

Figure 5.1   *Causality among transaction costs, economic growth and foreign trade*

4.2.2 Constructing the VAR model

The Granger test shows that there exists a relatively close relationship among the four variables: HPJY, HPGDP, HPJG, and HPXF. Accordingly, the VAR model with these four variables as the endogenous variables can be constructed.

It is of the utmost importance to determine the model's lag order in the process of constructing the VAR model and the lag length test result indicates that it will be relatively rational to construct a VAR (4) model. As a result, the VAR model which reflects the dynamic feedback mechanism among the four variables is constructed as follows:

$$
\begin{pmatrix} HPJY \\ HPGDP \\ HPXF \\ HPJG \end{pmatrix} = \begin{pmatrix} -0.0012 \\ -0.0013 \\ -0.0058 \\ -0.0057 \end{pmatrix} +
$$

$$
\begin{pmatrix} 0.866 & -0.823 & 0.423 & 0.059 \\ -0.122 & 0.363 & 0.359 & 0.009 \\ 0.702 & -0.566 & 0.233 & 0.051 \\ -5.955 & -0.520 & 1.764 & 0.163 \end{pmatrix} \begin{pmatrix} HPJY_{-1} \\ HPGDP_{-1} \\ HPXF_{-1} \\ HPJG_{-1} \end{pmatrix}
$$

$$
+ \begin{pmatrix} -0.667 & -0.076 & -0.056 & 0.054 \\ -0.500 & -0.242 & 0.036 & 0.063 \\ -0.607 & -1.093 & -0.002 & 0.090 \\ 4.449 & -2.874 & 0.427 & 0.689 \end{pmatrix} \begin{pmatrix} HPJY_{-2} \\ HPGDP_{-2} \\ HPXF_{-2} \\ HPJG_{-2} \end{pmatrix}
$$

$$
+ \begin{pmatrix} -0.198 & 1.047 & -0.142 & 0.019 \\ 0.284 & 0.779 & -0.232 & 0.012 \\ -0.177 & 1.952 & -0.011 & 0.019 \\ 3.372 & -1.089 & -1.133 & 0.001 \end{pmatrix} \begin{pmatrix} HPJY_{-3} \\ HPGDP_{-3} \\ HPXF_{-3} \\ HPJG_{-3} \end{pmatrix}
$$

$$+\begin{pmatrix} -0.190 & -0.397 & -0.002 & 0.021 \\ -0.055 & -0.480 & -0.207 & 0.013 \\ -0.719 & -0.048 & -0.375 & 0.013 \\ -4.277 & 0.693 & 0.412 & -0.041 \end{pmatrix}\begin{pmatrix} HPJY_{-4} \\ HPGDP_{-4} \\ HPXF_{-4} \\ HPJG_{-4} \end{pmatrix}$$

AIC $= -24.761$; $SC = -21.424$; **Log likelihood** $= 365.137$

In general, the fitting effect of the model is quite good and most of the coefficients are remarkable. Upon testing, all the characteristic roots of the model lie outside the unit circle, which shows that the system structure of the VAR model is stable.

4.2.3 Impulse response and variance decomposition

The reciprocal influences among the four endogenous variables in the VAR model can be investigated through impulse response function analysis (see Figure 5.2). Taking into consideration the causality shown in Figure 5.1 our research has focused on the corresponding effects of the one standard deviation random shock given by HPGDP, HPJG and HPXF to HPJY as well as HPJY to HPJG.

Figure 5.2(a) demonstrates, from left to right, the impulse response of the above-mentioned five relationships; the abscissa indicates the number of periods (year) of the shock effect, while the ordinate demonstrates the change range. The impulse response function analysis shows:

1. The influence that GDP, total retail sales of consumer goods, and export volume of processing trade have on transaction costs. When HPJY (the growth rate of macroscopic transaction costs relative to secular trends) is shocked by one standard deviation of HPGDP (GDP that deviates from the equilibrium trend), it will yield a sustained fluctuation when it is shocked by the total retail sales of consumer goods and export volume of processing trade. It will also yield a sustained fluctuation but in the long term the fluctuation range will be reduced thus suggesting that the influence these three variables have on transaction costs is relatively small. The data indicates that the standard deviation shock these variables have on macroscopic transaction costs relative to secular trends has a 0.01% fluctuation. In the cycle direction the shock of GDP and the reaction of the relative growth rate of transaction costs first declines then rises, while the reaction to the shock of both domestic and foreign trade rises at first and then declines afterwards. At the same time the effect export volume has on processing

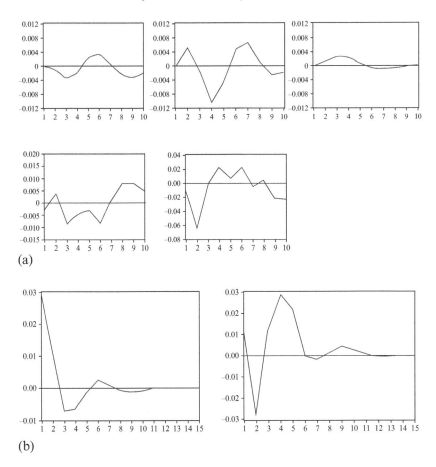

Figure 5.2   Impulse response function

trade and transaction costs is of a longer cycle between wave crest and wave trough. This effectively leads to a gap of four years which is twice the cycle length of the shock of total retail sales of consumer goods.

2.   The influence of transaction costs on GDP, domestic and foreign trade, and standard deviation of the growth in macroscopic transaction costs with respect to long-term equilibrium level leads the growth rate of total retail sales of consumer goods to increase slightly in the second year after the shock. However, in the mid-term negative effects occur. There is 0.01% negative growth of macroscopic transaction costs relative to the long-term equilibrium level for four years. Further research is needed in order to determine why the long-term effect of seven years later is positive. Moreover, the positive shock of macroscopic absolute

transaction costs leads to lower volume of processing trade compared to the secular trend in the short term.

In order to more explicitly reflect the effect of the relationship between transaction costs and China's domestic and foreign trade, Figure 5.2(b) shows the impulse response of the growth rate of total retail sales of consumer goods and the growth rate of export volume of processing trade being shocked by the growth rate of absolute transaction costs. As can be seen, the result in Figure 5.2(b) is slightly different from that of Figure 5.2(a). This is because when the growth rate of macroscopic transaction costs has given one standard deviation positive shock the total retail sales of consumer goods yield brief positive growth in the first and second year. From the third to fifth years, however, the growth is negative although in the next two years it has a slight positive rebound. Similarly, after being shocked in the second year the growth of export volume of processing trade is negative but from the third year it starts to increase significantly, reaching a peak in the fourth year and continuing to the sixth year before returning to zero.

In summary therefore, after filtering the data's mutual secular trends the growth of transaction costs stimulates the growth of export volume of processing trade in the mid-term and restrains the growth of total retail sales of consumer goods, while in the short term the situation is just the reverse. In order to show more accurately the differences in the contributions of the factors to the fluctuation of certain variables, Table 5.7 shows the variance decomposition result of the total retail sales of consumer goods.

In the long term, the deviation of the total retail sales of consumer goods

Table 5.7   Variance decomposition result of the total retail sales of consumer goods

Period	S.E.	HPJY	HPGDP	HPXF	HPJG
1	0.018536	2.32409	5.927619	91.74829	0
2	0.019068	6.057552	5.893475	87.7988	0.25017
3	0.022166	20.39373	12.21653	65.69274	1.697006
4	0.025967	17.94316	8.901716	71.487	1.668123
5	0.026991	17.93044	10.09692	70.36717	1.605475
6	0.030567	21.7008	9.242103	67.69718	1.359914
7	0.031115	21.102	9.568908	67.72504	1.604044
8	0.032302	26.05768	9.466205	62.87125	1.604865
9	0.033504	29.93319	9.975846	58.59916	1.491807
10	0.034355	30.44106	9.714563	58.42173	1.422646

from its own trend (over 60%) can be decided. However, it will become stationary at about 30% when the influence of macroscopic absolute transaction costs increases over time. This indicates that on the one hand total retail sales of consumer goods has a relatively strong self-accumulation effect and on the other the influence of macroscopic transaction costs far exceeds that of economic growth and foreign trade.

4.3 Analyses of Johansen Co-Integration Test and VEC Model

Since the short-term analysis of export volume of processing trade is the focus of this research we shall concentrate our analysis in this section of the chapter. Other foreign trade variables such as export volume of manufactured goods and export volume of general trade will be left out for future research. Since the VEC model does not require data to be stationary our analysis shall utilize the original data of JY, GDP, XF, and JG.

4.3.1 Johansen co-integration test

As has been mentioned in the preceding discussion, this group of variable series all represent a I (1) process, and consequently Johansen co-integration test can be conducted directly to investigate whether there exists a long-term equilibrium relationship between variables. Johansen test result is relatively sensitive to the selection of VAR lag order. Therefore, after repeated consideration the research constructs a VAR (1, 2, 4) to test the original data series. The co-integration test result[6] indicates that there exist co-integration relationships inside these four groups of data series and the standardized co-integration equation which contains all the four variables is:

$$JY = 3.007 + 0.321GDP - 0.08XF + 0.399JG^7$$

Since our research uses the logarithmized data, coefficients in the equation represent the elasticity. As a result, in the long term, 1% growth of GDP will cause macroscopic transaction costs to increase by 0.32%. This means that approximately 0.4% growth of macroscopic transaction costs will bring about 1% growth of export volume of processing trade; 0.08% growth of transaction costs will lead to a 1% reduction of the total retail sales of consumer goods. This result is consistent with the above short-term analysis. As a result it proves that within the sample interval the relationship between the level of China's macroscopic transaction cost and the volume of domestic trade has a reverse change and that the relationship between the level of China's macroscopic transaction cost and foreign trade (especially export volume of processing trade) is a positive change.

Table 5.8   Error correction coefficients

Equation	Error adjustment coefficient	Standard deviation	t-statistics
D(JY)	−0.282411	0.19734	−1.43108
D(GDP)	−0.020156	0.13258	−0.15203
D(XF)	−1.082018	0.33869	−3.19476
D(JG)	4.21501	0.60018	7.02289

4.3.2   VEC model

Although transaction costs have a long-term equilibrium relationship with GDP, domestic trade, and export volume of processing trade in the short term, there clearly exist imbalances in the relationship between the variables. The dynamic structure of these imbalances can be described by the VEC model. The regression result of the VEC model is satisfactory and the overwhelming majority of the coefficients at the significance level of 10% are remarkable. However, due to limited space the complete parameter estimation will not be provided. Rather, only the estimated result of error correction coefficients will be reported as shown in Table 5.8.

Error correction coefficients reflect the mechanism through which the VEC model corrects errors that represent deviation from equilibrium. Table 5.8 shows that there exist error correction mechanisms in both transaction costs and GDP with the adjustment speed of 28% and 2% respectively. The correction coefficients of the total retail sales of consumer goods and export volume of processing trade are inconsistent with the theoretical construct – i.e. the VEC model fails to correct the influence of long-term equilibrium error. On the contrary it intensifies the growth fluctuation of XF and JG.

5.   CONCLUSION

Currently, a significant part of the literature concerned with measuring macroscopic transaction costs in the Chinese economy focuses on the relationship between transaction costs and variables like economic growth and the degree of market orientation. There are very few research undertakings that utilize the concept of transaction costs (especially macroscopic transaction costs) to describe and interpret the actual economic phenomena through quantification. This is due to the fact that within the framework of the present national economic accounting system there are still great difficulties in measuring transaction costs since often data is inaccurate and incomplete. And this problem has been particularly acute over the last 30 years – i.e. since China adopted its market reforms and opening-up policy. The statistical caliber of the national economy has often changed which reflects the development and improvement of statistical work, but it has also undoubtedly brought relatively large obstacles to researchers.

As a result, the contribution of our research can be seen from two perspectives: (1) it fills the gap that exists in China's macroscopic transaction costs analysis since 2003; and (2) it analyzes the relationship between transaction costs, economic growth, and trade structure in detail by using dynamic econometric models. By utilizing VAR and VEC models our research has come to the following preliminary conclusions:

1. China's macroscopic transaction costs have a close relationship (and complicated causality) with economic growth and trade structure. In the short term, transaction costs have bidirectional causal relationships with both domestic and foreign trade. This effectively means that there exists a complicated interactive relationship between China's trade structure and transaction costs.
2. Among the different variables which describe foreign trade, the relationship between export volume of processing trade and macroscopic transaction costs is the closest. The impulse response function of the VAR model indicates that the growth of macroscopic transaction costs relative to its long-term equilibrium will reduce the growth of export volume of processing trade (i.e. lower than the equilibrium value) but that in the mid-term it will clearly increase export volume of the processing trade. The VEC model demonstrates that in the long term export volume of the processing trade and macroscopic transaction costs will move in the same direction.
3. The relationship between the total retail sales of consumer goods which describes domestic trade and macroscopic transaction costs is just the opposite of the relationship between macroscopic transaction costs and foreign trade. In the mid- and long term the rise in macro-transaction costs will have a negative effect on the growth of domestic trade.
4. The above three points suggest that there exists a potential relationship between the rise in transaction costs which are decided upon by economic growth and the degree of "marketization" (Jin Yuguo and Zhang Juan, 2009). Further, it stimulates the development of China's processing trade and, to some extent, restrains the growth of China's domestic consumption and trade which has consequently led to the continuous change in the country's trade structure leading to persistent accumulation of trade surplus. This conclusion could

not only enrich our understanding of the cause of China's enormous trade surplus, it could also provide some preliminary indications as to how the problem of China's persistent trade imbalances could be resolved.

In conclusion we believe that due to the rather modest sample size of our research the VEC model we have constructed may not be entirely adequate. In an ideal VEC model the number of the lag order should be four. However, the problem is that the Johansen test and coefficient estimates cannot be conducted within the parameters of an ideal model. Although our VEC model has presented the co-integration equation, as it currently stands, the regression result is not entirely satisfactory. This leads to the need to conduct further research in order to more adequately address the problem. Our future research shall address specifically this issue.

NOTES

1. In this chapter, short term is within three years, mid-term is three to seven years, long term is more than seven years.
2. The literature referred to in this chapter has not analyzed data related to macroscopic transaction costs from 2003 onwards.
3. The coefficient 0.5 before "transport, storage and postal services" refers to Lu Xianxiang and Li Xiaoping (2008); the coefficient 0.65 before "the other categories" is the proportion of the value-added sum of Leasing and business services, Services to households and other services, Education, culture, sports and entertainment, as well as Public management and social organization from 2005 to 2007 in the total value-added of "the other categories" from 2005 to 2007.
4. The data in Table 5.4 indicates that the relative transaction cost measured in this chapter is comparatively close to the external relative transaction cost measured by Jin Yuguo and Zhang Wei (2005).
5. Consumer Price Index (CPI) is replaced by Commodity Price Index from 1980 to 1985.
6. Due to limited space the detailed results of the co-integration test are not outlined in this chapter.
7. The changes of variable ordering in the co-integration equation will not affect the coefficients. This means that the results of the elasticity analysis are stationary.

REFERENCES

Benham, A. and Benham, L. (2001), 'The Costs of Exchange', *Ronald Coast Institute Working Papers Series*, No. 1, July, available at http://www.coase.org/workingpapers/wp-1.pdf.

Huang, Yue-se (2008), 'The Transaction Costs Measurement Based on Transaction Persons in Guangdong Province: 1993–2002', *Journal of South China Agricultural University (Social Science Edition)*, **2**, 53–60.

Jin Yuguo and Zhang Juan (2009), 'Comparison of Measure of Non-market

Transaction Costs Based on Factor Analysis – The Capital City as an Example', *Journal of Huaiyin Teachers College (Social Sciences Edition)*, **4**, 475–480, 485.

Jin Yuguo and Zhang Wei (2005), 'The Statistical Measuring of the External Transaction Cost in China: 1991–2002 and the Calculation of System Transition Performance', *China Soft Science*, **1**, 35–40.

Liao Renbin and Chen Zhi'ang (2002), 'The Measurement of Transaction Fee and the Economic Growth of China', *Statistical Research*, **8**, 14–21.

Lu Xianxiang and Li Xiaoping (2008), 'Institutional Transition, Economic Growth, and Transaction Cost: Empirical Analysis on Chinese Provinces and Cities', Working Paper, Zhongnan University of Economics and Law, Wuhan, Hubei.

Lu Xianxiang and Zhu Qiaoling (2006), 'A Summarizing of the Interrelation of Two Levels in Measuring the Transaction Cost', *The Journal of Quantitative and Technical Economics*, **7**, 97–108.

North, D.C. (1986), 'The New Institutional Economics', *Journal of Institutional and Theoretical Economics (JITE)*, **142** (1), March, 230–237.

Wallis, J.J. and North, D.C. (1986), *Measuring the Transaction Sector in the American Economy, 1870–1970, Long-Term Factors in American Economic Growth*, Chicago: University of Chicago Press.

Wang Zetian and Yao Yang (2008), 'An Estimation of the Equilibrium RMB Exchange Rate', *Journal of Financial Research*, **12**, 22–36.

Williamson, O.E. (1985), *The Economic Institutions of Capitals*, New York: The Free Press.

Xu Jianwei and Yao Yang (2010), 'Finance Manufacturing Comparative Advantage and Global Imbalances', Working Paper, China Center for Economic Research (CCER), Peking University.

6. MNCs' offshore R&D co-location strategies: comparison of Western and Asian firms in China

Pei Yu and Jean-Louis Mucchielli

1. INTRODUCTION

Traditionally, MNCs' innovation units were concentrated in the developed world, but in the last ten years offshore R&D has increasingly shifted towards developing countries (Bruche 2009, Liu and Chen 2012), and China is listed among the top destinations for future R&D expansion of the world's top 300 R&D investors (Hedge and Hicks 2008, UNCTAD 2005).

Research on MNCs' offshore R&D mainly focuses on Europe, the US and Japan (Alcacer and Chung 2007, Belderbos 2006, Cantwell and Piscitello 2003, Ito and Wakasugi 2007, Kumar 1996, 2001, Mariani 2002, Shimizutani and Todo 2008, Siedschlag et al. 2013, Todo and Shimizutani 2009). Less research, especially quantitative research, has been undertaken into the recent expansion of MNCs' offshore R&D in China (Sun et al. 2008). Dunning's eclectic paradigm predicts that MNCs' offshore R&D can be considered not only as a consequence of "ownership" advantages, but also as a channel for further augmenting a firm's competitive advantage through sourcing new knowledge (Cantwell and Piscitello 2005). Compared with Western countries, however, knowledge stock is limited in China, and moreover, MNCs encounter cross-cultural barriers when investing there (Magnmusson and Boyle 2009, Rugman and Li 2007). Therefore, as with China's integration in R&D globalization, it is essential to enrich current research, through discovering the strategic framework of MNCs' offshore R&D in China, by answering the questions: What factors drive the location choice of MNCs' R&D activities in a developing country? What locational advantages of a Chinese city affect MNCs' R&D location choice?

As it is usually the last step of internationalization, MNCs' offshore R&D follows offshore production with a certain time-lag (Cantwell and

Iammarino 2000, Cantwell and Piscitello 2002, 2005, Kumar 2001); thus, an R&D unit's internal linkage with production plants can help it to better adapt to a local market and save on transaction costs (Sun 2011). Nonetheless, the "knowledge capital model" raised by Markusen (2002) predicts that knowledge-intensive activities may be concentrated in small skill-intensive national economies, and in this case "local innovative milieu" (Camagni 1991), such as market sophistication and the innovation capacity of local universities, form firm-university linkages (Buckley and Ghauri 2004, Cantwell and Narula 2001, Park 2012). These internal and external linkages create co-location tendencies for MNCs' new R&D affiliates.

This study seeks to investigate and compare co-location strategies of US, European and Asian offshore R&D units across Chinese cities, and it brings three contributions to research on R&D globalization: firstly, it predicts internal and external linkages of MNCs by establishing a theoretical framework of R&D co-location strategies, on the basis of location theory and MNCs' R&D networks literature (Alcacer and Chung 2007, Helble and Chong 2004); secondly, in contrast to previous research focusing on Triad R&D flows (US, Europe and Japan), this chapter analyzes offshore R&D in China; thirdly, unlike previous case studies or those studies based on regional levels (Liu and Chen 2012), it verifies the framework by using firm-level data and quantitative methods by taking a Chinese city as a basic location unit, which accounts for regional heterogeneity within China and avoids aggregation bias (Siedschlag *et al.* 2013).

2. CONCEPTUAL FRAMEWORK: MNCS' R&D CO-LOCATION STRATEGIES

With the progress of R&D internationalization, MNCs' offshore R&D organizational structure has tended to be a multi-level network pattern (Gassmann and Zedtwitz 2004). The study defines an R&D affiliate's co-location strategy as it locates in close proximity to other firms or academic institutions, generally caused by localization economies or urbanization economies through various linkages (Cantwell and Iammarino 2005, Cantwell and Piscitello 2005).

In the case of localization economies, a path-dependence of technological accumulation in a particular industry calls for geographic proximity between R&D units and other affiliates, aimed at supporting local production or maintaining intra-/inter-firm knowledge flows (Cantwell and Narula 2001, Cantwell and Santangelo 2002, Gugler and Michel 2010, Sun 2011). At industry level, Marshallian industry specialization leads to

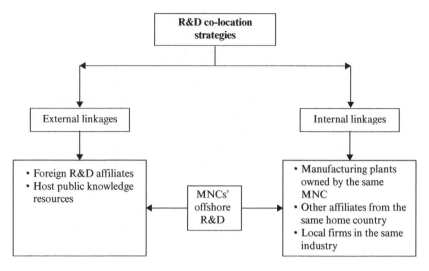

Source: Arranged by authors.

Figure 6.1   MNCs' R&D co-location strategies: a network perspective

R&D agglomeration in the same industry, which facilitates knowledge accumulation (Cantwell and Piscitello 2005). In relation to urbanization economies, local external resources, such as abundant human capital and public knowledge stocks, are crucial for promoting R&D co-location with local universities and institutions, in order to cumulate tacit knowledge (Alcacer and Chung 2007, Gugler and Michel 2010). Following the above discussions, Figure 6.1 presents a conceptual framework of MNCs' offshore R&D co-location strategies.

2.1   Internal Linkages

2.1.1   Co-location with manufacturing plants owned by the same MNC
Since MNCs' R&D global dispersion is first of all a consequence of their globalization of production activities (Gugler and Michel 2010), some previous research points out that if R&D activities mainly support local demand (i.e. home-based exploiting), its co-presence with production affiliates can feed a firm's adaptively innovative works (Cantwell and Santangelo 2002, Kumar 2001). This strategy is also called "home-based exploiting" (HBE) (Kuemmerle 1999). Hashai (2009) develops the internalization hypothesis by considering knowledge transfer costs, and he argues that the co-location of firms' activities is more likely to facilitate formal

and non-formal knowledge transfer. Brookfield and Liu (2005) build up a comprehensive production network associated with manufacturing plants and R&D units to explain Taiwan-based firms' location in China. Sun (2011) demonstrates that MNCs tend to locate their R&D units along with their manufacturing facilities in China, in order to share resources.

2.1.2 Intra-industry spillovers

Marshall (1890) firstly indicated three advantages of a "localized industry", including spillover effects, economy of scale and a constant market for skilled labor. Sector-specific or tacit knowledge needs face-to-face contacts (Cantwell and Iammarino 1998), and in the meantime, geographic agglomeration of firms within a common industry leads to further accumulation of relevant knowledge. A few empirical studies have used location quotient (LQ) to measure a location's industrial specialization, and they reveal that an MNC's R&D location is cumulative and path-dependent on intra-industry spillovers (Cantwell and Iammarino 2005), and, especially in information and communications technology (ICT) industries, firms tend to co-specialize in the same field, by co-locating in the same geographic area (Cantwell and Santangelo 2002). While receiving spillovers, firms also serve as potential knowledge sources, especially for their less technologically advanced competitors (Alcacer and Chung 2007). Therefore, in order to avoid knowledge leakage, technologically advanced firms may avoid co-locating with other firms in the same industry. Firms need to balance these two competing constraints when choosing an optimal location.

2.1.3 Home country linkages

"Liabilities of Foreignness" literature emphasizes foreign affiliates' disadvantages in host countries (Zaheer 1995). A number of studies have proven that cultural distance is an impediment to foreign investments (Flores and Aguilera 2007), and greater home-host cultural distance is associated with a lower probability that an innovation-oriented alliance will be formed (Kaufmann and O'Neill 2007). Traditionally, Kogut and Singh's (1988) index based on Hofstede (1991) has been used in international business research. However, Hakanson and Ambos (2010) emphasize that in entry mode decisions it is foremost psychic distance which is the deciding factor, and they prove by quantitative analysis that the subjectively perceived distance to a foreign country is influenced by a range of cultural, geographic, political and economic factors, and the use solely of Kogut and Singh's index is incorrect. On the basis of agglomeration economies, an affiliate's co-presence with other affiliates from the same home country will produce an "investment-stalk" or signaling effect (Dunning 1998), which provides an information network on host cities and reduces cross-cultural distance

(Cheng and Stough 2006, Crozet *et al.* 2004, Inui *et al.* 2008, Mataloni 2011, Mucchielli and Puech 2003, Mucchielli and Yu 2011). Brookfield and Liu (2005) also prove inter-firm ties between Taiwan-based firms in mainland China.

2.2   External Linkages

2.2.1   R&D agglomeration

Inter-firm networks through geographic co-presence with other R&D firms also amplify agglomeration effects, such as a cluster of innovative activities or specialized support services (Cantwell and Iammarino 1998). "Following your competitor's strategy" promotes R&D affiliates to co-locate in the same area, aiming to emulate the technological advantages of competitors and enhance their own knowledge base (Cantwell and Narula 2001, Cantwell and Santangelo 2002). When analyzing R&D location determinants across Europe, Siedschlag *et al.* (2013) underline that agglomeration economies from foreign R&D activities are particularly important. Firms' motivation in augmenting knowledge stock is also called "home-based augmenting" (HBA) strategy (Kuemmerle 1999).

2.2.2   Co-location in science cities

University–industry linkages form a center of excellence (or a science city, Park 2012), in which the public knowledge resources may largely enhance a firm's technology portfolio (Cantwell and Piscitello 2005). These external linkages promote firms' HBA motivation. Song *et al.* (2011) indicate that, since spillovers of intellectual capital are embedded in social relations or structure, R&D affiliates' "local embeddedness" with host scientific and engineering communities is important. In reality, innovative regions such as Silicon Valley, Hitachi's Cambridge Lab, Mitsubishi Electric's US laboratories, and research centers in Scotland and East Anglia, etc. are all examples of university–industry intensive research collaboration. The importance of R&D's co-locating with external knowledge resources has been proved in previous research (Belderbos 2006, Cantwell and Piscitello 2003, Ito and Wakasugi 2007, Kumar 1996, 2001, Liu and Chen 2012, Shimizutani and Todo 2008).

On the basis of Figure 6.1, it can be assumed that a foreign R&D affiliate pursues a city which can bring it maximum profit. Therefore, the study proposes the two main hypotheses as follows:

- **Hypothesis 1:** an MNC's offshore R&D affiliate, which aims to benefit from local production networks or to support local demand, tends to co-locate with internal resources.

- **Hypothesis 2:** a city with abundant public knowledge resources attracts MNCs' offshore R&D units, which pursue specialized human capital or advanced technology. In this case, R&D units are often technologically advanced and external linkage is dominant.

3. CHARACTERISTICS OF US, EUROPEAN AND ASIAN OFFSHORE R&D AFFILIATES IN CHINA

As among the first economies to invest in China, the US and the EU have augmented their R&D expenditures. For instance, US R&D expenditures in China rose from US$35 million in 1995 to US$565 million in 2003 (Gugler and Michel 2010). In relation to Asian MNCs, Japanese and Korean "white goods" producers, such as Panasonic, Hitachi, Samsung and LG, had more than 23 R&D units in China by the end of 2009. By 2005, China's growing role in the ICT global innovation network had resulted in part from the relocation of Taiwan-based firms' R&D functions (Liu and Chen 2012).

In general, Western MNCs encounter greater cultural and geographic barriers than Asian ones, and, therefore, their location strategies in relation to offshore R&D units are worth comparing. The research examines the study's conceptual framework by studying US, European and Asian R&D affiliates in China. The statistics at firm level come from a series of annual "*Report on Transnational Corporations in China*", edited by the Research Center of MNCs in China's Ministry of Commerce. The annual report of each MNC, e-mail and phone calls are also used to double-check and cross-examine the latest information. The sample is composed of 185 new R&D affiliates owned by 75 US MNCs, 107 European affiliates owned by 48 European MNCs, and 115 Asian R&D affiliates (including 47 Japanese, 25 Korean, 8 Singaporean, 30 Taiwanese and 5 Indian firms) owned by 58 Asian MNCs, located across 27 cities during the period 1992–2011. All the US and European sample MNCs and 60 percent of the Asian MNCs were listed in Fortune's *Global 500* magazine in the year of their investing in China.

Figure 6.2 shows home country distribution of the sample European firms. Germany and France are the top two countries with established offshore R&D units in China. Swedish and Swiss MNCs have already registered China as a "desirable location", followed by British firms. Besides geographic distance, different political systems and economic development levels also affect the psychic distance of a foreign investor when making location choices among different alternatives (Hakanson and Ambos 2010). Therefore, it is assumed that the psychic distance between an MNC's home country (economy) and China has impacts on R&D location strategies across China, and cross-country differences exist.

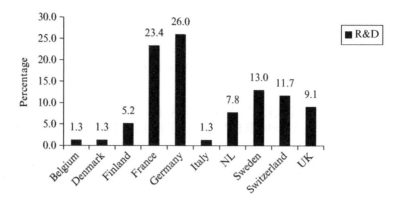

Source: Arranged by authors on the basis of a series of annual *"Report on Transnational Corporations in China"*, edited by the Research Center of MNCs in China's Ministry of Commerce.

Figure 6.2   *Home country distribution of EU R&D affiliates in China (unit: %)*

The statistics in Table 6.1 reveal that 70 percent of US R&D affiliates are in the electronic-communications industry, and 90 percent are in high-tech or medium-high tech industries. Industrial distribution of European R&D affiliates are more dispersed and 88 percent are in four industries: electronics-communications; chemicals; electrical machinery; and pharmaceuticals. The industrial distribution of Asian MNCs is similar to that of US firms. Nearly 70 percent of the sample R&D affiliates are fully foreign-owned. It is deduced that, due to psychic distance, MNCs want to reduce knowledge leakage or the management gap by fully controlling their R&D affiliates in China.

Table 6.2 firstly shows the geographic distribution of US, European and Asian R&D affiliates in each sample city at the end of 2011. By grouping these cities into five regions based on their geographic locations the research finds that Beijing and Shanghai have attracted nearly 65 percent of the sample R&D units, and their neighboring cities, such as Tianjin, Nanjing, Wuxi, Suzhou, etc., have benefitted from the spillover effects (for instance, Suzhou accounts for nearly 14 percent of Asian R&D units). Secondly, two south coast cities, Guangzhou and Shenzhen, are preferred by US and Asian firms. Thirdly, economically backward regions such as the west region also attract MNCs' interests, especially Chengdu and Xian. Therefore, unlike foreign manufacturing plants, which are highly agglomerated in developed regions of China (Mucchielli and Yu 2011), foreign R&D affiliates are more dispersed.

Table 6.1   *Industry distribution and investment mode of US, EU and Asian R&D affiliates in China (unit: %)*

MNC's home country	Industry distribution (%)					Investment mode (%)	
	Electronic–communications	Chemicals	Electrical machinery	Pharmaceuticals	Others	Fully owned	Others
US	70	7.7	8.8	3.8	9.7	76	24
EU	36.8	19.7	13.2	18	12.3	66	34
Asia	68.7	2.3	13.9	6.1	9	76.5	23.5

Source: Arranged by authors on the basis of a series of annual "*Report on Transnational Corporations in China*", edited by the Research Center of MNCs in China's Ministry of Commerce.

Table 6.2 Geographic distribution of US, EU and Asian R&D affiliates in China (2011) (unit: %)

Region	City	US firms	EU firms	Asian firms	Region	City	US firms	EU firms	Asian firms
Bohai	Beijing	29.73	20.78	16.52	Pearl River Delta	Guangzhou	3.78	1.30	2.61
	Dalian	1.08	1.30	2.61		Jiangmen	0.54	0.00	0.87
	Shenyang	0.54	0.00	0.87		Shenzhen	8.65	0.00	8.70
	Jinan	0.54	0.00	0.00		Xiamen	0.54	0.00	0.87
	Yantai	0.54	0.00	0.87		Haikou	0.54	0.00	0.00
	Tianjin	2.16	3.90	2.61	West	Chongqing	2.16	0.00	0.00
Yangtze River Delta	Shanghai	36.76	45.45	26.69		Xian	2.16	2.60	3.48
	Wuxi	1.62	1.30	1.74		Chengdu	2.16	3.90	1.74
	Xuzhou	0.54	1.30	0.00	Center	Ningjin	0.54	0.00	0.00
	Nanjing	2.70	6.49	0.00		Haerbing	0.54	0.00	0.00
	Nantong	0.00	1.30	0.87		Wuhan	0.00	1.30	0.87
	Changzhou	0.00	1.30	2.61		Taiyuan	0.00	1.30	0.87
	Suzhou	1.08	3.90	13.91	Total (%)		100	100	100
	Hangzhou	0.54	2.60	5.22	Total (absolute number)		185	107	115
	Hefei	0.54	0.00	0.00					

Source: Arranged by authors on the basis of a series of annual "Report on Translational Corporations in China", edited by the Research Center of MNCs in China's Ministry of Commerce.

Table 6.3   Geographic concentration of US and EU R&D affiliates in China (2011) (unit of GDP per capita: US$1; unit of FDI inflow: US$ billion)

Region	Average GDP per capita (2002–2011)	HHI of US R&D firms	Average US FDI inflow (2002–2010)	HHI of EU R&D firms	Average EU FDI inflow (2002–2010)	HHI of Asian R&D firms	Average Asian FDI inflow (2002–2012)
East	7672.59	2343.61	3.1727	2587.28	4.2511	1331.56	53.95
Center	3592.50	0.58	0.4982	3.37	0.4678	1.512	
West	2635.12	14.02	0.3128	21.93	0.1058	15.123	

Notes:
1. In the HHI's calculation formula, N is the number of cities, X_i is the number of sample affiliates in a given city i at the end of 2011, whereas X is the number of sample affiliates in the whole of China for the same period, and S_i is the ratio of the former to the latter. For the different sets of values of X_i and X, the study considers, separately, the number of US affiliates, the number of European affiliates and the number of Asian affiliates. The eastern region includes the Bohai, Yangtze River Delta and Pearl River Delta geographic regions; $(S_i)^2$ was calculated for each city and then added up for different regions (for simplicity only the numerator of the percentage in the formulation was considered).
2. Due to limitation of statistics, average US FDI inflow and average European FDI inflow cover the period 2002–2010; Asian FDI includes investment from Japan, Korea, Taiwan, Hong Kong, Singapore and Macao; the average Asian FDI inflow is the statistic in the whole of China.
3. Regional average GDP per capita is a weighted average of GDP per capita of all cities inside that region.

Source: Calculated by authors based on the "*Report on Translational Corporations in China*", "China FDI Reports", and the China Economic information network database.

The spatial distribution of innovation resource is not even in China. In Table 6.3, the Herfindahl-Hirschman Index (HHI) is employed to describe the geographical concentration of sample R&D facilities in China:

$$HHI = \sum_{i=1}^{N}\left(\frac{X_i}{X}\right)^2 = \sum_{i=1}^{N}(S_i)^2$$

Compared with the west region, although the center region has a better macro-economic performance, more foreign R&D activities are concentrated in the west, where the HHI is much higher than that in the center. The findings echo those of the OECD (2008), which states that high R&D intensity remains heavy in cities such as Beijing, Shanghai, Shanxi and Chengdu, and the "East-West" gap[1] is less evident than it is in respect of manufacturing plants' location. Therefore, it is very interesting to investigate foreign R&D location choices, by combining MNCs' co-location strategies and host geographic structure.

4.   METHODOLOGIES: DISCRETE CHOICE MODELS

The research adopts two discrete choice models – conditional logit model (CLM) and nested logit model (NLM) – to simulate MNCs' individual R&D location strategy. These models can transcend the limits of available quantitative statistics on the dependent variable, and also consider host geographic structure. The statistics on affiliates' ownership state that on average, 76 percent of R&D affiliates are fully foreign-owned. Thus, the sample MNCs make their location decisions without restrictions, satisfying the basic hypothesis of logit regressions.

Suppose that an R&D affiliate i chooses a region r from set $r = 1, 2, \ldots,$ R in which to locate, followed by the choice of a specific city j from a set of cities $j = 1, 2, \ldots, N_j$ belonging to region r. City j in region r can offer utility π_{jr} to affiliate i, with $\pi_{jr} = \beta X_{jr} + \alpha Y_r + \varepsilon_{jr}$, in which X_{jr} are observed attributes of the city inside the region r, Y_r are those only varying between regions, β and α are the vectors of estimated coefficients.

P_{jr}^i is denoted as the probability that i chooses city j inside of region r, satisfying:

$$P_{jr}^i = P_{j|r}^i \times P_r^i \tag{6.1}$$

$P_{j|r}^i$ is the probability of choosing city j being conditional on having chosen region r, thus:

$$P_{j|r}^i = \frac{e^{\beta X_{jr}}}{\displaystyle\sum_{k=1}^{N_j} e^{\beta X_{kr}}}, \text{ with } j \neq k \tag{6.2}$$

P_r^i is R&D affiliate i's probability of choosing region r, and so:

$$P_r^i = \frac{e^{\alpha Y_r + \sigma_r I_r}}{\displaystyle\sum_{m=1}^{R} e^{\alpha Y_m + \sigma_m I_m}}, \text{ with } m \neq r \tag{6.3}$$

According to McFadden (1984), I_r in equation (3) is the inclusive value representing an expected maximum utility brought about at regional level by the alternative cities inside the region, that is $I_r = \ln(\sum_{k=1}^{N_j} e^{\beta X_{kr}})$; σ_r is the coefficient of inclusive value, and $0 < \sigma_r < 1$ is the sufficient condition for justifying a nested model. If σ_r equals to 1, alternatives inside the nest are quite different, and the Independence of Irrelevant Alternatives (IIA) assumption is valid, and the choice of a region is totally dependent on the choice of city, thus, NLM equates to CLM at city level; if σ_r equals to 0, the choice of region is independent of inside cities' attributes, thus, NLM equates to CLM at regional level. The study substitutes equation (1) by (2) and (3), and then obtains:

$$P_{jr}^i = \frac{e^{\beta X_{jr}}}{\sum_{k=1}^{N_j} e^{\beta X_{kr}}} \times \frac{e^{\alpha Y_r + \sigma_r I_r}}{\sum_{m=1}^{R} e^{\alpha Y_m + \sigma_m I_m}} \quad (6.4)$$

Since $e^{I_r} = e^{\ln(\sum_{N_j k = 1} e^{\beta X_{kr}})} = \sum_{k=1}^{N_j} e^{\beta X_{kr}}$, equation (4) can be transformed as:

$$P_{jr}^i = \frac{e^{\beta X_{rz}}}{e^{I_r}} \times \frac{e^{\alpha Y_r + \sigma_r I_r}}{\sum_{m=1}^{R} e^{\alpha Y_m + \sigma_m I_m}} \quad (6.5)$$

Equation (5) is the basic study's regression model. The research concludes that foreign R&D affiliate i will choose a city j inside the region r maximizing its utility π_{jr}, and if $0 < \sigma_r < 1$, this probability is decided by both regional and city level attributes. The coefficients which make up vector β and α are estimated using the maximum likelihood estimation (MLE) method.

5.   VARIABLES AND HYPOTHESES

5.1   Dependent Variable

The study supposes that each R&D investment happens at the end of the year. The dependent variable (P_{jr}^i) is a binary variable equal to one if city j is chosen as a location by a US (or European or Asian) R&D affiliate, over the period 1992–2011, and zero if it is not. Since a firm will choose a location which can maximize its utility, therefore:

$$P_{jr}^i = \left\{ \begin{array}{l} 1, \text{ if } \pi_{jr} > \pi_{kr}, \forall j \neq k \\ 0, \text{ otherwise} \end{array} \right\}$$

5.2   Variables of Interests

5.2.1   Intra-firm co-location (INTRAF)

Following the idea of Cantwell and Santangelo (2002), Gugler and Michel (2010), Kumar (2001) and Sun (2011), the research uses *the number of manufacturing plants, owned by the same MNC and already located in city j before the entering of the R&D affiliate i*, to measure an MNC's intra-firm clustering strategy.

> **Hypothesis 1.1:** If intra-firm linkages between R&D affiliates with manu-facturing plants are important, an MNC should locate its R&D affiliates in a city which has been already chosen by manufacturing plants owned by the same parent firm. Thus, positive signs are expected.

5.2.2   Intra-industry co-location (INTRA_HLQ)

Guided by previous methods measuring industrial specialization (Mucchielli and Yu 2011), the research employs a city's Location Quotient $(LQ)^2$ in the host industry to capture Marshallian labor pooling effects: *INTRA_HLQ = (city j's employment in industry s/city j's employment in the manufacturing sector)/(China's employment in industry s/China's employ-ment in the manufacturing sector)*.

> **Hypothesis 1.2:** When a location's industrial specialized spillover domi-nates a firm's fear of knowledge leakage, an MNC will co-locate its R&D affiliates with local industry-specialized labor, in order to capture special-ized spillovers. Positive signs are expected.

5.2.3   Home country effect

Inter-firm co-location measures external linkages with other firms (Cantwell and Santangelo 2002, Inui *et al.* 2008). Cultural distance between home and host country may affect this linkage. Two variables are taken into account: Hakanson and Ambos' (2010) psychic distance is used to measure the distance between China and each sample country (or economy).

The study also considers an MNC's home country effect, which is cal-culated as follows: *INTERF_HOME = number of affiliates owned by other MNCs from the same home country and already located in city j before the entering of the R&D affiliate i*.

> **Hypothesis 1.3:** The more psychically distant the home country of an MNC from China, the less likely it will establish an R&D affiliate in a Chinese city; this impediment effect will be neutralized by an MNC's

home country effect in a Chinese city, which has already agglomerated other affiliates from the same home country.

5.2.4 External linkages

R&D agglomeration   INTERF_R&D = number of R&D affiliates owned by other MNCs and already located in city j before the entering of the R&D affiliate i.

> **Hypothesis 2.1:** If an MNC wants to expand its knowledge base, it will co-locate its R&D unit with other MNCs' R&D affiliates. Positive signs are expected.

Co-location with science cities   Gugler and Michel (2010) point out that access to local science and technology resources has increasingly promoted Swiss offshore R&D activities across China. The research respectively considers four variables to measure knowledge resources in a city:

HUMAN = number of higher education students per 10 000 people in j. Higher education students indicate the number of persons who are still studying in higher education institutions and universities, from BA to PhD candidates.

UNIVERSITY = number of higher education institutions and universities in j.

S&T = j's yearly expenditures on Science & Technology activities. S&T activities include science and technological research funded by local government, academic conferences and also research projects organized by local government.

SKILLED = number of scientists, engineers and technicians per thousand in manufacturing employment in j.

> **Hypothesis 2.2:** If external public knowledge resources are essential for firms' innovative activities, foreign R&D affiliates will choose a location with strong public R&D capabilities. Positive signs are expected for these four variables.

5.3   Control Variables

5.3.1   Market size

The pull of local market demand may have significant positive influence on market-seeking R&D (Cantwell and Piscitello 2002). Belderbos (2006) uses GDP per capita to measure a country's market sophistication, and the result shows that it has a positive effect on Japanese overseas R&D locations. Mariani (2002) obtains similar results. This study takes into account *yearly GDP per capita in a city j*, which evaluates local economic development and market demand.

Hypothesis 3: Market size has a positive impact on R&D location.

5.3.2 Labor costs

Motohashi (2005) detects that the higher average wages of science and technology employees in a Chinese province attract more FDI in R&D activities. Low wages in China are no longer a decisive factor for attracting FDI, and productivity has become a determinant (Gugler and Michel 2010, Mucchielli and Yu 2011). The research takes into account *Effective Wage = (average wages of manufacturing employment in city j/yearly total manufacturing output in j)*.

Hypothesis 4: As they are different from manufacturing plants, R&D affiliates attach more importance to labor quality. Thus, the influence of the *effective wage* variable is ambiguous.

5.3.3 Geographic position

In China, sources of innovation are unevenly distributed at regional level (Liu and Chen 2012). Mayer and Mucchielli (1998), Mucchielli and Puech (2003) and Crozet *et al.* (2004) take into account sub-national geographic units in Europe. In the Chinese case, Motohashi (2005), Cheng and Stough (2006) and Hong and Chin (2007) consider respectively the geographic factor's influence on FDI in R&D, production and logistical activities. This study considers *host geographic structure* when measuring a location's geographic position:

Host geographic structure: the research regroups sample cities into five regions based on their geographic positions: *Bohai, Yangtze, Pearl, West* and *Center*.

Hypothesis 5: The geographic position of a Chinese city affects an MNC's overseas R&D location. Location strategies vary with host geographic position.

All statistics at city level come from the *Urban Statistical Yearbooks of China*. Industrial data is collected from the *China Economic Industrial Statistical Yearbook*. All variables are in the form of natural logarithm except *INTRAF*, *INTERF_R&D* and *INTERF_HOME*, due to zero value in some cities. Table 6.4 summarizes the description of independent variables.

6. REGRESSION RESULTS

6.1 CLM and NLM Regression

At first, the study conducts a CLM estimation. In order to reduce the risk of violating the IIA assumption, the study adds a regional dummy to control invisible attributes in a city (Head and Ries 1999). Year dummies aim at controlling macro-economic shocks. The estimation results are reported in Table 6.5. The Hausman-McFadden test is used to examine whether the IIA assumption[3] is violated in the CLM estimations. In the case of US firms, a part of the p-values in the Hausman-McFadden test is very small and, thus, the IIA assumption can't be fully respected. Nonetheless, for the European and Asian firms, the majority of p-values are close to 1, which means the null hypothesis can't be rejected, and the CLM results are credible.

To cut down on the risk of IIA violation, the research conducts an NLM estimation, in which 27 sample cities are grouped into five nests based on their geographic locations. It is supposed that MNCs adopt a hierarchical location process, namely, they choose a region first and then a city inside the region chosen. The NLM regression results are presented in Table 6.6(a)–(c). At regional level, *S&T* and *HUMAN* are sums of these two variables in each city, belonging to the sample region.

6.2 Results Analysis: Cross-country Differences in R&D Co-location Strategies

In order to produce results with economic significance, the study adopts average probability elasticity (APE)[4] to measure the marginal magnitude of the coefficients (Cheng and Stough 2006, Mayer and Mucchielli 1998). By comparing regression results, the research obtains the following main findings, which reveal MNC's cross-country differences in R&D's co-location strategies.

6.2.1 Different decision-making processes

The validity of the nested structure of location choices should respect two criteria: firstly, the inclusive value (IV) lies within the (0, 1) range and is highly significant, especially when the IV is close to 0.5, which proves that

Table 6.4 *Summary of independent variables*

Groups	Variables	Definition	Source	Mean	Standard deviation	Min.	Max.
Internal linkages	INTRAF	Number of manufacturing plants owned by the same MNC and already located in city j before the entering of R&D affiliate i	Authors' own database on MNCs	0.395 (0.544, 0.411)	1.427 (1.874, 1.967)	0 (0, 0)	20 (22, 21)
	INTRA_HLQ	(City j's employment in industry S / city j's manufacturing employment)/ (China's employment in industry S / China's manufacturing employment)	*Urban Statistical Yearbooks of China; China Economic Industrial Statistical Yearbook*	−0.178	0.963	−4.605	2.424
	PSY_DIS	A scale from 0 to 100 by asking executive MBA students and alumni of the partner universities from 2003 to 2008. The scale depends on sum of factors (cultural, language difference, geographic distance, political rivalry, economic development and relative government quality) that affect the flow and interpretation of information to and from a sample economy	Hakanson and Ambos (2010) (see Appendix Table 6A.1)	3.769	0.496	2.564	4.190
	INTERF_HOME	Number of affiliates owned by other MNCs from the same home country and already located in that city j before the entering of R&D affiliate i	Authors' own database on MNCs	31.203 (31.665, 30.167)	34.325 (33.793, 35.912)	0 (0, 0)	291 (292, 275)

External linkages	INTERF_R&D	Number of R&D affiliates owned by other MNCs and already located in city j before the entering of R&D affiliate i	Authors' own database on MNCs	7.548	19.237	0	134
	S&T	j's yearly expenditures on science and technology activities	Urban Statistical Yearbooks of China	11.392	1.237	8.851	15.311
	HUMAN	Number of higher education students per 10000 people in city j	Urban Statistical Yearbooks of China	5.690	0.753	2.763	7.459
	UNIVERSITY	Number of higher education institutions and universities in city j	Urban Statistical Yearbooks of China	2.690	1.049	0	4.419
	SKILLED	Number of scientists, engineers and technicians per thousand employees in the manufacturing sector in city j	Urban Statistical Yearbooks of China	11.362	1.237	8.851	15.311
Control variables	Market size	City j's yearly GDP per capita	Urban Statistical Yearbooks of China	10.104	0.634	7.447	11.932
	Effective wage	Average wage in the manufacturing sector in city j / yearly total output in the manufacturing sector in j	Urban Statistical Yearbooks of China	2.284	0.749	−0.757	4.963
	Geographic position	Regroup sample cities into five regions based on their geographic positions: Bohai, Yangtze, Pearl, West and Center	China Statistical Yearbooks	Dummy variable			

Notes:
1. For the statistics of independent variables, the former data represents US sample firms and those in the brackets represent European and Asian ones respectively.
2. These statistics are calculated on the base of the natural logarithm value.

Table 6.5   US, European and Asian R&D locations: conditional logit model estimation results

Variables	US					EU
	M1	*M2*	*M3*	*M4*	*M5*	*M1*
GDPP	0.079	0.076	0.016	0.285	0.270	0.180*
	(0.339)	(0.237)	(0.106)	(0.343)	(0.535)	(0.098)
EW	−0.302**	−0.187**	−0.240**	−0.363**	−0.317**	−0.914**
	(0.143)	(0.092)	(0.109)	(0.171)	(0.156)	(0.397)
S&T	0.786***	0.772***	0.776***	0.727***	0.806***	0.591**
	(0.262)	(0.259)	(0.248)	(0.223)	(0.212)	(0.267)
HUMAN	0.625***	0.683***	0.676***			0.092*
	(0.193)	(0.198)	(0.248)			(0.050)
SKILLED				0.144***	0.166***	
				(0.047)	(0.047)	
UNIVERSITY				0.902**	1.061**	
				(0.451)	(0.480)	
INTRAF	0.093***	0.086***	0.091***	0.109**	0.103**	0.846***
	(0.029)	(0.026)	(0.028)	(0.049)	(0.046)	(0.250)
INTRA_HLQ	0.313**	0.321**	0.384**			0.568***
	(0.155)	(0.159)	(0.191)			(0.141)
PSY_DIS	−0.140*					−0.368**
	(0.079)					(0.173)
INTERF_ HOME	0.159**					0.782***
	(0.078)					(0.284)
PSY_DIS* INTERF_ HOME		0.015*		0.016*		
		(0.008)		(0.009)		
INTERF_R&D			0.139***		0.166***	
			(0.046)		(0.036)	
Year dummy	Yes	Yes	Yes	Yes	Yes	Yes
Region dummy	Yes	Yes	Yes	Yes	Yes	Dropped
Log likelihood	−376.169	−371.796	−370.293	−373.195	−378.730	−151.228
Pseudo R2	0.3831	0.3902	0.3925	0.3879	0.3789	0.4041
Observations	4070	4070	4070	4070	4070	3079

city and region attributes matter "equally"; secondly, the p-value is less than 0.05 in the IIA test. In Table 6.6(a)–(c), for US firms, the coefficients of IV in the *Bohai*, *Yangtze*, and *Pearl* regions lie within the range (0, 1) and are statistically significant at 5 percent level. This finding attests to Hypothesis 5. In the *West* region, IV is close to 1 and significant at 10 percent level, which reveals that US firms will consider a city's characteristics inside this region quite distinct. The p-value of IIA tests also affirms US firms' hierarchical decision-making processes. For European and Asian firms, regional dummies are dropped automatically in the CLM

				Asian				
M2	M3	M4	M5	M1	M2	M3	M4	M5
0.099*	0.093*	0.089*	0.103*	1.095***	1.092***	1.187***	1.224***	1.207***
(0.054)	(0.051)	(0.049)	(0.056)	(0.328)	(0.327)	(0.335)	(0.336)	(0.335)
−1.367***	−0.983 **	−1.020***	−1.013***	−0.928***	−0.980***	−0.895***	−0.904***	−0.897***
(0.430)	(0.489)	(0.390)	(0.257)	(0.294)	(0.295)	(0.294)	(0.293)	(0.281)
0.592**	0.527**	0.574**	0.553**	0.173*	0.159*	0.154*	0.170*	0.166*
(0.270)	(0.234)	(0.271)	(0.247)	(0.098)	(0.087)	(0.089)	(0.094)	(0.087)
0.080*	0.066*			0.054*	0.035*	0.027*		
(0.043)	(0.036)			(0.029)	(0.021)	(0.016)		
		0.189**	0.255**				0.218**	0.217**
		(0.094)	(0.128)				(0.107)	(0.108)
		0.010**	0.012**				0.005*	0.006*
		(0.005)	(0.005)				(0.003)	(0.003)
0.850***	0.643***	1.204***	0.974***	0.092*	0.082*	0.093*	0.091*	0.088*
(0.277)	(0.227)	(0.409)	(0.363)	(0.052)	(0.045)	(0.051)	(0.049)	(0.046)
0.640***	0.726***			0.217*	0.198*	0.182*		
(0.175)	(0.138)			(0.114)	(0.104)	(0.094)		
				−0.004				
				(0.125)				
				0.315**				
				(0.157)				
0.033**		0.035**			0.127		0.116	
(0.016)		(0.016)			(0.281)		(0.309)	
	0.008**		0.014**			0.021*		0.016*
	(0.004)		(0.006)			(0.012)		(0.009)
Yes	Yes	Yes	Yes	Yes	Yes	Yes	Yes	Yes
Dropped	Dropped	Dropped	Dropped	Dropped	Dropped	Dropped	Dropped	Dropped
−153.445	−150.825	−163.641	−156.530	−381.906	−379.289	−377.877	−377.171	−376.315
0.3954	0.4057	0.3552	0.3832	0.3061	0.3077	0.3062	0.3080	0.3089
3079	3079	3079	3079	3105	3105	3105	3105	3105

Note: Standard errors in brackets, *** $p<0.01$, ** $p<0.05$, * $p<0.1$.

regressions and the p-value is greater than 0.05 in the NLM estimations. Thus, European and Asian firms prefer to choose a city directly rather than use a hierarchical location process.

It can be deduced that MNCs' different location processes may be caused by "information searching costs". The study's database shows that the first US affiliate entered China in 1979 and the first European affiliate was consequently established five years later. US firms know more about regional characteristics when considering location processes of their R&D affiliates; however, to save on information searching costs, European firms

Table 6.6(a)   US and European R&D locations: nested logit model estimation results: Model 1

US

City variables	Internal linkages	External linkages			Control variables	
	INTRAF	INTRA_HLQ	HUMAN	INTERF_HOME * PSY_DIS	GDPP	EW
	0.289**	0.267**	1.439***	0.033**	0.706	−0.392**
	(0.128)	(0.124)	(0.211)	(0.016)	(0.758)	(0.196)

Regional variables	Bohai	Yangtze	Pearl	West	Center	IIA test Ch2 (Prob.>Ch2)
S&T	1.886**	1.867**	1.941	1.851***	1.659	33.24
	(0.811)	(0.801)	(1.790)	(0.575)	(1.870)	(0.000)
Inclusive value	0.422**	0.504**	0.117**	1.070*	1.097	
	(0.179)	(0.216)	(0.056)	(0.594)	(2.201)	

Observations	4070	Log likelihood	−356.601	Year dummy	Yes

EU

City variables	Internal linkages	External linkages			Control variables	
	INTRAF	INTRA_HLQ	HUMAN	INTERF_HOME * PSY_DIS	GDPP	EW
	0.849***	0.582***	0.091*	0.095**	0.265*	−0.637*
	(0.175)	(0.139)	(0.050)	(0.041)	(0.145)	(0.351)

Regional variables	Bohai	Yangtze	Pearl	West	Center	IIA test Ch2 (Prob.>Ch2)
S&T	1.450*	1.327*	1.964	1.740*	1.612	5.67
	(0.801)	(0.715)	(1.668)	(0.961)	(1.549)	(0.7123)
Inclusive value	0.590*	1.062*	0.321	1.044*	1.236	
	(0.325)	(0.587)	(0.631)	(0.576)	(1.239)	

Observations	3079	Log likelihood	−146.317	Year dummy	Yes

Note: Standard errors in brackets, *** p<0.01, ** p<0.05, * p<0.1.

Table 6.6(b) US and European R&D locations: nested logit model estimation results: Model 2

| | US | | | | | | EU | | | | | |
| | Internal linkages | External linkages | | | Control variables | | Internal linkages | External linkages | | | Control variables | |
City variables	INTRAF	INTERF_R&D	SKILLED	UNIVERSITY	GDPP	EW	INTRAF	INTERF_R&D	SKILLED	UNIVERSITY	GDPP	EW
	0.245** (0.118)	0.209** (0.093)	0.227* (0.125)	1.561** (0.723)	0.709 (0.705)	−0.343** (0.170)	0.805*** (0.152)	0.017* (0.009)	0.484*** (0.161)	0.011** (0.005)	0.244* (0.133)	−0.891* (0.489)
Regional variables	Bohai	Yangtze	Pearl	West	Center	IIA test Ch2 (Prob.>Ch2)	Bohai	Yangtze	Pearl	West	Center	IIA test Ch2 (Prob.> Ch2)
HUMAN	1.005** (0.436)	0.990** (0.420)	1.028 (0.781)	0.975*** (0.304)	0.776 (0.856)	29.73 (0.000)	0.093* (0.050)	0.096* (0.052)	0.025 (0.021)	0.108* (0.058)	0.061 (0.051)	3.35 (0.6456)
Inclusive value	0.272** (0.131)	0.321** (0.157)	0.135* (0.071)	1.050* (0.583)	1.042 (2.071)		0.445 (1.529)	0.755* (0.411)	0.380 (1.858)	0.802* (0.440)	1.377 (4.127)	
Observations	4070	Log likelihood −363.035		Year dummy	Yes		Observations 3079	Log likelihood −149.522		Year dummy	Yes	

Note: Standard errors in brackets, *** p<0.01, ** p<0.05, * p<0.1.

127

Table 6.6(c)   Asian R&D locations: nested logit model estimation results: Model 1 and 2

Model 1

City variables	Internal linkages	External linkages			Control variables	
	INTRAF	INTRA_HLQ	HUMAN	INTERF_HOME * PSY_DIS	GDPP	EW
	0.215*	0.227*	0.105*	0.017	0.987***	-0.721**
	(0.115)	(0.119)	(0.061)	(0.126)	(0.375)	(0.358)
Regional variables	Bohai	Yangtze	Pearl	West	Center	IIA test Ch2 (Prob.> Ch2)
						11.27 (0.5215)
S&T	0.325*	0.297*	0.199	0.217	0.208	
	(0.188)	(0.167)	(0.252)	(0.322)	(0.353)	
Inclusive value	0.486*	1.033*	0.372	1.012*	1.152	
	(0.266)	(0.537)	(0.824)	(0.533)	(3.987)	
Observations	3105	Log likelihood −321.523	Year dummy	Yes		

Model 2

City variables	Internal linkages	External linkages			Control variables	
	INTRAF	INTERF_R&D	SKILLED	UNIVERSITY	GDPP	EW
	0.209*	0.018*	0.542**	0.013**	1.008***	-0.698**
	(0.109)	(0.010)	(0.269)	(0.007)	(0.361)	(0.345)
Regional variables	Bohai	Yangtze	Pearl	West	Center	IIA test Ch2 (Prob.> Ch2)
						13.79 (0.6214)
HUMAN	0.103*	0.125*	0.019	0.355*	0.075	
	(0.058)	(0.066)	(0.125)	(0.205)	(0.251)	
Inclusive value	0.462	1.015*	0.391	0.975*	1.158	
	(0.315)	(0.557)	(0.742)	(0.567)	(3.523)	
Observations	3105	Log likelihood −322.836	Year dummy	Yes		

Note: Standard errors in brackets, *** p<0.01, ** p<0.05, * p<0.1.

may prefer to locate directly in big metropolises such as Shanghai and Beijing. Thus, hierarchical location structure of European firms is not evident. For Asian firms, especially those from Taiwan and Singapore, due to geographic proximity and cultural links, they shortlist alternative cities instead of considering the "region-city" structure.

6.2.2   Different R&D co-location strategies of Western MNCs

US R&D affiliates: external linkages   In Table 6.5, three public knowledge variables, *S&T, HUMAN, UNIVERSITY*, and inter-firm R&D, have positive impacts on US R&D location choice. The study's findings affirm Hypothesis 2.2 and Hypothesis 2.3. US R&D affiliates are driven by China's public knowledge stocks and foreign R&D clustering. Motohashi (2005), Alcacer and Chung (2007) and Siedschlag *et al.* (2013) have obtained similar results.

Model 2 in Table 6.6(b) shows that, for a US R&D, the coefficient of *INTERF_R&D* at city level is amplified from 0.166 in the CLM to 0.209 in the NLM estimation, and its magnitude is much bigger than that of European firms and Asian firms. In reality, HP, Alcatel-Lucent, Intel and Microsoft have co-located their R&D affiliates in the Haidian District of Beijing, and the electronics technology park in Chengdu is another "center of excellence", which is chosen by foreign R&D labs, such as Alcatel, IBM and Intel, etc. US firms do not worry about knowledge leakage to their competitors.

European R&D affiliates: internal linkages   Table 6.5 shows that, for European firms, the APE of *INTRAF* is at least seven times as big as that of US and Asian firms; thus, a European R&D prefers to locate near the manufacturing plants owned by the same parent firm. Hypothesis 1.1 is confirmed. Taking European R&D affiliates in Shanghai as an example, Alcatel, Siemens, BASF, Schneider, Philips and Saint-Gobain all adopt intra-firm co-location strategies. European R&D affiliates pay attention to "forward linkages" on the value chain of the firm.

At industry level, Hypothesis 1.2 is true for European firms. Model 3 in Table 6.5 and Model 1 in Table 6.6(a) demonstrate that the positive impact brought about by a city's industry specialization (*INTRA_HLQ*) on a European firm is three times as big as that of US and Asian ones. Some previous research also attests that intra-industry specialization promotes MNCs' location in France and in other European countries (Cantwell and Piscitello 2003, Mayer *et al.* 2010). It can be inferred that European R&D firms may take charge of applied research, supporting local production and market demand. Therefore, they need to benefit from localized spillovers, such as high productivity, skilled labor or some special technology in a host industry. For example, Lipton engaged in R&D on the basis of Chinese consumers' special tastes, by launching green tea and Jasmine tea products in 2004, and in 2005 a herbal tea series with Chinese characteristics was also put on the market.

6.2.3   Asian firms: traditional market-seeking and cost-seeking

The coefficients of a city's GDP per capita are significant at 1 percent level and positively affect Asian R&D affiliates' location decisions. However, this variable is less important for Western firms. The finding echoes with that of Belderbos (2006), which indicates that Western MNCs investing in Asia are less responsive to this market sophistication variable.

In addition, the coefficients of *EW* for Asian firms are on average twice as big as those of US firms. Therefore, Asian R&D affiliates are more "cost-seeking" than US ones. A few previous studies have also proved that, firstly, foreign R&D in China is, for a large part, driven by the motive to reduce R&D costs (Belderbos 2006, Liu and Chen 2012).

The positive and significant coefficients of *SKILLED* affirm Asian firms "efficiency-seeking" strategy (see Model 4, 5 in Table 6.5 and Model 2 in Table 6.6(b) and 6.6(c)). A city's skilled labor intensity in the manufacturing sector is supposed to increase local productivity, and has a greater magnitude for new Asian R&D affiliates than Western firms. Liu and Chen (2012) also prove that the availability of effective local engineers has attracted Taiwanese ICT firms to establish R&D units in China. The findings correlate with Kojima's hypothesis, which indicates that due to a lack of labor, East Asian firms tend to transfer their production units to countries with abundant labor resources.

6.2.4   Psychic distance and home country effect

The coefficients of *PSY_DIS* in Table 6.5 reveal home-host psychic distance has a significantly negative impact on US and European R&D location, and especially so for European firms, with the magnitude being nearly twice that of US firms. However, psychic distance doesn't prevent Asian investors in establishing R&D units in China. Hakanson and Ambos (2010) reveal that, when making foreign entry decisions, two countries' geographic distance has a significantly positive impact on their psychic distance. Since Asian firms have a geographic proximity to China, they don't take psychic distance as an important location factor. Chinese firms' failures in M&A with Western MNCs have demonstrated cultural barriers within management. For example, in TCL Group's M&A with Thomson TV the post-acquisition difficulties, ranging from building effective working relationships with host country stakeholders to reconciling disparate national- and corporate-level cultures (i.e. difference in labor practices between China and France), challenged Chinese managers' cross-cultural management skills (Luo and Tung 2007, Rugman and Li 2007).

Model 1 in Table 6.5 and Table 6.6(a) shows that the "home country" effect is more evident in European R&D affiliates than in US and Asian ones. The findings are supported by Mucchielli and Yu (2011) and prove that due to "risk aversion" (tendency to avoid risks caused by an unfamiliar market environment, law system, or culture distance, etc.) home country agglomeration effects are significant for the European affiliates' location in China. When the interaction variable *PSY_DIS* INTERF_HOME* is considered, interesting results are obtained: this interaction variable has a significantly positive impact on US and European firms, and the magnitude for European firms is nearly three times as large as that of US firms. The more evident the home country effect is, the weaker the psychic distance's negative impact has on European R&D location choice. This finding satisfies Hypothesis 2.1. Being agglomerated with affiliates from the same country, a European firm can benefit from useful information about the host city, establish a network with another "home country" firm, and consolidate its immunity from risk in an overseas location. In practice, the French industrial park in Wuhan city is a typical example. Due to the location of a Citroën manufacturing plant in the early 1990s, the French government intends to promote Wuhan as a "French Cultural Center", by setting up a French Consulate and an Alliance Française, constructing a French Cultural Commercial Street and a French industrial park, and also by promoting academic and educational exchange programs. In April 2012, Air France was the first European airline to open a direct flight route from Paris to Wuhan. As of the end of 2010, there were more than 80 French firms located in Wuhan and more than 1500 French citizens living there. The home country agglomeration's neutralization effects on psychic distance are not evident in Asian firms.

7. DISCUSSION AND MANAGEMENT IMPLICATIONS

The empirical results find consistent support for the study's predictions on MNCs' cross-country differences in R&D co-location strategies across Chinese cities. On the basis of these findings, the study highlights business and policy implications aimed at helping MNCs to better penetrate into China by adjusting their strategies, while also helping the Chinese local government to combine foreign R&D activities with local comparative advantages, in order to strengthen local competitiveness and realize an upgrading in their position on the global value chain (GVC).

Firstly, a city's innovation system is the foundation for establishing R&D labs and sustainable development. The research reveals that the inputs of innovation systems, such as yearly S&T expenditures, promote MNCs' technologically advanced R&D in knowledge-intensive regions. The OECD (2008) indicates that China has several "bottlenecks" in attracting new FDI in R&D, such as shortages in specialized human capital at various stages of the innovation process, especially at the manufacturing stage, with an underdeveloped regional innovation system for translating R&D efforts into innovative outcomes being another obstacle.

Secondly, knowledge cities in China's economically backward regions are suitable for establishing external innovation networks with academic research labs, by being specialized in a particular high-tech industry.

The empirical findings attest that public knowledge resources in the west region largely improve its attractiveness for US R&D centers. Wuhan and Chengdu, located in economic low order regions, have comparative advantages in new energies and/or high technologies. Optics Valley in Wuhan, which agglomerates 48 universities, 56 academic institutions, 11 state-owned major labs and ten National Engineering and Technology Centers, has abundant human capital specialized in fiber-optical communication and botanic genetics (i.e. 200000 skilled technicians and engineers and 400000 university students), and it is also one of China's top three intelligence centers. By 2012, more than 400 European firms had invested 2 billion euro in Wuhan. The majority of these investments concern the low-carbon economy and energy conservation. Moreover, in April of 2012, Lenovo moved its R&D center of mobile internet work to Wuhan with an investment of 16 billion Yuan, due to its rich external knowledge resources in fiber-optical communications.

Thirdly, a city can use the "home country" effect to rationally attract high-quality FDI in R&D activities. The results clearly prove the existence of a "home country" effect for European firms; therefore, a city can take advantage of a location of an affiliate, owned by one of the world's biggest MNCs, which works as a "flag firm" or a "seeding firm" and continually attracts new FDI from the same country. PSA-Citroën first established a joint venture in Hubei province (the center region of China) in 1992, and by 2010 this group had opened four manufacturing plants in the same province. The entrance of PSA has also stimulated other French automobile parts MNCs to invest in Hubei, such as Electricfil Automotive, Faurecia and Valéo, including an R&D center of Valéo. Another example is electronic communications in Chengdu (west region). After Motorola opened an R&D lab in 1993, by 2006 the "snowball" effect had encouraged five MNCs – Ericsson, Nokia, Siemens, Microsoft and Alcatel – to construct their R&D labs in Chengdu.

Fourthly, MNCs can reduce psychic distance by clustering their R&D affiliates with other firms from the same home country, especially European MNCs, and Chinese local government can also establish special organizations for guiding new entrants.

A yearly National Image Survey organized by the BBC revealed that globally, in 2012, 39 percent of interviewees held a negative impression of China, and that French people had the worst opinions *vis-à-vis* China, with a negative ratio of 68 percent. Consequently, there is still a long road ahead for China to decrease its cross-cultural distance with developed countries. In recent years, construction of central business districts (CBDs) which agglomerate MNCs' headquarters and consular services, and also the development of cultural and creative industries in Beijing are good examples of this being pursued. With these culture-promoting channels, foreign investors can better access the Chinese market.

8. CONCLUSIONS

This chapter aims to enrich the current understanding of R&D globalization towards a developing market by both theoretical and empirical sides. Firstly, focusing on US, European and Asian offshore R&D affiliates located in China, it establishes a framework on MNCs' R&D co-location strategies by combining location theory and R&D networks literature. Secondly, due to China's substantial regional variations, and to avoid the aggregation bias of a national level study, it uses "city" as the basic geographic unit and considers a city's heterogeneity in geographic location. Thirdly, it takes advantage of published statistics by the Chinese government and adopts discrete choice models, which better simulate MNCs' individual location strategies than an aggregate model.

In summarizing the key findings, the empirical evidence proves MNCs' cross-country differences in clustering strategies: US firms tend to favor conducting a "region-city" hierarchical location process approach, and seem to pay particular attention to external innovation linkages, through co-locating with public knowledge resources or other R&D firms, especially in the Bohai and the Western regions. However, European R&D firms, which are "efficiency-seeking", prefer internal linkages, including intra-firm forward linkage, agglomeration of affiliates from the same home country, or local industry specialization. Furthermore, unlike Western MNCs, Asian MNCs adopt traditional market- and cost-seeking strategies rather than co-location strategies. China's geographic structure's impact on European firms is therefore not significant.

ACKNOWLEDGMENTS

This research received financial support from P.R. China's 2013 National Social Science Foundation (Young Researchers' Program: No. 13CJY052) and the Fundamental Research Funds for the Central Universities (WUT: 2015VI003).

NOTES

1. The "East-West" gap indicates the imbalance of regional economic development between east coast provinces (cities) and hinterland provinces (cities) in China.
2. Due to the limitation of statistics, the employment data by industry is only available at provincial level. The majority of sample cities are capital cities, which are the economic and industrial centers of provinces. The study supposes that, in a province, a city's proportion of employment in an industry s is similar to that of the manufacturing sector at provincial level. Thus, a city j's employment in industry $s = j$'s share of yearly manufacturing employment in province $p \times p$'s employment in industry s.
3. The principle of the Hausman-McFadden test is to compare the estimated coefficient of a sub-sample, in which an alternative is omitted, to those of the full sample. The null hypothesis is that the Independent Irrelevant Alternatives (IIA) is not violated and the results of the CLM are credible. Thus, when the p-value is very small, the null hypothesis can't be accepted and the CLM estimations are not credible.
4. According to p. 157 in Mayer and Mucchielli (1998), the coefficients obtained by CLM and NLM estimations are slightly greater than APE: in NLM estimations, since variables at city level will influence those at regional level through inclusive values (IVs), the scaling factor is the same for the city and region; in CLM estimations, the APE of an independent variable k equals to $\beta_k(\frac{J-1}{J})$, in which J is the total number of administrative units considered in estimations and β_k is the estimated coefficient of variable k. In this study, J equals to 27. Thus, the coefficients obtained by CLM should be multiplied by 0.963 for the sample firms.

REFERENCES

Alcacer, J. and Chung, W. (2007), 'Location strategies and knowledge spillovers', *Management Science*, **53**(5), 767–776.

Belderbos, R. (2006), 'R&D activities in East Asia by Japanese, European, and US multinationals', Japan Center for Economic Research Working paper, 1 June.

Brookfield, J. and Liu, R. (2005), 'The internationalization of a production network and the replication dilemma: building supplier networks in Mainland China', *Asia Pacific Journal of Management*, **22**(4), 355–380.

Bruche, G. (2009), 'The emergence of China and India as new competitors in MNCs' innovation networks', *Competition and Change*, **13**(3), 267–288.

Buckley, P. and Ghauri, P. (2004), 'Globalisation, economic geography and the strategy of multinational enterprises', *Journal of International Business Studies*, **35**(2), 81–98.

Camagni, R. (1991), 'Local milieu, uncertainty and innovation networks: towards a new dynamic theory of economic space', in Camagni, R. (ed.), *Innovation Networks: Spatial Perspectives*, London: Belhaven Press, pp. 121–142.

Cantwell, J. and Iammarino, S. (1998), 'MNCs, technological innovation and regional systems in the EU: some evidence in the Italian case', *International Journal of the Economics of Business*, **5**(3), 383–408.

Cantwell, J. and Iammarino, S. (2000), 'Multinational corporations and the location of technological innovation in the UK regions', *Regional Studies*, **34**(4), 317–332.

Cantwell, J. and Iammarino, S. (2005), 'The technological innovation of multinational corporations in the French regions', *Revue d'économie industrielle*, **10**, 9–28.

Cantwell, J. and Narula, R. (2001), 'The eclectic paradigm in the global economy', *International Journal of the Economics of Business*, **8**(2), 155–172.

Cantwell, J. and Piscitello, L. (2002), 'The location of technological activities of MNCs in European regions: the role of spillovers and local competencies', *Journal of International Management*, **8**(1), 69–96.

Cantwell, J. and Piscitello, L. (2003), 'The recent location of foreign R&D activities by large MNCs in the European regions. The role of different sources of spillovers', R-Papers submitted to ERSA 2003 Congress.

Cantwell, J. and Piscitello, L. (2005), 'Recent location of foreign-owned research and development activities by large multinational corporations in the European regions: the role of spillovers and externalities', *Regional Studies*, **39**(1), 1–16.

Cantwell, J. and Santangelo, G. (2002), 'The new geography of corporate research in information and communications technology (ICT)', *Journal of Evolutionary Economics*, **12**(1–2), 163–197.

Cheng, S. and Stough, R. (2006), 'Location decisions of Japanese new manufacturing plants in China: a discrete-choice analysis', *The Annals of Regional Science*, **40**(2), 369–387.

Crozet, M., Mayer, T. and Mucchielli, J.L. (2004), 'How do firms agglomerate? A study of FDI in France', *Regional Science and Urban Economics*, **34**(1), 27–54.

Dunning, J.H. (1998), 'Location and the multinational enterprise: a neglected factor?', *Journal of International Business Studies*, **29**(1), 45–66.

Flores, R. and Aguilera, R.V. (2007), 'Globalization and location choice: an analysis of US multinational firms in 1980 and 2000', *Journal of International Business Studies*, **38**(7), 1187–1210.

Gassmann, O. and Zedtwitz, H. (2004), 'Motivations and barriers of foreign R&D activities in China', *R&D Management*, **34**(4), 423–437.

Gugler, P. and Michel, J. (2010), 'Internationalization of R&D activities: the case of Swiss MNEs', *International Business & Economics Research Journal*, **9**(6), 65–80.

Hakanson, L. and Ambos, B. (2010), 'The antecedents of psychic distance', *Journal of International Management*, **16**(3), 195–210.

Hashai, N. (2009), 'Knowledge transfer considerations and the future of the internalization hypothesis', *International Business Review*, **18**(3), 257–264.

Head, K. and Ries, J. (1999), 'Attracting foreign manufacturing: investment promotion and agglomeration', *Regional Sciences and Urban Economics*, **29**(2), 197–218.

Hedge, D. and Hicks, D. (2008), 'The maturation of global corporate R&D: evidence from the activity of U.S. foreign subsidiaries', *Research Policy*, **37**(3), 390–406.

Helble, V.R. and Chong, L. (2004), 'The importance of internal and external R&D network linkages for R&D organizations: evidence from Singapore', *R&D Management*, **34**(5), 605–612.

Hofstede, G. (ed.) (1991), *Culture and Organizations*, New York: McGraw-Hill.

Hong, J. and Chin, A. (2007), 'Modeling the location choices of foreign investments in Chinese logistics industry', *China Economic Review*, **18**(4), 425–427.

Inui, T. *et al.* (2008), 'The location of Japanese MNC affiliates: agglomeration, spillovers and firm heterogeneity', CEPII working paper, 2008(24).

Ito, B. and Wakasugi, R. (2007), 'Factors determining the model of overseas R&D by Multinationals: Empirical Evidence', RIETI discussion paper series 07-E-004.

Kaufmann, J. and O'Neill, H. (2007), 'Do culturally distant partners choose different types of joint ventures?', *Journal of World Business*, **42**(4), 435–448.

Kogut, B. and Singh, H. (1988), 'The effect of national culture on the choice of entry mode', *Journal of International Business Studies*, **11**(1), 35–55.

Kuemmerle, W. (1999), 'The drivers of foreign direct investment into research and development: an empirical investigation', *Journal of International Business Studies*, **30**(1), 1–24.

Kumar, N. (1996), 'Intellectual Property Protection, market orientation and location of overseas R&D activities by multinational enterprises', *World Development*, **24**(4), 673–688.

Kumar, N. (2001), 'Determinants of location of overseas R&D activity of multinational enterprises: the case of US and Japanese corporations', *Research Policy*, **30**(1), 159–174.

Liu, M. and Chen, S. (2012), 'MNCs' offshore R&D networks in host country's regional innovation system: the case of Taiwan-based firms in China', *Research Policy*, **41**, 1107–1120.

Luo, Y. and Tung, R.L. (2007), 'International expansion of emerging market enterprises: a springboard perspective', *Journal of International Business Studies*, **38**(4), 481–498.

Magnmusson, P. and Boyle, B. (2009), 'A contingency perspective on psychic distance in international channel relationships', *Journal of Marketing Channels*, **16**(1), 77–99.

Mariani, M. (2002), 'Next to production or to technological clusters? The economics and management of R&D location', *Journal of Management and Governance*, **6**(2), 131–152.

Markusen, J. (ed.) (2002), *Multinational Firms and the Theory of International Trade*, Cambridge, MA and London: MIT Press.

Marshall, A. (ed.) (1890), *Principles of Economics*, London: Macmillan and Co., Ltd.

Mataloni, R.J. (2011), 'The structure of location choice for new U.S. manufacturing investments in Asia-Pacific', *Journal of World Business*, **46**, 154–165.

Mayer, T. and Mucchielli, J.L. (1998), 'Strategic location behavior: the case of Japanese investments in Europe', in J.L. Mucchielli, P. Buckley and V. Cordell (eds.), *Globalization and Regionalism: New Strategies for Multinational Firms*, New York: Hartworth Press.

Mayer, T., Mejean, I. and Nefussi, B. (2010), 'The location of domestic and foreign production affiliates by French multinational firms', *Journal of Urban Economics*, **68**(1), 115–128.

McFadden, D.L. (1984), 'Economic qualitative response models', in Z. Griliches and M. Intrilligator (eds.), *Handbook of Econometrics, Vol. II, 1396–1456*, Amsterdam: Elsevier.

Motohashi, K. (2005), 'R&D of multinationals in China: structure, motivations and regional difference', RIETI discussion paper series 06-E-005.

Mucchielli, J.-L. and Puech, F. (2003), 'Internationalisation et localisation des firmes multinationales: l'exemple des entreprises françaises en Europe', *Economie et Statistique*, **363**(1), 129–144.

Mucchielli, J.-L. and Yu, P. (2011), 'MNC's location choice and agglomeration: a comparison between US and European affiliates in China', *Asia Pacific Business Review*, **17**(4), 1–24.

OECD (2008), *Reviews of Innovation Policy: China*, Paris: OECD.

Park, S. (2012), 'Competitiveness of East Asian science cities and role of innovative SMEs', International Council for Small Business. World Conference Proceedings, June 2012.

Rugman, A. and Li, J. (2007), 'Will China's multinationals succeed globally or regionally?', *European Management Journal*, **25**(5), 333–343.

Shimizutani, S. and Todo, Y. (2008), 'What determines overseas R&D activities? The case of Japanese multinational firms', *Research Policy*, **37**(3), 530–544.

Siedschlag, I. *et al.* (2013), 'What determines the location choice of R&D activities by multinational firms?', *Research Policy*, **42**, 1420–1430.

Song, J., Asakawa, K. and Chu, Y. (2011), 'What determines knowledge sourcing from host locations of overseas R&D operations?: a study of global R&D activities of Japanese multinationals', *Research Policy*, **40**, 380–390.

Sun, Y. (2011), 'Location of foreign research and development in China', *GeoJournal*, **76**(6), 589–604.

Sun, Y., von Zedtwitz, M. and Simon, D. (eds.) (2008), *Global R&D and China*, Oxford: Routledge.

Todo, Y. and Shimizutani, S. (2009), 'R&D intensity for innovative and adaptive purposes in overseas subsidiaries: evidence from Japanese multinational enterprises', *Research in International Business and Finance*, **23**(1), 31–45.

UNCTAD (2005), *World Investment Report 2005*, Geneva: UNCTAD.

Zaheer, S. (1995), 'Overcoming the liability of foreignness', *The Academy of Management Journal*, **38**(2), 341–363.

APPENDIX

Table 6A.1   Psychic distance between China and the sample economy

Country	US	France	Germany	Italy	Belgium	Denmark	Finland	Netherlands
China	44	48	52	56	63	60	66	62
Country	Sweden	Switzerland	UK	Japan	Korea	Singapore	India	Taiwan
China	64	65	48	29	25	13	48	18

Note: Hakanson and Ambos (2010)'s survey does not include the score of Finland, Singapore and Taiwan. Due to similar geographic distance, economic development and cultural distance, China's psychic distance of Singapore (and also Taiwan) is replaced with that of Korea, and that of Finland is replaced with that of Switzerland.

Source: Refer to Table 2 on p. 202 of Hakanson and Ambos (2010).

7. Chinese outward direct investment to the European Union against the background of the euro crisis

Bernadette Andreosso-O'Callaghan and Christopher Dathe

INTRODUCTION

The euro crisis that has been unfolding since 2008 manifested itself by financial stress, liquidity problems and low investment rates in the euro area and in the European Union (EU) as a whole. By contrast, the economy of the People's Republic of China (PRC) has been relatively resilient, and the weakened EU economy might have therefore represented an opportunity for relatively cash-rich Chinese firms. The opportunity is palpable through the speeding up of financial reforms (with the aim of RMB internationalization for example) and also through the large increase in research and development (R&D) expenditure in China since 2008.

In terms of direct investment, which is meant to refer to cross-border capital flows leading to a significant management influence and a long-term investment relationship (with the common threshold for a direct investment being 10 percent of voting shares), a natural question that springs to mind is whether the euro crisis represents a turning point for Chinese outward direct investment (ODI) in the EU and in particular in the distressed euro area. Have Chinese investment deals been opportunistic in the euro area, in particular in its distressed periphery?

By analyzing Chinese investment deals in the EU with an emphasis on inflows since the euro crisis, this chapter attempts at bringing some elements of response to this central question. By doing so, section 1 reviews the institutional framework supporting overseas direct investment since the implementation of the Chinese economic reforms in 1979. This institutional framework led to the emergence of the Chinese global multinational corporation (MNC) and it culminated with the 'going global strategy'. Section 2 reviews Chinese direct investment trends in the EU before and after the euro crisis. Section 3 analyzes the extent to which the euro crisis can be seen as an opportunity for the Chinese MNC. Some concluding remarks will be provided in a final section.

1. INSTITUTIONAL FRAMEWORK UNDERPINNING THE EMERGENCE OF THE CHINESE GLOBAL MNC

Up until China joined the World Trade Organization (WTO) in November 2001 leading to its transformation into a major world economic player, several regulations and laws had already been in place that facilitated *outward* direct investment from the country. Much has been written about the different laws permitting and governing the establishment and operations of foreign economic entities on China's territory since Deng Xiaoping's reforms (see Naughton, 2007) – laws decided at the 3rd Plenary Session of the 11th Central Committee of the Communist Party of China (CPC) in 1978 (for example the *Law of the PRC on Joint Ventures Using Chinese and Foreign Investment*) – but substantially less is known about the institutional framework encouraging foreign direct investment (FDI) from China since that same time period. According to the Beijing-based Development Research Center of the State Council (see Gang, 2002), four different stages can be identified in the modern history of the PRC outward investment regulatory framework up until the country's member-ship to the WTO.[1] During the first stage covering the period 1979–1985, the State Council allowed for the first time in the PRC history the establish-ment of businesses overseas. At the time, outward trading and investment activities by only a few enterprises were only marginal since, between 1979 and 1983, the annual total amount of overseas investment was roughly US$9.2 million (Gang, 2002). During the second stage (1986–1991) appli-cation procedures for enterprises undertaking business overseas on either a joint-venture or a wholly-owned enterprise basis were fine-tuned (except for those investing in Hong Kong and Macao). The new legislative frame-work stipulated different application procedures for 'large' investments, i.e. those above US$1 million. Application for these large projects had to be made to the people's government of each province (autonomous region and municipality) first, and then to the Ministry of Foreign Trade and Economic Cooperation (MOFTEC) for its further application to the cor-responding embassy of the relevant country.[2] The annual average invested amount reached US$208 million during this period. Further procedural fine-tuning characterizes the third stage (1992–1998) with an upper limit set at US$30 million for large-scale projects involving bodies such as the State Development Planning Commission and the State Council.

During this period, annual direct outward investment amounted to about US$705 million. The fourth stage started in 1999 with the issuing of a circular by MOFTEC; this circular was aimed at encouraging enterprises processing and assembling overseas through the supplying of their own material inputs.

All four stages culminated in October 2000 with the central government decision to make the 'going out strategy' one of the four key pillars in terms of economic and social development, together with the Western development strategy, the Urbanization strategy and the Human Resource (talent) strategy (CCPIT, 2008). These priorities were to become subsequently enshrined in the 10th Five Year Plan (FYP) covering the period 2001–2005. The year 1999 can therefore be considered as an important critical juncture in China's ODI strategy as other pieces of legislation, such as the 'Administrative Regulation of the Discount Interest Rate for Loans for Working Foreign Exchange for Overseas Enterprises of Raw-Processing Trade', effectively created a fund of foreign exchange managed by Chinese banks to lend to the selected overseas investing enterprises (processing trade). From that time, ODI became increasingly a key topic in China's policy making. The year 1999 coincided broadly with China's accession to the WTO in November 2001, and this marked a new era of capital- and technology-intensive exports and of outward Chinese international flows (Chen, 2009).

Key to the Chinese ODI strategy is the element of diversification of host markets by investing also for example in the emerging international markets of Latin America, Africa, Middle East, Eastern Europe and Southeast Asia. Chinese ODI in many of these emerging markets is in mining and this is seen from the part of the State Council as crucial, with the aim of diversifying China's energy sources from coal to nuclear power and to renewable energy (State Council, 2003). In developed countries, ODI is encouraged to further expand overseas processing and assembly trade and the Chinese institutions also encourage Chinese companies to take part in overseas engineering, overseas agriculture production and processing as well as promoting the cooperation of Chinese companies with foreign financial institutions. The aim here is to transform the Chinese manufacturing base from a labor- to a technology-intensive industrial base, in line with its technology and research policy.

In terms of the evolving institutional framework, larger direct investment projects and lighter administrative procedures for many of the projects became gradually the rule. For example, from 2003, the streamlining of the examination and approval procedures for ODI became more decentralized, with local government departments gaining more authority with regard to processing trade.[3] The 'Verification and

Approval Procedures for OFDI/Interim Measures for the Administration of Examination and Approval of the Overseas Investment Projects' (National Development and Reform Commission, 2004) gave enterprises under the administration of the central government the right to invest independently overseas without obtaining prior approval from the central government, if the investment is below US$30 million in the area of raw materials and resources or below US$10 million in the other approved sectors and industries. These investments are possible in all countries having restored diplomatic relations with China, excluding Taiwan up until the signing of the Economic Cooperation Framework Agreement (ECFA) with China in 2012.

2. CHINESE DIRECT INVESTMENT TRENDS IN THE EU

This section opens with an overview of China's increasing global positioning as an outward direct investor. It then goes on to depict, using descriptive statistics, Chinese ODI in the EU alongside a number of dimensions including geographical and sectoral distribution, as well as mode of entry.

2.1 Overview – General Trends

According to the latest figures released by UNCTAD (2015), some 55 percent of ODI originates from developing and emerging countries. The analysis of global investment flows does show that the share of direct investment from mainland China in total global direct investment has significantly grown, from 0.08 percent in 2000 to 8.6 percent in 2014 of total global direct investments. In 2012, mainland Chinese ODI grew by about 18 percent and became for the first time higher than Hong Kong ODI flows. In 2014, Hong Kong overtook China again in terms of ODI flows, and this is explained by a strong outflow of ODI from Hong Kong (at 77 percent) during that year (UNCTAD, 2015).

By 2013, Chinese firms had invested in more than 60 countries, with Australia, the USA and Canada having been the major hosts in value terms. Other large host countries are Iran, Brazil, Indonesia and Nigeria (EIU, 2013). According to forecasts by the Economist Intelligence Unit (EIU) based on UNCTAD figures, China's direct investment outflows are expected to equate direct investment inflows for the first time by the end of 2015, ceteris paribus. The EIU forecast places the turning point in terms of outflows surpassing inflows to happen in 2017 (EIU, 2014).

It should be noted that an exact picture of direct investment flows between China and the EU is blurred by a number of limitations, namely: (1) the rising use of offshore financial centers and tax havens; for example Luxembourg stands out as one of the largest historical recipients of inward investment in the EU. This is explained by the fact that Chinese companies, among others, choose Luxembourg to incorporate legal entities due to its lax tax regime (European Union Chamber of Commerce in China, 2013; Hanemann and Rosen, 2012); (2) the role of Hong Kong in rerouting Chinese investment towards different destinations including the EU. About 85 percent of Chinese ODI is from Hong Kong and from Caribbean tax havens (Hanemann and Rosen, 2012). The Chinese government's measurement of the overseas activities by its companies' offshore subsidiaries is rather tentative, thereby rendering the official data on Chinese direct investment notoriously unreliable; (3) relatedly, a growing number of Chinese direct investments are channeled through offshore equities and complex financial vehicles and according to Hanemann and Huotari (2015), this is explained partly by strong financial market regulations in China which many enterprises try to bypass; (4) considerable delays in publishing the figures with a lag of about nine months in the case of Chinese statistics and 1.5 years in the case of Eurostat data; and (5) added to these limitations, is the issue of confidentiality under the cover of data protection, hiding some of the transfers.

Consequently, and not surprisingly, there is considerable variation between the figures reported by the different official agencies. For example, Eurostat put Chinese inward direct investment in the EU as low as $0.98 billion in 2010, whereas according to MOFCOM the figure is $5.96 billion, or six times greater (Hanemann and Rosen, 2012).

These limitations are somewhat minimized by some of the data released by private think-tanks and research institutes who base their measurements on individual transactions or enterprises (Hanemann and Huotari, 2015). The China Global Investment Tracker (CGIT) from the American Enterprise Institute and Heritage Foundation (2015) is one such source of information upon which we will rely here as much as possible. This source measures all Chinese investments above US$100 million (or about €74 million) by using corporate information to determine the final destination of Chinese investments. This is especially important for Hong Kong, which officially receives about 40 percent of Chinese direct investment.

By reconciling all the different sources and even though the accuracy of the resulting figures is subject to heated debate, the trends suggest a unique pattern: there has been a recent shift of Chinese investment from mineral resource-rich countries such as the developing countries of Africa to partnerships in advanced economies countries, such as those of the EU, and therefore there has been a substantial increase in Chinese direct investment to the EU. According to Deutsche Bank figures (which seem to accord with MOFCOM figures), the total stock of Chinese direct investment in the EU was slightly greater than €6.1 billion in 2010, and by the end of 2012 these stocks had quadrupled to reach nearly €27 billion (Hansakul and Levinger, 2014). These preliminary figures indeed suggest a shifting trend of Chinese ODI in the EU since the global financial crisis, or a 'crisis effect'.

2.2   Statistical Analysis of Chinese ODI in the EU

After the crisis hit the world economy, global FDI flows fell by about 34 percent between 2007 and 2014, and global FDI inflows contracted by another 16 percent in 2014, reaching US$1.23 trillion, which is below the pre-2008 crisis level. Over the 2007–2014 period, the share of global investment inflows into the EU shrank by about 22 percentage points to reach 17 percent of total inward investment in 2014. It was however during that time that Chinese ODI started to surge worldwide, growing from 4 percent in 2007 to 19 percent in 2014 of all global direct investment flows. Despite or perhaps because of the global decline of investment flows, this stable growth makes Chinese investment special for the European economies (UNCTAD, 2015).

While Chinese ODI in the EU declined at the beginning of the financial crisis, Chinese investment increased again after 2009 leading to a surge in 2014 of nearly €13 billion. Figure 7.1 shows that Chinese ODI in the EU does not look like a short-lived bubble, but that it tends rather to signal a lasting interest in the European economy.

Indeed, between 2006 and the first half of 2015, Chinese firms invested €41 billion in the EU, representing about 22 percent of all Chinese ODI (American Enterprise Institute and Heritage Foundation, 2015). Chinese investment flows to the EU grew indeed from a low €462 million in 2006 to €12 billion in 2014, with an average annual growth of 50 percent. For the year 2014, China's ODI flows to the EU represented about 40 percent of its total ODI.

Rhodium Group data, which include investment projects that are smaller than US$100 million, show a big surge in investment after the crisis hit from about €1 billion in 2008 to €10 billion in 2012. After a decline to €7 billion in 2013, the inflow reached a historical high of €14 billion in 2014 (Hanemann and Huotari, 2015; Hanemann and Rosen, 2012).

2.2.1   Type of Chinese investor and mode of entry
A first striking characteristic of Chinese ODI in the EU is its concentration on high value-added (VA) deals. This logically implies that these investments are mainly driven by government-controlled investors such as

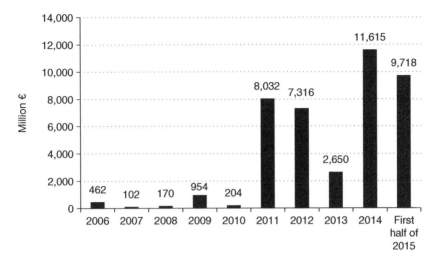

Note: The exchange rate USD–EUR has been calculated based on Eurostat figures.

Sources: American Enterprise Institute and Heritage Foundation (2015), China Global Investment Tracker for Chinese outward investments, own calculation.

Figure 7.1   Chinese ODI to the EU (million €, 2006–2015)

the Chinese State-Owned Enterprises (SOEs) followed by the Sovereign Wealth Funds (SWFs). Chinese SOEs such as China National Offshore Oil Company (CNOOC) and Sinopec have been the first movers and are still the main direct outward investors from China. SOEs and SWFs invested together €12.5 billion or 72 percent of the inflowing Chinese investment in the EU between 2000 and 2011 (Hanemann and Rosen, 2012), and they were responsible for about 18 of the top 20 deals in Europe (Macdonald and Yan Lin, 2012). SWFs alone are responsible for 17 percent of the value of all Chinese ODI, and their investments are mainly aimed at ensuring financial diversification in China's currency reserves as well as the procurement of resources for the Chinese manufacturing sector (Macdonald and Yan Lin, 2012).

However, SOEs are far less important to Europe than they are to the rest of the world. Even if SOEs accounted for 55 percent of the value of all Chinese ODI between 2000 and 2011, most deals (359 or 63 percent) in Europe were done by private entities with a government ownership below 20 percent. In particular, private investment by small and medium-sized enterprise (SMEs) in green-field projects and in the services sector (Hanemann and Rosen, 2012) are aimed at securing operational advantages in the areas of branding and technology.

In terms of entry mode in the EU, some 69 percent of all invested projects over the period 2000–2014 were green-field investments leaving 31 percent to the mergers and acquisitions (M&A) category.

2.2.2   Geographical distribution of Chinese ODI in the EU

Over the long period 2000–2014, more than 50 percent of all Chinese investments were concentrated in the European core countries such as the UK, Germany and France. Some of these investments have been widely reported in the national press, such as for example the acquisition of a top-tier German company of the Putzmeister Group by a Chinese company eager to acquire Western know-how and technology, in the area of concrete pumps (Klawitter and Wagner, 2012). Other much discussed deals have been Geely's US$1.5 billion purchase from Ford of Volvo in 2010, the US$600 million acquisition of Germany's Medion AG (multimedia products) by Lenovo in 2011, the controversial inroad by the SWF China Investment Corporation (CIC) in buying a 30 percent stake in the French Gaz de France in August 2011, as well as the China Ocean Shipping Company's (Cosco Pacific) planned purchase of a majority stake in Athens' port of Piraeus.

A rising amount of Chinese ODI has been flowing into the EU peripheral countries, Cyprus and East European countries since 2012. Indeed, the share of EU peripheral countries in total Chinese ODI in the EU went from below 10 percent prior to 2011 to 30 percent between 2012 and 2014 (Hanemann and Huotari, 2015). In particular, Italy and Portugal have increasingly been sought after by Chinese investors since 2010, with total Chinese investments of €19 billion and €6 billion respectively up to the first half of 2015. In 2014, Italy was China's second biggest target in Europe after the UK with a surge of investment in the first half of the year, since approximately 85 percent of the €7 billion cumulated Chinese investment in Italy by the end of 2014 was made in the year 2014 alone. Portugal saw a jump in 2011 and in 2014, and Spain has experienced steady increases since the euro crisis (American Enterprise Institute and Heritage Foundation, 2015). In short, even though the UK remains the top recipient of Chinese investment in the EU on a cumulative basis, Chinese investors have been diversifying more and more their ODI strategy in the EU (Hanemann and Huotari, 2015).

2.2.3   Sectoral distribution of Chinese ODI in the EU

The sectoral distribution of Chinese ODI in the EU also shows a great degree of increasing diversification. Rising investment trends have been noted in financial intermediation since 2012, a broad sector undergoing a contraction in the EU between 2008 and 2012. An increasing share of these

Table 7.1   *Chinese direct investment stock in Europe (2005–first half of 2015, million €)*

	Agriculture	Energy	Finance	Real estate	Technology	Transport	Other	Sum
Austria						101		101
Belgium		202	233					436
Britain	2669	2413	519			1351	1089	10155
France	382	2694			233	1370	2241	6921
Germany		397	105	1655	481	783	93	3516
Greece							86	86
Hungary							1193	1193
Italy		2303			357	6261		8921
Luxembourg						166		166
Netherlands	941		1334		204	296	1089	3863
Poland		727				78		804
Portugal		3289	1024		444		75	4827
Spain							233	233
Sum	3992	12021	3716	4126	1362	10405	6100	41222

Note: The exchange rate USD–EUR has been calculated based on Eurostat figures.

Sources: American Enterprise Institute and Heritage Foundation (2015), China Global Investment Tracker, own calculation.

ODIs has been made in the broad category of business services (25 percent of all Chinese FDI in 2013) according to Eurostat (2015). Consequently, the share of manufacturing has been declining but this sector is still considered as representing a business opportunity given the eagerness of Chinese investors to acquire superior skills, technology and other modern strategic assets. Table 7.1 depicts the sectoral distribution of Chinese ODI between 2005 and June 2015 on a cumulated basis, and it shows clearly the still-predominant role of broad sectors such as energy and transport (representing 29 percent and 25 percent of the total respectively). Interestingly and although the UK is still the main recipient in 2015 it has largely been caught up by peripheral countries such as Italy (representing 22 percent of inward Chinese investment in the EU) and Portugal (12 percent). Note that other statistical sources put Greece at the same level as Portugal in 2014, whereas Spain remains a very marginal recipient (Nodé-Langlois, 2014). As discussed above, the German and French shares have been diminishing slightly, but it is important to highlight the relative importance of these two countries for real estate and transport (Germany) as well as for energy and transport (France). In the energy sector, the acquisition of a 21 percent stake in Energias de Portugal in 2011 by the Chinese Three Gorges Corporation was one early example of Chinese inroads into the power utility sector of an EU country. Finally, the agricultural sector has been the fifth most sought after sector with 10 percent of Chinese total ODI in the EU by June 2015. Since most of these investments have flown to the UK, a country which is not particularly characterized by a relatively large agricultural sector in output terms, it can be conjectured easily that these investments have been mostly in food commodities-related stocks, food companies as well as in the food retail sector (including catering). Of specific note are the US$1.5 billion Chinese investment in the restaurant chain PizzaExpress and the US$1.9 billion stake in Weetabix (manufacturer of breakfast cereals) (American Enterprise Institute and Heritage Foundation, 2015). Chinese direct investment in the broad agricultural sector of other EU countries includes the US$940 million deal in Nidera, a Dutch food commodity distributor.

Other alternative statistical sources, to both Eurostat and the National Bureau of Statistics of China, such as the Rhodium Group data, place the energy sector as the key targeted sector for Chinese ODI in the EU over the years. Fossil fuel and metal assets are strong in the EU because many global mining firms are listed in London while their assets are often located outside of the EU (Hanemann and Rosen, 2012). The transport sector has been the second highest recipient, especially the automotive sector with €8.2 billion. The Rhodium Group data tend to minimize the extent of ODI in the banking sector by putting it at scarcely 4 percent of total Chinese ODI in the EU, against 13 percent according to other sources.

An interesting, contrasting, picture emerges in terms of entry mode and sectoral distribution when appraised together. SOEs tend to invest mainly in mineral resources and in the energy sector, while private investors prefer to invest in technologies and brands. The first strategy is in line with the central government objective to secure energy from abroad whereas the second strategy espouses the motives of asset (i.e. knowledge) seeking. In that regard, the EU is an ideal investment location. According to recent surveys by the EIU (2013 and 2014), some 22 percent of all surveyed potential Chinese investors mentioned acquiring brands and technology as their main motivation for future direct investment in the EU. Four EU countries feature prominently as top preferences, namely Germany, France, the UK and Sweden, although all EU countries slipped to lower ranks according to the 2013 survey (EIU, 2014).

Increasing sectoral diversification is therefore a feature of Chinese ODI in the EU. As noted by Hanemann and Rosen (2012) and by Hanemann and Huotari (2015), Chinese firms' strategies in the areas of distributive trades, logistics, marketing and also R&D are aimed at creating a network of Chinese firms in Europe, something which is very much reminiscent of Japanese firms' strategies in Europe in the 1980s–1990s

(Andreosso-O'Callaghan, 1996). This increasing sectoral diversification promotes, and in turn is stimulated by, China's changing position in the global value chain owing to a great deal of structural change in the country. China is still relatively strong in the middle segment of the value chain which has relatively low profit margins, and it is relatively weak in those segments of the value chain characterized by high profit margins, such as upstream research and development, branding, as well as distribution and retail (in downstream activities). Rising domestic production costs have been an important push factor leading to the relocation of Chinese manufacturing sites in low-cost countries such as Vietnam, whereas an appreciating RMB has been putting pressures on low VA light manufacturing activities, forcing Chinese producers to move up the value chain into higher VA products.

3. ANALYSIS: THE EURO CRISIS AS AN OPPORTUNITY FOR CHINESE ODI?

The above review leads to a number of specific insights.

First, Chinese ODI in the EU does not conform to standard FDI theory (with the ownership-location-internalization or OLI paradigm at its core) but rather it follows a logic that has been noted before in the case of other East-Asian countries in the past, namely Japan and South Korea. A combination of push factors and pull factors together explain this ODI. With regard to push factors, they are entirely represented by the changing institutional framework since 1978 (and this is a major distinguishing factor with standard ODI models which involve Western economies such as the USA, Germany or Japan). As seen in section 1, the evolving institutional framework created incentives for investing abroad and this culminated with the 'going global' policy. The only 'specific' asset (*à la* Dunning) is the financial assets of cash-rich and heavily controlled Chinese firms. Deprived of any other assets emanating from the firm itself, it has been and still is thus imperative for the Chinese firm to seek a long-lasting involvement in advanced markets abroad, such as that of the EU, in order to acquire specific assets such as technology, marketing know-how (branding) and superior managerial capabilities. Chinese investors have therefore been largely opportunistic by investing at the same time in natural resources as well as in highly praised assets. There is also some evidence of market seeking behavior, although this has been rather marginal so far (Richet, 2013) given the large qualitative distance existing between the sophisticated EU average consumer and the average Chinese producer.

Second, Chinese ODI in the EU has shown a remarkable ability to adapt to the rapidly evolving global circumstances. The severe contraction of economic activity in the EU since 2008 and the inability to bring timely and adequate responses to the euro crisis in the EU area until the autumn of 2012 explain to some extent the cautious approach with regard to Chinese investment in the EU financial and insurance sector up to that date. Increasingly, larger stakes are being invested in the EU (Scissors, 2015). As discussed earlier, Hansakul and Levinger (2014)[4] note a change in ownership of Chinese investors since the late 2000s with Chinese private firms playing a bigger role. Their share in Chinese M&A activity in Europe rose to more than 30 percent between 2011 and 2013, compared to 4 percent in the previous three years. These considerations show again the increasing assertiveness of Chinese investors in a mature and advanced market such as the EU.

Third, owing to the EU external policy designed along the lines of it being a 'principled actor', antagonism and extreme caution on the part of certain EU recipient countries are important considerations when studying ODI emanating from a one-party rule and non-democratic country. Two main types of obstacles (socio-environmental and technological protection) have been noted. In terms of labor laws and environmental protection, a survey led by the European Union Chamber of Commerce in China found that Chinese companies in the EU saw labor laws, labor costs, immigration rules and cultural differences in management style as the main obstacles to doing business in Europe. Despite these obstacles, some 97 percent of the Chinese companies that have invested in Europe planned to invest even more in the years to come (European Union Chamber of Commerce in China, 2013).

Finally, the West (including the EU) is notorious for its reluctance to accept deals in technology-based sectors from countries such as China. Although evidence shows (Helwer, 2013) that the technology distance between, say, a typical German manufacturing firm in the motor-vehicle industry and a Chinese equivalent has shrunk over time, the EU and EU firms are still not willing to sell China their key technologies (Scissors, 2015).

CONCLUSION

The Chinese economic reforms decided at the 11th CPC Central Committee in 1978 opened a new vista not only for firms investing in China but also for Chinese firms contemplating direct investment abroad. An array of procedures and laws formed a strong (and strengthening) outward investment regulatory framework culminating in October 2000 with the 'going global strategy'. An analysis of Chinese ODI brings to the fore a number of revealing remarks: first, the fast speed at which this ODI is growing, increasing for example one-hundredfold in relative terms between 2000 and 2014; second, a diversification in terms of host countries at the global level; and, third, a turning point between being a passive recipient of ODI and being a sender of direct investment in around 2015/2016.

Despite the difficulties measuring the real extent of Chinese FDI flows in the EU, in particular because of the increasing use of offshore financial centers and of tax havens such as Luxembourg, a close examination of the data shows an indisputable increase of Chinese ODI in the EU since the euro crisis, with a quadrupling of Chinese direct investment stocks in the EU between 2010 and 2012. Chinese investment was quite hesitant at the beginning of the crisis period (until 2010), but it surged afterwards and remained consistently high, suggesting therefore a more lasting (new) trend. Increasing confidence over time on the part of Chinese investors can also be seen in relation to their entry mode and geographical location in the EU. Whereas high VA deals from SOEs and SWFs were common at the beginning of the period, the specific case of the EU is characterized by a relatively large share of deals done by private entities (SMEs) with a government ownership below 20 percent. Indeed, the predominance of this type of investor suggests the aim of securing advantages in the areas of branding and technology/knowledge (asset-seeking). The wait-and-see policy and cautious attitude of Chinese investors and institutions *vis-à-vis* the EU is also visible from the evolving choice of host countries in the EU. Whereas the UK is still the main recipient of Chinese ODI in 2015, peripheral countries such as Italy and Portugal have increasingly been sought after. Diversification is also visible in terms of industrial sectors with a shift from energy and transport into services, in particular business services and real estate.

This analysis shows that Chinese ODI does not follow the prescribed dominant FDI theory, and that the Chinese case, although close enough to the cases of Japan and South Korea, is rather different because of the paramount importance of the institutional factors, in particular of the CPC. Given its remarkable ability to adapt to evolving macroeconomic circumstances and in particular to some of the responses proffered to the euro crisis, Chinese ODI in the EU can be seen as opportunistic. The conditional rescue programs orchestrated by the EU, the European Central Bank and the International Monetary Fund have been putting pressure on crisis-stricken countries such as Greece, Portugal and Italy to privatize and to sell off large minority stakes in utilities and infrastructure. As a result, Chinese investors have seized the opportunity, and they have turned more systematically towards the EU distressed periphery. What this ultimately shows is that the euro area crisis has not only allowed these peripheral EU economies to gain some credibility in the eyes of Chinese investors, but that Chinese ODI in the EU, although still small, has grown formidably in the space of only a few years, and this is what needs to be focused on in the future.

ACKNOWLEDGEMENTS

The authors would like to thank Guilhem Fabre for very valuable comments on an early version of this chapter.

NOTES

1. Another similar breakdown can be found in CCPIT (2008, p. 3) where the breakdown in different stages is made on the basis of the Five Year Plan (FYP).
2. Several institutions are involved in today's 'going out' strategy. These are the Ministry of Commerce (MOFCOM), the National Development and Reform Commission (NDRC), the State Administration of Foreign Exchange (SAFE), and the State-owned Assets Supervision and Administration Commission (SASAC). The approval of projects is subject to examination by the NDRC, the approval of companies falls under the remit of MOFCOM, whereas records are mostly kept by SAFE (JunHe Law Firm, 2014).
3. See the Circular on the Pilot Work Concerning the Examination and Approval of Overseas Investments released by MOFCOM in April 2003 and the Circular on Issues Relating to Simplifying the Examination and Approval Procedures for the Projects of Overseas Processing Trade and Delegating the Authority released by both MOFCOM and SAFE in June 2003.
4. As reported by the *Financial Times* in a 2014 article entitled 'Chinese investors surged into EU at height of debt crisis' by Jamil Anderlini in Beijing, 6 October 2014, accessed on 15 June 2015 at http://www.ft.com/cms/s/2/53b7a268-44a6-11e4-ab0c-00144feabdc0.html#axzz3zJQOBuiO.

REFERENCES

American Enterprise Institute and Heritage Foundation (2015), 'China Global Investment Tracker', accessed on 17 August 2015 at https://www.aei.org/data/China-Global-Investment-Tracker.

Andreosso-O'Callaghan, B. (1996), 'The Spatial Impact of Japanese Direct Investment in France', in Darby, J. (ed.), *Japan and the European Periphery*, London: Macmillan, pp. 111–131.

CCPIT (China Council for the Promotion of International Trade) (2008), '2007 Discussion Research Paper', China Council for the Promotion of International Trade ('我国 '走出去' 战略的形成及推动政策体系分析'), Beijing, accessed on 24 July 2015 at http://aaa.ccpit.org/Category7/Asset/2007/Jul/24/onlineeditimages/file71185259698809.pdf.

Chen, C. (2009), 'Characteristics of FDI firms in China after WTO accession', in Chen, C. (ed.), *China's Integration with the Global Economy*, Cheltenham, UK and Northampton, MA, USA: Edward Elgar Publishing, pp. 101–125.

Economist Intelligence Unit (2013), 'China Going Global Investment Index – A report from The Economist Intelligence Unit', London: Economist Intelligence Unit.

Economist Intelligence Unit (2014), 'China Going Global Investment Index – A report from The Economist Intelligence Unit', London: Economist Intelligence Unit.

European Union Chamber of Commerce in China (2013), 'Chinese Outbound Investments in the European Union', January, accessed on 17 August 2015 at http://www.kpmg.de/docs/Chinese_Outbound_Investment_European_Union.pdf.

Eurostat (2015), 'Balance of Payment International Transaction', last updated on 16 July, accessed on 15 August 2015 at http://ec.europa.eu/eurostat/data/database.

Gang, L. (2002), 'Reform of the Administrative System for Promoting a Healthy Outward Investment Development' (改革行政审批制度促进境外投资健康发展), Policy Research Group for Major Enterprises Going-Out Studies (大企业 '走出去' 政策研究" 课题组), Development Research Center of the State Council, accessed on 24 July 2015 at http://www.drc.gov.cn/dcyjbg/20020509/75-224-30360.htm.

Hanemann, T. and M. Huotari (2015), 'Chinesische Direktinvestitionen in Deutschland und Europa – Eine neue Ära chinesischen Kapitals', Mercator Institute for China Studies and the Rhodium Group, June, accessed on 17 August 2015 at http://www.merics.org/fileadmin/templates/art/aktuelles/COFDI/COFDI-DE-Web.pdf.

Hanemann, T. and D.H. Rosen (2012), 'China Invests in Europe – Patterns, Impacts and Policy Implications', Rhodium Group, June, accessed on 17 August 2015 at http://rhg.com/wp-content/uploads/2012/06/RHG_ChinaInvestsInEurope_June2012.pdf.

Hansakul, S. and H. Levinger (2014), 'China-EU Relations: Gearing up for Growth', Deutsche Bank Research, 31 July, accessed on 7 September 2015 at http://www.dbresearch.com/PROD/DBR_INTERNET_EN-PROD/PROD0000000000339508/China-EU+relations%3A+Gearing+up+for+growth.PDF.

Helwer, K. (2013), 'German Technology Transfer to China in the Automotive Industry', Masters Thesis at the Ruhr-Universität Bochum Faculty for East Asian Studies, June.

JunHe Law Firm (2014), 'The Review of China's Outward Investment Policy for the Last 10 years and Interpretation of the New Policy', Beijing.

Klawitter, N. and W. Wagner (2012), 'Buying Germany's Hidden Champions: Takeover Could Signal New Strategy for China', *Spiegel Online*, 9 February, accessed on 6 September 2015 at http://www.spiegel.de/international/business/buying-germany-s-hidden-champions-takeover-could-signal-new-strategy-for-china-a-813907.html.

Macdonald, M. and Y. Lin (2012), 'China-Europe-China Deal Flow: A Perspective on the Trends', in *China Deals – A Fresh Perspective*, PricewaterhouseCoopers LLP, pp. 10–22, October, accessed on 12 August 2015 at http://www.pwc.co.uk/industries/emerging-markets/insights/china-deals-a-fresh-perspective.html.

National Development and Reform Commission (2004), 'Verification and Approval Procedures for OFDI/Interim Measures for the Administration of Examination and Approval of the Overseas Investment Projects', 9 October, trans. by Bernasconi-Osterwalder, N., L. Johnson and J. Zhang (eds.) (2013),

Chinese Outward Investment: An Emerging Policy Framework – A Compilation of Primary Sources, The International Institute for Sustainable Development and the Institute for International Economic Research, pp. 43–48, accessed on 7 August 2015 at http://www.iisd.org/pdf/2012/chinese_outward_investment.pdf.

Naughton, B. (2007), *The Chinese Economy – Transition and Growth*, Cambridge, MA: MIT Press.

Nodé-Langlois, F. (2014), 'Les capitaux chinois déferlent sur l'Europe', *Le Figaro Economie*, 15 October, accessed on 12 August 2015 at http://www.lefigaro.fr/conjoncture/2014/10/15/20002-20141015ARTFIG00316-les-capitaux-chinois-deferlent-sur-l-europe.php.

Richet, X. (2013), 'L'internationalisation des firmes chinoises: croissance, motivations, stratégies', Fondation Maison des Sciences de l'Homme, February, accessed on 15 June 2015 at https://halshs.archives-ouvertes.fr/halshs-00796197.

Scissors, D. (2015), 'China's Investment in the World Increasing, Not Soaring', American Enterprise Institute, July, accessed on 17 August 2015 at https://www.aei.org/wp-content/uploads/2015/07/Chinas-investment-in-the-world-increasing-not-soaring.pdf.

State Council (2003), 'China's Policy on Mineral Resources', December, trans. by Bernasconi-Osterwalder, N., L. Johnson and J. Zhang (eds.) (2013), *Chinese Outward Investment: An Emerging Policy Framework – A Compilation of Primary Sources*, The International Institute for Sustainable Development and the Institute for International Economic Research, pp. 119–133, accessed on 7 August 2015 at http://www.iisd.org/pdf/2012/chinese_outward_investment.pdf.

United Nations Conference on Trade and Development (UNCTAD) (2015), 'World Investment Report – Reforming International Investment Governance', 24 June, Geneva: United Nations Publications.

8. Expatriation policies of Chinese emerging MNCs

Feng Wei and Jacques Jaussaud

INTRODUCTION

China has been growing dramatically after the implementation of the "open door policy" from the end of the 1970s, and is now one of the most powerful emerging countries. A significant number of foreign companies entered into China in the form of various kinds of foreign direct investment (FDI), equity joint ventures with local partners at first, but also as wholly owned subsidiaries from 1986. In doing so, foreign firms were looking for low production costs on the one hand, and for huge market potential on the other hand. According to a report of the United Nations Conference on Trade and Development (UNCTAD, 2013), China attracted FDI of US$121 billion in 2012, and became the second largest favorite inward FDI location in the world after the United States.

At the same time, intense competition at home pushes Chinese companies to develop their businesses at an international level, in order to benefit from foreign market opportunities and to develop economies of scales. By 2013, according to *Fortune* magazine, Chinese companies including those from Hong Kong and Taiwan occupied 95 places in the world's top 500 list, their total annual revenue being US$5200 billion, which is 17 percent of the total annual revenue of the world's top 500 companies. Among these 95 companies, 85 were from mainland China, 4 were from Hong Kong, and 6 were from Taiwan. These 95 Chinese firms had overseas employees of 624 000, which is 28.58 percent higher than the 485 000 overseas employees of the *Fortune* 500 list in 2012. What's more, according to UNCTAD's 2013 worldwide FDI report, China became the third largest outward FDI country in the world. Chinese FDI amounted to US$4 billion, behind the United States and Japan. Such growing FDI requires, on the part of Chinese companies, the despatch of more and more expatriates abroad, as one may imagine.

However, Chinese multinational companies do not have much experience as far as international management and particularly international human resource management are concerned. China is still a new participant in international markets when compared to the multinational corporations (MNCs) of the industrialized countries. For instance, in 2014 the average transnationality index of the top 100 Chinese MNCs, as the arithmetic mean of the ratio of their foreign assets to total assets, the ratio of their foreign sales to total sales, and the ratio of their foreign employment to total employment, was only 13.6 percent,[1] far lower than the transnationality index of the world's top 100 MNCs at 64.55 percent, and even much lower than the transnationality index of the top 100 MNCs of developing countries at 54.22 percent. Thus one may fear that international human resource management by Chinese MNCs might be neither mature nor implemented according to systematical systems in most cases.

As far as the academic literature is concerned, the vast majority of the published papers are devoted to expatriation management by the MNCs from the industrialized countries, such as West European countries, the United States and Japan (Schaaper *et al.*, 2012; Tung, 1981). Some papers, but not so many, have been published on Asian-Pacific MNCs, such as those from Singapore, Taiwan and South Korea (Calantone and Zhao, 2000; Cheng and Lin, 2009; Hailey, 1996; Lin *et al.*, 2012). But to the best of our knowledge very few papers have been published on the cases of Chinese mainland MNCs. It is thus essential to investigate Chinese MNCs in order to discover the ways in which they manage their expatriates and to identify the problems they are facing on expatriation management. We may wonder too whether successful western experiences may inspire them to improve their expatriation management systems and to strengthen their capabilities in international business. Based on a qualitative investigation of expatriation practices by 18 Chinese MNCs, this research finds that the expatriation policies of Chinese emerging MNCs present both common features and differences with expatriation policies of more experienced MNCs from western industrialized countries and Japan.

The structure of this chapter is as follows. Section 1 investigates the academic literature on the question of expatriation, underlying the possible specificities of Chinese MNCs. Then, in order to check the nature and extent of such specificities, section 2 is devoted to our empirical investigation.

1.   LITERATURE REVIEW

The general research question of this chapter is as follows: How do emerging Chinese mainland MNCs manage their expatriates? Do they conform with the practices that are suggested by the academic literature, ranging from a rigorous selection of candidates to pre-departure training, implementation of an enticing compensation system and a fair and motivating evaluation system, and career planning management (Belderbos and Heijltjes, 2005; Feldman and Thomas, 1992; Hiltrop and Janssens, 1990; McEvoy and Buller, 2013; Tung, 1984)? What specific problems might Chinese MNCs face as far as expatriation is concerned, and what particular solutions might they implement?

In order to answer such questions, the academic literature on expatriation may be of some help, although it is devoted mainly to other countries than China, particularly industrialized countries, as already stated.

When firms develop their business abroad, particularly through the creation of subsidiaries, staffing key management positions with expatriates is almost always necessary, for several reasons (Edström and Galbraith, 1997; Perlmutter and Heenan, 1974; Schaaper *et al.*, 2013). Developing a subsidiary abroad requires a high degree of interaction with managers at headquarters, which is easier for an expatriate who previously worked in the MNC's country of origin, and possibly at the headquarters itself. Expatriates often share similar cultural backgrounds, both national and corporate, with headquarters' managers. They will have developed informal networks within the MNC, prior to their assignment, which are particularly useful for recently created subsidiaries. Furthermore, expatriation is an instrument of control by headquarters over overseas subsidiaries (Ando *et al.*, 2008; Edström and Galbraith, 1997; Lam and Yeung, 2010; Perlmutter and Heenan, 1974). Thus MNCs often appoint expatriates as general managers or chief financial officers in subsidiaries abroad, while they may assign local managers to more locally oriented functions, such as human resource management (HRM) and marketing (Harzing, 2001).

Expatriation is extremely costly however, as in addition to their wages expatriates usually receive extra payments depending on the geographic distance and cultural and standard-of-living differences between the host country and their own (Latta, 1999). For western MNCs, it has been estimated that the costs of sending a manager to Asia can be tenfold the cost of employing him or her at home, if not more (Selmer, 2003; Wong and Law, 1999).

Furthermore, even good managers can underperform when expatriated, as the context may differ significantly from home (Black *et al.*, 1991; Claus *et al.*, 2011; Tung, 1981). According to Tung (1981), the expatriation failure rate (the expatriate being recalled or dismissed) reaches between 10 to 20 percent for US firms and around 5 percent for European and Japanese firms. With a broader definition of expatriation failure, Black *et al.* (1991) estimate failure rates of 16 to 50 percent. In the 1990s in

China, the expatriation failure rate by foreign MNCs reached some 25 to 30 percent (Melvin and Sylvester, 1997).

The costs of expatriation failure are extremely high. The MNC has to repatriate and replace the failed manager, with huge moving expenses for both, and undertake the selection and training of the new expatriate. The MNC has also to bear the hidden costs of subsidiary underperformance when the first expatriate fails to meet business objectives. The costs and difficulties linked to expatriation lead MNCs to favor short-term assignments of managers or technicians if the problems to be solved do not require long stays, on the one hand, and to develop training and promotion of local managers for key management positions when possible (Fayol-Song, 2011; Jaussaud and Schaaper, 2006, 2007; Selmer, 2003; Wong and Law, 1999). Training and promotion of local managers for key management positions, however, requires a lot of effort and the accumulation of experience in the country, as a comprehensive system of local HRM should be developed in order not to train managers who would subsequently leave to a competitor (Fayol-Song, 2011; Kühlmann and Hutchings, 2010; Schaaper *et al.*, 2013).

According to Lee (2007), three major issues may cause expatriation failure, two of them being lack of formal cross-culture training on the one hand and family issues on the other hand. Trained candidates should be better equipped to face the challenges arising from the overseas assignment. In addition, Carlson (2005) found globally that companies which spent money on language training for expatriates and their spouses had an increased success rate from 34 percent in 1999 to 42 percent in 2005. Referring to the family issues, we can easily imagine that the spouses of the expatriates have to give up their own jobs in order to accommodate the move. They have also to deal with the daily household affairs in a foreign language and a new environment, a different culture and different ways of dealing with everyday problems. The same may apply for their children, as they may have to give up their familiar studying environment and leave their close friends to live in a place where they have to go to school in which a foreign language is spoken and be surrounded by foreign faces. If the expatriates receive complaints rather than support when they return home after work, they might feel stressed and become anxious, which might negatively influence their performances on the overseas missions. On the other hand, a supportive family environment has a significantly positive influence on the expatriate's quality of work life, and on his or her ability to accomplish the overseas assignment successfully (Hays, 1974).

As China has a different culture and different values from those of western countries, and as Chinese MNCs are at the very initial stage of their internationalization, we wonder whether the same problems which were identified by McEvoy and Buller in 2013 are also being faced by Chinese MNCs. For instance, do Chinese international human resources managers encounter the same difficulties in persuading the most suitable candidates to accept international assignments? Are they facing the same problems, such as the expatriates and their families not being interested in participating in the pre-departure training programs? Are they also confronted with complaints relating to the inequity of the income differential between the expatriates and host country employees who feel that they deal with roughly the same work as the expatriates?

As mentioned above, in 2013 95 Chinese companies were ranked in the world's top 500 *Fortune* list, and 85 of those were from mainland China. It appears however that 78 of the 95 MNCs are controlled by the mainland Chinese government, which poses the following question: Is the expatriation management in the state-owned Chinese mainland MNCs the same as that in the private Chinese mainland MNCs? It is often assumed that Chinese state-owned companies invest more on training and compensation than private firms do, for example. Do they also do this as far as expatriation is concerned? Do they invest more in the training, settling abroad and compensation programs to make sure that the expatriates and their family members would better adapt to the foreign, unfamiliar environment and would be more satisfied, which could contribute to the further success of the overseas assignments?

Additionally, the repatriation policy in the state-owned MNCs could be different from that in private Chinese MNCs. The former would provide greater certainty in terms of repatriation, as in some of the state-owned companies the lifetime employment system still exists. Some previous research indicates that the lifetime employment system explains to some degree the reason why in the Japanese MNCs the failure rate is relatively lower than the MNCs of other western countries (Belderbos and Heijltjes, 2005). Our empirical research will check whether such repatriation policies differ from Chinese state-owned and private firms, and whether this may affect their expatriation failure rate.

Thanks to China's "open door policy" since 1978, and to its admission to the WTO (World Trade Organization) in 2001, China now has become the second largest economy in the world. Although Chinese MNCs are still new participants in the worldwide business scene they have been growing and developing internationally at an incredible speed. This is not easily done. The President of the Center for China & Globalization (CCG), Wang Huiyao, estimated that at the beginning of the present century China needed approximately 75 000 executive managers with international experience, when only 3000–5000 were able to meet those needs (from *China Daily*, 12 November 2013).

Thus, much research is currently needed on the expatriation management of Chinese MNCs in order to discover how they manage their expatriates and about their strategies on expatriation management. We need to investigate precisely their practices, the problems they face in the process, and solutions they may find to address the problems. Therefore, we undertook an empirical investigation on a sample of 18 Chinese MNCs, focusing on their expatriation policies, outcomes, and difficulties faced.

2.   METHODOLOGY

This study is based on a qualitative investigation, as Chinese firms are still reluctant to answer large questionnaire surveys when not administrated by supervising authorities. Furthermore, Collings *et al.* (2009, p. 1263) call for more qualitative research in international HRM, to "shed light on some of the underlying factors behind specific phenomena and a more nuanced understanding of global staffing decisions." This is particularly relevant in the case of China, which involves a number of specificities still not addressed rigorously by the academic literature. In 2014 and 2015, we conducted semi-structured, in-depth interviews with international human resources managers of 18 major Chinese MNCs.

On the basis of the academic literature that has been presented in section 1 above, we prepared a semi-structured interview guide in English and Chinese. Seven open-ended questions and several sub-questions invited the manager respondents to describe the HRM practices in their subsidiaries, as well as any changes they expected in these practices. We asked about a wide variety of HRM practices, to gain extended insights into the actual situation and any difficulties they may have faced when implementing these practices. Those interviewed were managers working in China, following one or several international assignments.

Through personal contacts we have with people working in Chinese firms, we contacted the people in charge of international HRM in a carefully selected sample of major Chinese companies. When they agreed to participate in our research, we sent them our questionnaire, which was either filled in face to face, or on the phone, or we received their answers by mail. In all cases, we could get additional explanations from them if and when needed. We eventually received comprehensive answers from 18 companies. Table 8.1 contains an overview of the sample. At the request of the interviewees, we do not provide the names of the MNCs, allowing the respondents to answer more freely. For the same reason we indicate the industry sector in very broad terms only. All the MNCs in our sample are major players in China in their industry sector.

Table 8.1   Sampled Chinese MNCs interviewed in 2014 and 2015

Chinese MNC Identification Code	Industry	HQ localization	Main countries of settlement*	State-owned vs private
CA	Equipment for telecommunications	Shenzhen	Most countries in the world	Private
CB	Building	Shenyang	Most countries in the world	State-owned
CC	Education services	Hangzhou	Australia	Private
CD	Trucks manufacturer	Beijing	Russia, India, Middle East	State-owned
CE	Railway construction	Beijing	African countries, Latin America	State-owned
CF	Furniture industry	Dalian	African countries	Private
CG	Electricity generation	Guangzhou	Middle East, African countries, European countries	State-owned
CH	Electricity generation	Guangzhou	Middle East, African countries, Europe, North America	State-owned
CI	Iron and steel	Chongqing	African countries	State-owned
CJ	Banking and finance	Beijing	Most countries in the world	State-owned
CK	Banking and finance	Beijing	European countries, South America	State-owned
CL	Hydraulic engineering	Chongqing	African countries	State-owned
CM	Trading company	Shanghai	African countries	Private
CN	Trading company	Chongqing	African countries	Private
CO	Construction and civil engineering	Beijing	African countries	State-owned
CP	Human resource management services	Beijing	European countries, North America	State-owned
CR	Construction	Chongqing	African countries	State-owned
CS	Electricity generation	Hubei	African countries, Asia, America	State-owned

Note: * Some of the respondents did not wish the cities in which they are located to be released, so we only cite the provinces in which they are located.

Among the 18 Chinese MNCs that we interviewed, five are on the list of the world's top 500 companies, and nine belong to the Chinese top 500 companies. As can be seen in Table 8.1, there is a certain amount of diversity in the sample in order that the results are not biased by industry specificity or headquarter location, for instance. Furthermore, we had enough cases to reach the so-called saturation point, in the sense that we did not receive any more crucial information on our research question when carrying out the last interviews (Symon and Cassel, 1998).

In order to investigate the whole process of expatriation management by the Chinese MNCs, our questions ranged from candidate selection, to training, compensation, evaluation, incentive mechanisms, and to repatriation. We also asked questions on the positions held by the expatriates, the main difficulties they might encounter, solutions which were implemented if any, localization of management positions as an alternative to expatriation, and so on. Questions were of an open nature, as our approach is a qualitative one, in an exploratory perspective. Additional data have been found on the internet (including company websites), and from other sources, including, for example, newspapers. Carefully selected secondary data have been added to primary data collected by questionnaire as a basis for our analysis.

The content of the interviews was fully transcribed and then translated into English for analysis. We entered the transcripts into a thematic content analysis grid, with one column per MNC, and one line per topic drawn from answers to our question or sub-question in the interview guide. We then carefully reduced the answers to key words, numbers and short sentences. Reduced in this way, the content analysis grid reveals systematic regularities and contrasts in HRM practices by our sample of Chinese MNCs.

3.   MAIN RESULTS

Most of the Chinese MNCS in our sample do not have difficulties in persuading their staff to travel abroad for an international assignment. Our respondents mention the following reasons. First, in most cases there are more candidates who are willing to work in industrialized countries than opportunities available, because of the current difficulties in China with regard to, for example, rather low salaries, air pollution in major cities, food safety issues, and so on. Some respondents also mentioned limited opportunities for personal development in China, constraining "relationship" issues in Chinese society, and even fascination with western culture. Second, young staff members are often ready to work in "hard condition" countries, because of the potential for an increased salary and a rapid promotion upon returning from such an international assignment. Third, even those who do not want to be assigned abroad have to comply when asked to do so by their employer; if they do not, sooner or later they will have to leave the company.

Most of the managerial positions of subsidiaries abroad are occupied by expatriates from the mother company. According to our respondents, this is in order to keep control over the subsidiaries in an unknown environment and to better develop businesses in close relationship with the headquarters in China. This is in line with what has been explained in the literature review section (Edström and Galbraith, 1997; Perlmutter and Heenan, 1974; Schaaper *et al.*, 2013). As they lack experience in foreign countries, Chinese firms find it difficult to trust "strangers" with their different language, culture, customs and habits. Thus they send a lot of expatriates to their subsidiaries abroad, according with the "ethnocentric" approach identified by Perlmutter (1969) and Perlmutter and Heenan (1979). However, some experienced MNCs also hire or promote local managers when staffing even the highest positions in certain departments which require a precise knowledge of the local environment, such as the marketing or HRM departments. In doing so they follow a "polycentric" approach, in the words of Perlmutter (1969) and Perlmutter and Heenan (1979).

In terms of compensation, expatriates receive their basic salary plus a daily allowance for working in the foreign country they have been assigned to, plus an accommodation allowance, plus other incentives. The basic salary is determined by the mother company in China according to the number of working years completed and the position level held by the expatriate. The daily allowance varies from country to country according to the local working and living conditions. The accommodation allowance and other allowances are also strongly related to the host country. All things considered, not surprisingly it appears that compensation principles for expatriates do not differ very much when comparing Chinese MNCs and other countries' MNCs, particularly mature ones. That said, the amounts of the various components of the compensation may differ greatly.

According to our respondents, however, it seems that expatriates of Chinese MNCs feel that they are not sufficiently supported by their parent company during their international assignments. In particular, they call for more support in terms of personal life support, working support, psychological counseling, family issues, and so forth.

Nevertheless, those who were expatriated to industrialized countries asked their companies to extend the expatriation period, which in most of the cases was two to three years' duration. Better living conditions than those in China, significantly higher salaries than can be earned in China, more personal development opportunities in working abroad than when working in China, are the most significant reasons for them wanting to extend the length of their stay. This is in line with Edström and Galbraith (1997) who emphasize expatriation as a way to improve the expatriates' capabilities.

On the basis of information provided by our respondents, it appears that Chinese MNCs clearly follow the same method as that of western companies in selecting suitable candidates. They select candidates both from inside and outside of the company, but the latter case is much rarer. The employers favor candidates they are familiar with in terms of their professional abilities and their personalities, which they consequently can trust. Candidates from outside the company are generally invited to apply only when no suitable candidate from inside has been found, which, as previously mentioned, happens rarely. The candidates are generally selected by both the human resources department and by the immediate supervisor, or at least by one of them. Overall, the selection process of candidates for expatriation in Chinese MNCs does not differ greatly from that of other MNCs, such as described by the academic and professional literature.

Most of the MNCs in our sample mention some problems regarding the selection of candidates for expatriation. They often lack suitable candidates in terms of the ability to speak foreign languages and the ability to adapt. They have many candidates certainly, but most of them do not have the right capabilities to be expatriated successfully. It is not easy, respondents insist, to be accepted by local staff in the subsidiaries abroad, and to adapt to foreign laws and practices. In many countries where Chinese MNCs are engaged, safety issues are crucial because of political instability and social unrest, not to mention wars and terrorism. Candidates are scarcely prepared nor scarcely able to face such situations. Another problem that has been raised by several of our respondents is the lack of strong employee loyalty.

In all of our sample MNCs, those selected attend a training program before departure. In all cases, the program is focused on language and professional knowledge more than any other aspects. For those who are to be sent to countries characterized by dangerous conditions, safety training is also provided. According to our respondents, training the candidates to behave morally by respecting the people, the regulations and the culture of the host country would be very useful, but often such training is not provided. In addition to the technical competences, special training programs on intercultural issues – in order to help candidates for expatriation to understand the differences in the way Chinese people behave compared to people from the host country – would help to reduce misunderstandings between the Chinese expatriates and the locals.

As mentioned in section 1 above, the academic literature has recently addressed the importance of family issues in expatriation and expatriation failure (Carlson, 2005; Cole, 2012; Lee, 2007), emphasizing the need for training for the spouse too, and support when settling in the host country. In our sample of Chinese MNCs, such training and support for spouses and children abroad is not provided. Two-thirds of the MNCs in our sample discourage expatriates settling abroad with their family – which would be both a source of problems and huge costs – and thus do not provide any support to family members, except for high-ranking managers and in specific situations. The remaining MNCs in our sample allow the expatriates to bring their family members with them, with funding support (flight tickets, increased accommodation allowance, and so on), but with strict conditions in order to limit the costs.

The dual career couple is not a problem in the Chinese case, compared with expatriated families from western countries. One reason for this, according to our respondents, is that there is a great number of working opportunities in China. So when spouses have to give up their existing job they find it very easy to secure a new one when they return to China. Furthermore, the purchasing power of the family when abroad – even when only one of the couple is expatriated – is so huge compared to the purchasing power of the family when both work in China that spouses usually do not hesitate to give up their own job in order to support their husband or wife in accepting the international assignment.

In addition, it should be emphasized that Chinese MNCs enjoy an almost zero failure rate in expatriation according to most of our respondents. This is in huge contrast to western and Japanese MNCs, as mentioned in section 1 of this chapter. The main reason, according to our respondents, is that expatriation failure would, in the present Chinese context, lead to the loss of one's job in the company, even in China. Another reason they mention is that expatriation, as already stated, not only provides excellent living conditions compared with those in China, but also provides great potential for promotion prospects and wage increases on returning to China.

Repatriation, in Chinese as in western MNCs, seems to be a difficult issue in some cases. In most of the MNCs in our sample, the expatriates' career development planning has actually been made prior to departure. However, when the expatriates return, a few years later, conditions have often changed, so much so sometimes that promises made to the employee by their companies cannot be realized. A few lucky expatriates may be placed in the same – or a higher – position as the one they held before departure, but this is not the case for the majority, whose positions may have been taken by other people during their absence. When not properly (from the expatriates' point of view) reintegrated, a feeling of "being forgotten" often forces them to leave the company for a better post with a higher salary elsewhere. For the MNCs it is a huge loss in terms of human resources. Chinese MNCs should reconsider repatriation programs to be pivotal, in a context where staff with international experience and capabilities are lacking, as mentioned previously above.

CONCLUSION

Following their rapid development in China, some Chinese firms emerged recently as major MNCs expanding in worldwide markets. Expatriation in such a process is an essential device, both for development and for control objectives. Compared to the well-documented cases of MNCs from western industrialized countries and Japan, Chinese MNCs were, at the beginning of our research, supposed to have specific approaches to expatriation, both because of lack of experience and because of particular conditions at home. On the basis of an investigation with 18 carefully-selected, major Chinese MNCs, we find that the expatriation policies of emerging Chinese MNCs present features common with those of more experienced MNCs from western industrialized countries and Japan, and also present several specificities.

Common features relate first to the structure of the compensation schemes offered to expatriates, although the amounts of each component may differ greatly. A second similarity is that in Chinese MNCs, as in most western and Japanese MNCs, high-ranking positions in subsidiaries abroad are almost always held by expatriates, again both for control and development reasons. Furthermore, in Chinese MNCs, as in most western and Japanese MNCs, repatriation is a difficult issue to manage, which is particularly damaging for Chinese MNCs in a context in which experienced international managers are lacking.

However, our investigation also sheds light on some particularities of expatriation of Chinese MNCs. Because of the peculiar context in China, characterized by high pollution in its large cities, strong social control and difficult working conditions, Chinese MNCs have plenty of candidates for expatriation, although they may face difficulties in finding enough experienced and capable candidates. In addition, Chinese MNCs experience very low expatriation failure rates as there is a very strong incentive for the expatriates to do whatever they can to avoid a situation which would lead to the loss of the advantages related to expatriation, and which would ultimately oblige the expatriates to leave the company. Another issue is that in most Chinese MNCs expatriates are not supported to settle abroad with spouses and children (who are supposed to stay in China), in order to minimize problems to be solved, risks to be faced, and costs. To some extent, this is a little surprising, as spouses wouldn't find it difficult to secure a new job on their return to China, given the current conditions in the Chinese labor market.

This very preliminary and exploratory research provides some direction for the improvement of the expatriation policies of Chinese MNCs, based on the experiences of MNCs from western industrialized countries and Japan, taking into account Chinese specificities however. In particular, according to our respondents, training should be improved – before both the expatriation and the repatriation processes. Further research is needed before more accurate conclusions can be drawn on these issues, and to shed light more broadly on expatriation as one of the dimensions of international HRM by emerging Chinese MNCs.

NOTE

1. The transnationality index of China's top 100 MNCs has been calculated by the China Enterprise Confederation (CEC), on the basis of the data provided by the top 500 Chinese companies, the top 500 Chinese manufacturing companies and the top 500 Chinese service companies, according to the standard proposed by the United Nations Trade and Development Organization. The top 100 Chinese companies are the non-financial companies who possess foreign assets, foreign revenue and employees working overseas, ranked in the light of total foreign assets. The transnationality index is calculated according to the following formula: [(foreign revenue/total revenue + foreign assets/total assets + employees working overseas/total number of employees)/3].

REFERENCES

Ando, N., Rhee, D.K. and Park, N.K. (2008), 'Parent Country Nationals or Local Nationals for Executive Positions in Foreign Affiliates: An empirical study of Japanese affiliates in Korea', *Asia Pacific Journal of Management*, **25**, 1, 113–135.

Belderbos, A. and Heijltjes, R.G. (2005), 'The Determinants of Expatriate Staffing by Japanese Multinationals in Asia; Control, Learning and Vertical Business Groups', *Journal of International Business Studies*, **36**, 3, 341–354.

Black, J., Mendenhall, M. and Oddou, G. (1991), 'Toward a Comprehensive Model of International Adjustment: An Integration of Multiple Theoretical Perspectives', *Academy of Management Review*, **16**, 2, 291–317.

Calantone, R.J. and Zhao, Y.S. (2000), 'Joint Ventures in China: A Comparative Study of Japanese, Korean and U.S. Partners', *Journal of International Marketing*, **9**, 1, 1–23.

Carlson, L. (2005), 'Complications Abound in Managing Expatriate Benefits', *Employee Benefit News*, **19**, 15 June, 28–39.

Cheng H.-L. and Lin, C.Y.Y. (2009), 'Do as the Large Enterprises Do? Expatriate Selection and Overseas Performance in Emerging Markets: The Case of Taiwan SMEs', *International Business Review*, **18**, 1, 60–75.

Claus, L., Lungu, A. and Bhattacharjee, S. (2011), 'The Effects of Individual, Organizational and Societal Variables on the Job Performance of Expatriate Managers', *International Journal of Management*, **28**, 1.2, 249–271.

Cole, N.D. (2012), 'Expatriate Accompanying Partners: The Male Speak', *Asia Pacific Journal of Human Resources*, **50**, 308–326.

Collings, D.G., Scullion, H. and Dowling, P. (2009), 'Global Staffing: A Review and Thematic Research Agenda', *The International Journal of Human Resource Management*, **20**, 6, 1253–1272.

Edström, A. and Galbraith, J.R. (1997), 'Transfer of Managers as a Coordination and Control Strategy in Multinational Organizations', *Administrative Science Quarterly*, **22**, 248–263.

Fayol-Song, L. (2011), 'The Reasons Behind Management Localization: A Case Study of China', *Journal of Asia Pacific Business Review*, **17**, 4, 455–471.

Feldman, D.C. and Thomas, D.C. (1992), 'Career Management Issues Facing Expatriates', *Journal of International Business Studies*, Second Quarter, **23**, 2, 271–293.

Hailey, J. (1996), 'The Expatriate Myth: Cross-Cultural Perceptions of Expatriate Managers', *The International Executive*, **38**, 2, 255–271.

Harzing, A.W. (2001), 'Who's in Charge? An Empirical Study of Executive Staffing Practices in Foreign Subsidiaries', *Human Resource Management*, **40**, 2, 139–158.

Hays, R.D. (1974), 'Expatriate Selection: Insuring Success and Avoiding Failure', *Journal of International Business Studies*, **5**, 1, 25–37.

Hiltrop, J.M. and Janssens, M. (1990), 'Expatriation: Challenges and Recommendations', *European Management Journal*, **8**, 1, 19–26.

Jaussaud, J. and Schaaper, J. (2006), 'Control Mechanisms of their Subsidiaries by Multinational Firms: A Multidimensional Perspective', *Journal of International Management*, **12**, 23–45.

Jaussaud, J. and Schaaper, J. (2007), 'European and Japanese Multinational Companies in China: Organization and Control of Subsidiaries', *Asian Business and Management*, **6**, 223–245.

Kühlmann, T. and Hutchings, K. (2010), 'Expatriate Assignments Versus Localization of Management in China; Staffing Choices of Australian and German Companies', *Career Development International*, **15**, 1, 20–38.

Lam, S.K. and Yeung, J.C.K. (2010), 'Staff Localization and Environmental Uncertainty on Firm Performance in China', *Asia Pacific Journal Management*, **27**, 677–695.

Latta, G.W. (1999), 'Expatriate Policy and Practice: A Ten Year Comparison of Trends', *Compensation and Benefits Review*, **31**, 4, 35–39.

Lee, H.-W. (2007), 'Factors that Influence Expatriate Failure: An Interview Study', *International Journal of Management*, **24**, 3, 403–413.

Lin, C.Y.Y., Lu, T.-C. and Lin, H.-W. (2012), 'A Different Perspective of Expatriate Management', *Human Resource Management Review*, **22**, 189–207.

McEvoy, G.M. and Buller, P.F. (2013), 'Research for Practice: The Management of Expatriates', *Thunderbird International Business Review*, **55**, 2, 213–226.

Melvin, S. and Sylvester, K. (1997), 'Shipping Out', *China Business Review*, **24**, 3, 30–34.

Perlmutter, H.V. (1969), 'The Tortuous Evolution of the Multinational Corporation', *Columbia Journal of World Business*, **4** (January–February), 9–18.

Perlmutter, H.V. and Heenan, D.A. (1974), 'How Multinational Should Your Top Managers Be?', *Harvard Business Review*, **52**, 6, 121–132.

Perlmutter, H.V. and Heenan, D.A. (1979), *Multinational Organization Development: A Social Architectural Perspective*, Reading, MA: Addison-Wesley Publishing Company.

Schaaper, J., Amann, B., Jaussaud, J., Mizoguchi, S. and Nakamura, H. (2012), 'Human Resource Management in Asian Subsidiaries: Comparison of French and Japanese MNCs', *International Journal of Human Resources Management*, **24**, 7, 1454–1470.

Selmer, J. (2003), 'Staff Localization and Organizational Characteristics: Western Business Operations in China', *Asia Pacific Business Review*, **10**, 1, 43–57.

Symon, G. and Cassel, C. (1998), *Qualitative Methods and Analysis in Organizational Research*, Newbury Park, CA: Sage Publications.

Tung, R.L. (1981), 'Selection and Training of Personnel for Overseas Assignments', *Columbia Journal of World Business*, **16**, 1, 68–78.

Tung, R.L. (1984), 'Strategic Management of Human Resources in the Multinational Enterprise', *Human Resource Management*, Summer, **23**, 2, 129–143.

UNCTAD (2013), *World Investment Report 2013: Global Value-Chains, Investment and Trade for Development*, Geneva: UNCTAD.

Wong, C. and Law, K.S. (1999), 'Managing Localization of Human Resources in the PRC: A Practical Model', *Journal of World Business*, **34**, 1, 26–40.

PART III

Emerging MNCs from other Asian countries

9. The Transatlantic Free Trade Area: ASEAN's perspective

Utai Uprasen

1. INTRODUCTION

The European Union (EU) is a crucial export destination for both the Association of Southeast Asian Nations (ASEAN) countries and the United States (the U.S.). The similarity in export structures between ASEAN and the U.S. leads ASEAN countries to be confronted with severe export competition from the U.S. in the EU market. Since the size of exports from the U.S. is larger than that of ASEAN, products from ASEAN might be displaced by U.S. commodities, i.e. the so-called displacement effect. The existing studies on displacement effect usually assume the exports from the larger country as an exogenous variable in their studied framework, typically based on the gravity model. This notion is reasonable if the size of exports of the larger competitor is substantially greater than that of the smaller one, such as in the case of China and Sudan, where China's exports were 605 times those of Sudan in 2012. In addition, the displacement effect in the existing studies is detected through the coefficient of the export variable of the larger competitor. No explanation has been provided for the cause of displacement and determinant factors which determine the degree of the displacement effect.

Accordingly, it can be argued that the above idea is not applicable in a study on the displacement effect on exports of machinery and transport equipment (SITC7) between ASEAN and the U.S. in the EU market as the size of exports from the U.S. is just two times greater than those from ASEAN. Therefore, this study proposes an alternative research methodology by endogenizing the export variable of the larger competitor in the framework. Furthermore, the displacement effect is derived in the model, which enables the study to explain the cause and the factor which determines the degree of the displacement effect. The simultaneous equation model is employed in the study to examine the displacement effect in five major industries at the 2-digit level of SITC7 (machinery and transport equipment). The period of study covers 2003 Q1–2013 Q4. The empirical results, based on the two-stage least square (2SLS) technique, reveal that three ASEAN countries encounter displacement effects emanating from exports of the U.S. in two studied industries. This has the important policy implication that the ASEAN countries need to find a way to improve the export competitiveness of the industries in which the displacement effect is found.

The rest of the chapter is organized as follows. Section 2 describes the trade relationship between ASEAN, the U.S. and the EU. Section 3 reviews the literature on displacement effect. Section 4 outlines the methodology upon which this study is based, while the estimation results are presented in Section 5. Section 6 contains the concluding remarks.

2. PATTERNS OF TRADE: ASEAN, THE U.S. AND THE EU

Section 2 illustrates patterns of trade between the U.S., the EU and ASEAN countries in detail. According to Table 9.1, the EU is the second largest export destination of ASEAN (accounting for 13.6 percent of total exports), behind China (16.5 percent). The EU is also the second largest export destination of the U.S. (16.7 percent of total exports), behind Canada (19.0 percent). According to Table 9.2, the export structure from ASEAN to the EU is similar to the export structure from the U.S. to the EU market. The main export products from both ASEAN and the U.S. to the EU destination are machinery and transport equipment (SITC7).

Table 9.1   Patterns of trade: U.S., EU and ASEAN, 2013 (percent)

EU as importer		U.S. as exporter		ASEAN as exporter	
Partner	%	Partner	%	Partner	%
China	16.6	Canada	19.0	China	16.5
Russia	12.3	EU	16.7	EU	13.6
U.S.	11.7	Mexico	14.3	Japan	13.0
Switzerland	5.6	China	7.7	U.S.	12.2
Norway	5.4	Japan	4.1	Hong Kong	8.6
Japan	3.4	Brazil	2.8	Korea	5.7
Turkey	3.0	Hong Kong	2.7	Australia	4.8
India	2.2	Korea	2.6	India	4.5
Korea	2.1	Singapore	1.9	U.A.E.	1.8
Row	37.7	Row	28.2	Row	19.3
Total	100.0	Total	100.0	Total	100.0

Source: Author's calculations based on the data from Eurostat ComExt.

Table 9.2   Export structures, classified by industry, average value during 2003–2013

SITC	Industry	Value (€ millions)		%		Ratio
		ASEAN	U.S.	ASEAN	U.S.	
0	Food and live animals	5037	4481	6.8	2.6	0.9
1	Beverages and tobacco	149	1211	0.2	0.7	8.1
2	Crude materials, inedible, except fuels	3012	7235	4.1	4.3	2.4
3	Mineral fuels, lubricants and related materials	1810	8511	2.4	5.0	4.7
4	Animal and vegetable oils, fats and waxes	3172	179	4.3	0.1	0.1
5	Chemicals and related products, n.e.s.	7664	35890	10.4	21.2	4.7
6	Manufactured goods classified chiefly by material	5029	10900	6.8	6.4	2.2
7	Machinery and transport equipment	32629	73479	44.1	43.3	2.3
8	Miscellaneous manufactured articles	14972	22899	20.2	13.5	1.5
9	Commodities not classified elsewhere in the SITC	550	4757	0.7	2.8	8.6
	Total	74023	169543	100.0	100.0	2.3

Notes:
ASEAN comprises six member countries: Indonesia, Malaysia, Philippines, Thailand, Singapore and Vietnam.
Ratio = export value of U.S./export value of ASEAN.
n.e.s. = not elsewhere specified.

Source: Author's calculations based on the data from Eurostat ComExt.

SITC7 products alone account for approximately 43 percent of the U.S.'s total exports to the EU and 44 percent of ASEAN's total exports to the same destination. Based on the EU being a crucial export destination and the similarity between export structures of ASEAN and the U.S., this situation implies that the degree of export competition in the EU market between these two entities is substantially high. Although the portion of SITC7 commodities of exports from the U.S. is similar to that of ASEAN, the value of exports from the U.S. is approximately twice as high as exports from ASEAN.

In addition, the EU and the U.S. have launched free trade agreement (FTA) negotiations since 2013 to establish the Transatlantic Trade and

Investment Partnership (TTIP), the so-called EU-U.S. FTA. The agreement aims to remove trade barriers in a wide range of economic sectors to facilitate trade in goods and services between the EU and the U.S.

Given the significance of the EU market for ASEAN and the high degree of similarity in export structure between the U.S. and ASEAN countries, the FTA agreement will have a considerable impact on exports of ASEAN to the EU market. The potential increase in trade between the EU and the U.S. emanating from the FTA enforcement may reduce exports from ASEAN countries to the EU market, especially in the product group of machinery and transport equipment (SITC7). This study aims to investigate the potential reduction on exports from ASEAN countries to the EU market emanating from the potential increase in exports from the U.S. to the same destination after the EU-U.S. FTA comes into force. The potential reduction on exports is scrutinized through the displacement effect.

3. LITERATURE REVIEW

The current literature related to the estimation of the displacement effect on exports can be described as follows. The displacement effect on exports has been examined by scholars from 2005–2015. The displacement effect tends to exist when two countries compete to export the same product to the same destination. The traditional assumption about displacement effect posits that if the size of export volume of the same commodity from two exporters into the third market is not identical, the exports of the smaller exporter may be crowded out (the so-called displacement effect) by the exports of the bigger country. Many studies have tried to explore whether the growth of China's exports displaces exports of other countries to third markets. The impact of China on African exports to their main trading partners, the U.S. and the EU, and to other African countries, was investigated for the period 1995–2005 (Giovannetti and Sanfilippo, 2009; Montinari and Prodi, 2011). Significant evidence on the existence of a displacement effect was found both for the whole set of products exported and for the manufacturing sector. An increase of 1 percent of exports from China reduced exports from African countries by 0.12 percent in exports of machinery and equipment. Moreover, Geda and Meskel (2008) found that China displaced African manufacturing exports to third markets by −2.25 percent. Currently, exports from China are crowding out exports from developed countries as China's export structures have changed from labor-intensive to high-tech products (Wang and Wei, 2008; Berger and Martin, 2013). Silgonera *et al.* (2015) also asserted that China crowded out exports from Central, Eastern and Southeastern Europe to the old 15

EU member states in the sector of capital goods and transport equipment. A displacement effect on exports to the world market from other regions such as North America, Central America, Mexico and South America during 2000–2009 was also found (Módolo and Hiratuka, 2012).

Studies on the displacement effect on exports between China and ASEAN countries and other non-ASEAN Asian countries to third markets have been completed (Bhattacharya *et al.*, 2001; Eichengreen *et al.*, 2004). The empirical results showed that China's surge in exports did appear to displace its neighbors' exports to third markets, with a 1 percent increase leading to a 0.06 percent drop in Asian countries' exports on average during 1990–2003 (Eichengreen *et al.*, 2007). The degree of displacement effect on total exports of Asian countries *vis-à-vis* China is higher (0.34 percent) in the study of Greenaway *et al.* (2008). An investigation at industry level has been conducted by Athukorala (2009). The study illustrated that East-Asian countries encountered the displacement effect on exports emanating from China in the world market in machinery and transport equipment (SITC7) during 1992–2005. A 1 percent increase in Chinese exports of final goods of SITC7 products (excluding parts and components) leads to a 0.08 percent drop in Asian countries' exports of the same commodities. However, the displacement effect was not found for Malaysia, the Philippines, Singapore and Thailand.

The research methodology of the existing empirical studies on the displacement effect, as mentioned above, is usually based on the gravity model (Anderson, 1979; Anderson and Wincoop, 2003). Although each study focuses on different cases, these studies typically estimate a variant of the simplified gravity equation, as follows:

$$\ln X_{ijt} = \alpha + \beta \ln X_{China, jt} + \gamma \ln Z + \varepsilon_{ijt}$$

where X_{ijt} denotes the value of exports from country i to destination country j at time t, while $X_{China, jt}$ refers to exports from China to the same destination and Z stands for a vector of other control variables. The displacement effect emanating from Chinese exports on a certain exporter to the third market is captured through the value of β. The negative value of β implies the existence of the displacement effect. In addition, the factor determining the degree of displacement effect (the value of β) has never been explained in previous studies. The variable $X_{China, jt}$ is treated as an exogenous variable in other studies. This idea may be reasonable if the model is employed to study the displacement effect in cases where the difference in the size of exports to the third market of two exporters is extremely large. For instance, in 2012, exports from China ($2.04 \times 10^{12} usd$) to the world market were 605 times greater than exports from Sudan

$(3.34 \times 10^9 usd)$. Therefore, it is true that Sudan will take exports from China as a predetermined variable.

However, the above concept may not be applicable if one wants to study the displacement effect in cases where the difference in size of exports between two competitors is not considerably high. For example, according to Table 9.2, the value of exports of machinery and transport equipment (SITC7) from the U.S. to the EU market is 2.30 times greater than exports from ASEAN to the same destination. This indicates that although the U.S. may create a displacement effect on exports from ASEAN, treating U.S. exports as an exogenous variable for ASEAN in the model may not be logical. U.S. exports do not unilaterally determine exports from ASEAN, but together both countries' exports affect each other.

Based on the above literature reviews, two major points are worth mentioning. First, estimations of displacement effect on exports have usually been conducted through the gravity equation. The export variable of the bigger exporter is considered as an exogenous variable in the model. This notion may be rational for studies that center on cases where the difference in size of exports between two competitors to the third market is considerably high. Still, this concept may not apply to cases where the difference in size of exports between two exporters is not significantly high. Second, the degree of displacement effect usually reveals itself through the value of the coefficient β. However, the factor that determines the value of β has never been established.

Accordingly, this chapter proposes an alternative approach that explicitly endogenizes the export variable of both competitors in the model, in order to examine the displacement effect on the exports between ASEAN countries and the U.S. into the EU market by focusing on exports of machinery and transport equipment (SITC7). The simultaneous equation model will be employed instead of the gravity model in our research, making the estimated results more reliable. Furthermore, the factor determining the value of the degree of displacement effect (β) will be delineated. The details of research methodology are described in the next section.

4.   METHODOLOGY

To examine the displacement effect and export competition between members of ASEAN and the U.S. in the EU market, we resort to a well-known simultaneous equation model. The derived displacement effect on exports is based on it.

4.1   Model Specification: Simultaneous Equation Model

When there is a two-way or simultaneous relationship between independent and explanatory variables in an equation, a simultaneous equation model is suitable for estimation in the study. The model used in the present study assumes imperfect substitution between exported goods and domestic ones based on the idea of Goldstein and Khan (1978, 1985). The model represents a system of equations for export supply and export demand, which simultaneously determine the export price and the export quantity. Their model has been modified extensively for estimating the import and export demand functions in various cases (Athukorala and Riedel, 1994; Abbott and De Vita, 2002). While Muscatelli *et al.* (1992) took wages as an exogenous variable, Riedel (1988) treated the manufacturing wage as an endogenous element. Edwards and Alves (2006) added infrastructure costs and skilled labor costs into the model to investigate South African manufacturing exports in the 1990s. Koukouritakis (2006) added export subsidies into the equation to test Greek export performance. Rahmaddi and Ichihashi (2012) separated the real income variable in their model to allow for a distinction between secular and cyclical movements' effects on the level of exports.

Following previous studies, this model is synthesized as follows. The displacement effect will be scrutinized from the ASEAN perspective. Since exports from ASEAN and the U.S. compete in the EU market, the quantity and price variables of both should be correlated. The supply and demand equations of exports from each country are shown below. The demand function for each country's exports has the following form:

$$Q_{it}^{j} = f\left(\frac{P_{it}^{as}}{P_{it}^{eu}}, \frac{P_{it}^{us}}{P_{it}^{eu}}, C_{it}^{eu}, V_{it}^{eu}, X_{it}^{eu}\right)$$

where Q_{it}^{j} denotes the quantity of commodity at time t exported from ASEAN to country i of the EU if j is ASEAN or exported from the U.S. to each member state of the EU if j is the U.S. The two price variables: P_{it}^{as}, P_{it}^{us} are export prices of ASEAN commodities and the export price of the U.S. which exports to country i of the EU, respectively. Goldstein and Khan (1985) suggest using the prices of foreign goods relative to domestic prices in the export demand function; therefore P_{it}^{eu} is the price of domestic products in country i of the EU.

The standard demand function of imports postulates that import demand is determined by relative prices and domestic income level. Baak (2014) and Narayan and Narayan (2010) set up their demand equations accordingly. However, many previous studies decomposed the domestic income (GDP) into its main components in order to observe the role of each element (Tang, 2005; Fosu and Magnus, 2008; Constant and Yue, 2010; Durmaz and Lee, 2012; Khan *et al.*, 2013). Therefore, the study also makes the same major modification to the basic import demand function by dividing the GDP into three main parts: $C_{it}^{eu}, V_{it}^{eu}, X_{it}^{eu}$. The variable C_{it}^{eu} is real consumption expenditures: the sum of private and public consumption expenditures in country i of the EU. The variable V_{it}^{eu} is expenditure on investment goods including gross domestic fixed capital formation in the member state i of the EU and X_{it}^{eu} is export expenditure of country i.

The export supply function of each country has the following form, where the superscript j is either ASEAN's member country or the U.S. as before:

$$Q_{it}^j = f(P_{it}^j, P_{it-1}^{as}, P_{it-1}^{us}, E_{it}^{j-eu}, W_t^j)$$

Besides the current export price, the lagged prices of ASEAN and the U.S. $(P_{it-1}^{as}, P_{it-1}^{us})$ are included since they may influence the current prices and a decrease in one country's price may exert some pressure on its competitor to lower their price as well. The E_{it}^{j-eu} is the exchange rate between exporting country j to each member state i of the EU. The W_t^j denotes nominal wages of the exporting country.

The above export demand function can be expressed in the log-linear form in the case of the ASEAN country as an exporter as follows:

$$\ln Q_{it}^{as} = \alpha_0 + \alpha_1 \ln P_{it}^{as} + \alpha_2 \ln P_{it}^{us} + \alpha_3 \ln C_{it}^{eu} + \alpha_4 \ln V_{it}^{eu} + \alpha_5 \ln X_{it}^{eu} + \varepsilon_{it} \ (9.1)$$

The study follows Goldstein and Khan (1985) by using the prices of foreign goods relative to domestic prices. As a matter of convenience, let P_{it}^{as} which normally represents the export price from ASEAN mean that the ASEAN export price has already been adjusted by dividing it by the EU domestic price throughout this chapter. The same idea is also applied to the U.S. export price, P_{it}^{us}. The expected sign of α_1 is negative while the expected sign of the rest of the coefficients ($\alpha_2, \alpha_3, \alpha_4, \alpha_5$) is positive.

The export supply function in the log form for ASEAN as an exporter can also be written as below:

$$\ln Q_{it}^{as} = \pi_0 + \pi_1 \ln P_{it}^{as} + \pi_2 \ln P_{it-1}^{as} + \pi_3 \ln P_{it-1}^{us} + \pi_4 \ln E_{it}^{as-eu} + \pi_5 \ln W_t^{as} + \varphi_{it}$$
$$(9.2)$$

A positive sign is expected from π_1, π_2 while a negative sign is anticipated from π_3, π_4, π_5, respectively. As a matter of convenience in the estimation of simultaneous equation systems, the model is usually normalized. The study follows the same method used by previous studies by normalizing the export demand function with export quantity and export supply function with export price in order to have the two endogenous variables on the left-hand side of the two equations. Therefore, equation (9.2) as rewritten, yields:

$$\ln P_{it}^{as} = \beta_0 + \beta_1 \ln Q_{it}^{as} + \beta_2 \ln P_{it-1}^{as} + \beta_3 \ln P_{it-1}^{us} + \beta_4 \ln E_{it}^{as-eu} + \beta_5 \ln W_{it}^{as} + \varphi_{it}$$
(9.3)

where, $\beta_0 = -\pi_0/\pi_1$, $\beta_1 = 1/\pi_1$, $\beta_2 = -\pi_2/\pi_1$, $\beta_3 = -\pi_3/\pi_1$, $\beta_4 = -\pi_4/\pi_1$, $\beta_5 = -\pi_5/\pi_1$

Accordingly, the expected sign of the new coefficient, β_i, depends on the sign of π_i: the positive sign is expected from β_1, β_3, β_4, β_5, while the β_2 should give the negative value, respectively. For simplicity, let the lowercase represent the log form of the uppercase: $q_{it}^j = \ln Q_{it}^j$. Hence, the equation of export demand and export supply of ASEAN in (9.1) and (9.3) are transformed into (9.4) and (9.5):

$$q_{it}^{as} = \alpha_0 + \alpha_1 p_{it}^{as} + \alpha_2 p_{it}^{us} + \alpha_3 c_{it}^{eu} + \alpha_4 v_{it}^{eu} + \alpha_5 x_{it}^{eu} + \varepsilon_{it} \qquad (9.4)$$

$$p_{it}^{as} = \beta_0 + \beta_1 q_{it}^{as} + \beta_2 p_{it-1}^{as} + \beta_3 p_{it-1}^{us} + \beta_4 e_{it}^{as-eu} + \beta_5 w_t^{as} + \varphi_{it} \quad (9.5)$$

The supply and demand of U.S. exports to the EU can be obtained in the same way, as presented in equations (9.6) and (9.7):

$$q_{it}^{us} = \gamma_0 + \gamma_1 p_{it}^{as} + \gamma_2 p_{it}^{us} + \gamma_3 c_{it}^{eu} + \gamma_4 v_{it}^{eu} + \gamma_5 x_{it}^{eu} + \eta_{it} \qquad (9.6)$$

$$p_{it}^{us} = \lambda_0 + \lambda_1 q_{it}^{us} + \lambda_2 p_{it-1}^{as} + \lambda_3 p_{it-1}^{us} + \lambda_4 e_{it}^{us-eu} + \lambda_5 w_t^{us} + \Theta_{it} \quad (9.7)$$

The expected sign of coefficient γ_i, λ_i in equation (9.6) and (9.7) is considered in similar fashion to the case of ASEAN in equation (9.4) and (9.5). Owing to the fact that this study examines the displacement on exports from ASEAN and the U.S. to the EU market, two demand equations and two supply equations of each exporter constitute the system of simultaneous equations in the work: (9.4), (9.5), (9.6) and (9.7). Consequently, the estimation is based on four equations and four endogenous variables: $q_{it}^{as}, p_{it}^{as}, q_{it}^{us}, p_{it}^{us}$. The remaining variables are considered as predetermined variables. The order and rank condition of identifiability affirms that each equation is over-identified (Gujarati and Porter, 2008). Accordingly, the system of equations (9.4) to (9.7) will be estimated by using the 2SLS technique.

4.2   Derivation of Displacement Effect

This section derives the displacement effect based on the system of simultaneous equations, seen above. For simplicity, equations (9.4) to (9.7) are rearranged into equations (9.4-1) to (9.7-1) as follows:

$$q_{it}^{as} = \alpha_1 p_{it}^{as} + \alpha_2 p_{it}^{us} + \aleph_{it} \tag{9.4-1}$$

$$p_{it}^{as} = \beta_1 q_{it}^{as} + \hbar_{it} \tag{9.5-1}$$

$$q_{it}^{us} = \gamma_1 p_{it}^{as} + \gamma_2 p_{it}^{us} + \wp_{it} \tag{9.6-1}$$

$$p_{it}^{us} = \lambda_1 q_{it}^{us} + \Im_{it} \tag{9.7-1}$$

where,

$$\aleph_{it} = \alpha_0 + \alpha_3 c_{it}^{eu} + \alpha_4 v_{it}^{eu} + \alpha_5 x_{it}^{eu} + \varepsilon_{it}$$

$$\hbar_{it} = \beta_0 + \beta_2 p_{it-1}^{as} + \beta_3 p_{it-1}^{us} + \beta_4 e_{it}^{as-eu} + \beta_5 w_t^{as} + \varphi_{it}$$

$$\wp_{it} = \gamma_0 + \gamma_3 c_{it}^{eu} + \gamma_4 v_{it}^{eu} + \gamma_5 x_{it}^{eu} + \eta_{it}$$

$$\Im_{it} = \lambda_0 + \lambda_2 p_{it-1}^{as} + \lambda_3 p_{it-1}^{us} + \lambda_4 e_{it}^{us-eu} + \lambda_5 w_t^{us} + \theta_{it}$$

By substituting (9.5-1) and (9.7-1) into (9.4-1), to remove the price variable, yields:

$$q_{it}^{as} = \alpha_1 \beta_1 q_{it}^{as} + \alpha_2 \lambda_1 q_{it}^{us} + \Lambda_{it} \tag{9.4-2}$$

where, $\Lambda_{it} = \alpha_1 \hbar_{it} + \alpha_2 \Im_{it} + \aleph_{it}$

Likewise, equation (9.5-1) and (9.7-1) plugged into (9.6-1), yields:

$$q_{it}^{us} = \gamma_1 \beta_1 q_{it}^{as} + \gamma_2 \lambda_1 q_{it}^{us} + Z_{it} \tag{9.6-2}$$

where, $Z_{it} = \gamma_1 \hbar_{it} + \gamma_2 \Im_{it} + \wp_{it}$

Subtracting (9.6-2) from (9.4-2), yields:

$$q_t^{as} = \left(\frac{1 + \alpha_2 \lambda_1 - \gamma_2 \lambda_1}{1 + \gamma_1 \beta_1 - \alpha_1 \beta_1} \right) q_t^{us} + \Psi_t \tag{9.8}$$

where, $\Psi_t = \dfrac{\Theta_t}{(1 + \gamma_1 \beta_1 - \alpha_1 \beta_1)}$ and $\Theta_t = A_t - Z_t$

As a result, Ψ_t is a group of exogenous variables in the model. Let's define Ω as a percentage change in the quantity of exports from ASEAN to the EU market in response to percentage changes in the quantity of exports from the U.S. to the same destination. Based on equation (9.8), Ω can be expressed as follows:

$$\Omega = \frac{dQ^{as}}{dQ^{us}} \cdot \frac{Q^{us}}{Q^{as}} = \frac{d\ln Q^{as}}{d\ln Q^{us}} = \frac{dq^{as}}{dq^{us}} = \left(\frac{1 + [\alpha_2 - \gamma_2]\lambda_1}{1 + [\gamma_1 - \alpha_1]\beta_1} \right) \qquad (9.9)$$

According to equation (9.9), the displacement effect on exports from ASEAN to the EU market emanating from exports of the U.S. to the same destination is equal to Ω having a negative value.

Consequently, the study explains that the degree of displacement effect depends on the value of six factors: α_2, γ_2, λ_1, γ_1, α_1 and β_1, where,

α_2 = cross-price elasticity of export demand for q_{it}^{as} with respect to p_{it}^{us}

γ_2 = price elasticity of export demand for q_{it}^{us} with respect to p_{it}^{us}

λ_1 = inverse of price elasticity of export supply of q_{it}^{us} with respect to p_{it}^{us}

γ_1 = cross-price elasticity of export demand for q_{it}^{us} with respect to p_{it}^{as}

α_1 = price elasticity of export demand for q_{it}^{as} with respect to p_{it}^{as}

β_1 = inverse of price elasticity of export supply of q_{it}^{as} with respect to p_{it}^{as}

The displacement effect will be calculated based on equation (9.9) in the next section.

4.3   Data

The following are data descriptions taken from quarterly data. The sample period of the study covers 2003 Q1–2013 Q4 for the estimation of a system of four simultaneous equations: (4)–(7). Each industry of SITC7 – machinery and transport equipment at 2-digit level (SITC71–SITC78) – is estimated separately. There are eight industries in total as follows: SITC71 – power-generating machinery and equipment, SITC72 – machinery specialized for particular industries, SITC73 – metalworking machinery, SITC74 – general industrial machinery and equipment, SITC75 – office machines and automatic data-processing machines, SITC76 – telecommunications and sound-recording equipment, SITC77 – electrical machinery, apparatus and appliances, and SITC78 – road vehicles (including air-cushion vehicles). The products of SITC79 (other transport equipment) are excluded from the study due to incomplete data.

Due to the different economic structures between the old EU member states (EU15) and those which have joined the EU since 2004, there may be an impact on the import structure of machinery and transport equipment. Accordingly, the study excludes the new member states. Due to lack of availability of data, the EU as an importer is composed of only seven member states: Belgium, France, Germany, Italy, the Netherlands, Spain and the United Kingdom. Likewise, only four major members of ASEAN countries are selected as an exporter: Malaysia, the Philippines, Singapore and Thailand. Given that the data of Brunei, Burma, Cambodia and Laos are not available, the data on exports of machinery and transport equipment (SITC7) from the four selected countries are good statistics to represent ASEAN. This is because the four selected countries account for 86 percent of exports of SITC7 products of the six major members (Indonesia, Malaysia, the Philippines, Singapore, Thailand and Vietnam) during 2003–2013.

Therefore, the empirical estimations constitute 308 observations per industry. The data on the quantity of exports (q_{it}^j, kg) are obtained from the Eurostat database. The data of the unit value of exports are not available. Hence, they are constructed by dividing export values by export volumes (p_{it}^j, euro per kg). The domestic price of EU products is proxied by the producer price in the domestic market which is obtained from the Eurostat database. Data on export values together with other related statistics of the EU countries, i.e. total consumption (c_{it}^{eu}, euro), real domestic capital formation (v_{it}^{eu}, euro) and real export value (x_{it}^{eu}, euro) are also obtained from the Eurostat database. The nominal exchange rate statistics of each member state of ASEAN and the U.S. *vis-à-vis* each member state of the EU ($e_{it}^{as-eu}, e_{it}^{us-eu}$: EU national currency/each ASEAN national currency and EU national currency/ USD) are acquired from the International Monetary Fund (IMF) International Financial Statistics (IFS). The wage rates in ASEAN countries and the U.S. (w_t^{as}, w_t^{us}) are proxied by the Manufacturing Wage Rates Index (2010 = 100). The data are collected from the IMF IFS for the Philippines and Singapore, from the Bank of Thailand for Thailand and from the Malaysian National Employment Return (NER), Ministry of Human Resource, for Malaysia.

5.   ESTIMATION RESULTS

Section 5 shows the empirical results from the study. The article aims to estimate regressions for eight major industries of SITC7 products at 2-digit level. The data which are used for running the panel data model should be stationary to avoid the spurious estimation problem. Therefore, unit root tests should be performed. The model contains both time series and panel data. The test for panel unit root is performed by adopting the method of Levin *et al.* (2002), while the test for time series rests on an augmented Dickey-Fuller (ADF) test. For the panel data, the results indicate that three variables – q_{it}^{as} of industry SITC71 and SITC73 of the Philippines and Thailand, and p_{it}^{us} of industry SITC72 of the U.S. – contain a unit root. Although these three variables pass the test at the 1 percent level of significance when expressed in first difference, it was decided to drop these three industries from the study. The main reason is that the estimated coefficient of the first difference cannot be employed in the calculation for the displacement effect. Excluding these three industries does not affect the significance of the study since only five studied industries (SITC74–78) account for 92 percent of exports of SITC7 products from ASEAN to the EU market during 2003–2013. The τ-statistics indicate that there is no unit root problem for the time series data (additional information for unit root test can be obtained from the author upon request). The empirical results are presented in Tables 9.3 and 9.4.

According to Table 9.3, in each industry the estimated coefficients are presented in the first row, while the second row shows the standard errors of the coefficient, respectively. Regression results indicate that most of the explanatory variables have the expected signs, even though there are differences in the magnitude of the respective effect across industries. The export price of a commodity turns out to have significant effects on the export quantity both from ASEAN and the U.S.

In relation to industry SITC77 – electrical machinery, apparatus and appliances – in the Thai export demand function, if the export price (p_{it}^{as}) increases by 1 percent, the export quantity from Thailand to the EU decreases by 0.32 percent. Similarly, if the export price of the U.S. product (p_{it}^{us}) increases by 1 percent, the export quantity from the U.S. reduces by 0.83 percent.

The price elasticities of the product from both the ASEAN countries and the U.S. are highly significant in almost all of the five industries studied.

The cross-price elasticities are also reported simultaneously. For office machines and automatic data-processing machines (SITC75) of Malaysia, if the price of the U.S. product rises by 1 percent, the export of the same

Table 9.3   Empirical results of demand equations: (4) and (6)

Variable	p_{it}^{as}	p_{it}^{us}	c_{it}^{eu}	v_{it}^{eu}	x_{it}^{eu}	R^2
Malaysia						
SITC-74						
q_{it}^{as}	−0.93*	1.27	0.42*	0.69	0.45***	0.63
	(0.54)	(0.90)	(0.23)	(0.58)	(0.14)	
q_{it}^{us}	1.03	−0.51**	0.65*	0.24***	2.03	0.72
	(0.93)	(0.22)	(0.35)	(0.08)	(1.57)	
SITC-75						
q_{it}^{as}	−0.33**	0.35*	−1.02	0.60**	1.22*	0.78
	(0.13)	(1.88)	(0.78)	(0.25)	(0.73)	
q_{it}^{us}	0.48***	−0.81**	1.07*	−1.36	1.01	0.66
	(0.15)	(0.40)	(0.61)	(0.92)	(0.68)	
SITC-76						
q_{it}^{as}	−0.27**	0.21**	0.73*	0.64	0.21**	0.83
	(0.11)	(0.09)	(0.39)	(0.48)	(0.10)	
q_{it}^{us}	0.32*	−0.69***	0.95	0.56*	−1.67	0.64
	(0.24)	(0.24)	(0.79)	(0.31)	(1.07)	
SITC-77						
q_{it}^{as}	−0.21***	0.29*	0.32*	1.24	0.26*	0.62
	(0.06)	(0.15)	(0.17)	(0.91)	(0.15)	
q_{it}^{us}	0.83*	−0.82*	0.33**	0.81	0.63	0.54
	(0.48)	(0.45)	(0.15)	(0.66)	(0.45)	
SITC-78						
q_{it}^{as}	−0.29*	0.12***	1.37	0.29*	0.40*	0.74
	(0.16)	(0.04)	(0.91)	(0.16)	(0.21)	
q_{it}^{us}	0.61*	−1.35**	0.85***	0.75	0.66*	0.63
	(0.32)	(0.58)	(0.26)	(0.49)	(0.37)	
Philippines						
SITC-74						
q_{it}^{as}	−0.24**	0.21*	0.58*	−1.13	0.06***	0.82
	(0.12)	(0.11)	(0.33)	(0.80)	(0.01)	
q_{it}^{us}	0.47*	−1.53**	−1.02	0.52	0.42*	0.77
	(0.26)	(0.66)	(0.70)	(0.37)	(0.23)	
SITC-75						
q_{it}^{as}	−0.32*	0.22*	0.83	0.57**	0.35**	0.71
	(0.17)	(0.12)	(0.61)	(0.23)	(0.15)	
q_{it}^{us}	0.69**	−0.91**	1.13	0.72*	2.24	0.69
	(0.28)	(0.38)	(0.83)	(0.40)	(1.44)	
SITC-76						
q_{it}^{as}	1.06	0.74*	0.06***	1.44	0.88*	0.75
	(0.81)	(0.42)	(0.02)	(1.17)	(0.50)	
q_{it}^{us}	0.23**	−0.39*	0.74	0.41**	0.25**	0.86
	(0.11)	(0.21)	(0.49)	(0.17)	(0.10)	

Table 9.3   (continued)

Variable	p_{it}^{as}	p_{it}^{us}	c_{it}^{eu}	v_{it}^{eu}	x_{it}^{eu}	R^2
SITC-77						
q_{it}^{as}	−0.54	1.35	1.23*	0.20*	−0.28	0.47
	(0.49)	(0.94)	(0.69)	(0.12)	(0.18)	
q_{it}^{us}	0.17**	0.38	0.52**	−0.61*	1.37	0.58
	(0.08)	(0.34)	(0.22)	(0.38)	(0.91)	
SITC-78						
q_{it}^{as}	−0.18***	0.23*	−1.18	0.61	0.86	0.61
	(0.06)	(0.12)	(0.89)	(0.44)	(0.71)	
q_{it}^{us}	0.31*	−1.54**	0.85*	−0.93	0.48**	0.57
	(0.17)	(0.51)	(0.46)	(0.66)	(0.19)	
Singapore						
SITC-74						
q_{it}^{as}	−0.85*	0.71*	1.34	1.99	0.31**	0.49
	(0.46)	(0.40)	(1.10)	(1.38)	(0.13)	
q_{it}^{us}	0.74**	−1.03	0.66**	0.73*	0.52*	0.55
	(0.32)	(0.90)	(0.31)	(0.42)	(0.29)	
SITC-75						
q_{it}^{as}	−0.22**	0.44*	0.29*	2.07	0.39	0.51
	(0.10)	(0.23)	(0.16)	(1.32)	(0.33)	
q_{it}^{us}	0.49***	−0.67**	−0.35	0.47*	1.07**	0.65
	(0.13)	(0.31)	(0.31)	(0.27)	(0.43)	
SITC-76						
q_{it}^{as}	−0.71*	0.82**	0.29**	0.25	0.74**	0.72
	(0.38)	(0.36)	(0.12)	(0.18)	(0.31)	
q_{it}^{us}	0.93	−0.34*	0.17***	0.51*	−1.87	0.63
	(0.83)	(0.19)	(0.05)	(0.27)	(1.35)	
SITC-77						
q_{it}^{as}	−0.33**	0.33**	0.21*	0.56**	1.53	0.65
	(0.15)	(0.13)	(0.12)	(0.24)	(1.37)	
q_{it}^{us}	0.77**	−0.98*	0.34**	−1.30	0.18*	0.73
	(0.33)	(0.56)	(0.14)	(0.86)	(0.10)	
SITC-78						
q_{it}^{as}	−0.25*	0.09***	0.61*	0.23	0.07**	0.79
	(0.14)	(0.03)	(0.32)	(0.16)	(0.03)	
q_{it}^{us}	0.42**	−1.61*	1.22	0.24*	0.61*	0.66
	(0.18)	(0.90)	(0.84)	(0.13)	(0.34)	
Thailand						
SITC-74						
q_{it}^{as}	−0.40**	0.28**	0.53*	1.14	0.77**	0.54
	(0.17)	(0.12)	(0.29)	(0.76)	(0.31)	
q_{it}^{us}	0.58***	−0.67*	1.25**	0.78	0.39	0.42
	(0.18)	(0.37)	(0.59)	(0.57)	(0.44)	

Table 9.3   (continued)

Variable	p^{as}_{it}	p^{us}_{it}	c^{eu}_{it}	v^{eu}_{it}	x^{eu}_{it}	R^2
SITC-75						
q^{as}_{it}	−0.31**	0.30*	−1.36	0.25***	0.17*	0.76
	(0.13)	(0.17)	(1.11)	(0.08)	(0.09)	
q^{us}_{it}	0.85**	−0.91*	0.55	1.01*	0.33***	0.69
	(0.37)	(0.49)	(0.41)	(0.55)	(0.10)	
SITC-76						
q^{as}_{it}	−0.36*	0.35**	0.65**	−1.22	0.27*	0.84
	(0.20)	(0.14)	(0.28)	(0.89)	(0.15)	
q^{us}_{it}	0.74**	−0.96**	0.28*	0.60**	1.88	0.81
	(0.31)	(0.44)	(0.14)	(0.28)	(1.21)	
SITC-77						
q^{as}_{it}	−0.32**	0.65***	1.17	0.51	−0.46*	0.77
	(0.14)	(0.19)	(0.75)	(0.41)	(0.25)	
q^{us}_{it}	0.62**	−0.83*	0.32***	0.26*	0.94	0.82
	(0.31)	(0.47)	(0.11)	(0.13)	(0.85)	
SITC-78						
q^{as}_{it}	−0.68**	1.25	0.41*	0.86**	−0.67	0.60
	(0.30)	(0.87)	(0.30)	(0.35)	(0.50)	
q^{us}_{it}	1.16	−0.34*	0.77**	−0.24	0.74*	0.58
	(0.95)	(0.18)	(0.32)	(0.18)	(0.41)	

Note: Statistical significance is denoted as *** 1%, ** 5%, * 10%. (Standard errors are in parentheses.)

product from Malaysia also increases by 0.35 percent, implying that Malaysian commodities can replace U.S. commodities. Likewise, when the Malaysian price increases by 1 percent, demand for the U.S. product in the EU market increases by 0.48 percent. The sign of cross-price elasticities is consistent with the prediction in most industries. The empirical results show that the value of cross-price elasticity of the U.S. is higher than that of ASEAN countries, in general, except for products of telecommunications and sound-recording equipment (SITC76) of the Philippines and electrical machinery and apparatus (SITC77) of Thailand. These findings imply that if export prices of the competitor decline, ASEAN exports are more adversely affected than those of the U.S.

Table 9.3 also shows that U.S. and ASEAN exports respond positively to economic activity in Europe in total consumption (c^{eu}_{it}), domestic capital formation (v^{eu}_{it}) and exports (x^{eu}_{it}), in general. However, exports and total consumption play more obvious roles than domestic capital formations on increases in imports from both ASEAN and the U.S., based on the number of industries which display statistically significant coefficients from the estimations. Nevertheless, U.S. products are used for domestic capital formation of the EU rather than products from ASEAN countries. On the other hand, products from ASEAN are used as elements of exports of the EU compared to the U.S. products.

The empirical results of supply equations are obtained based on equations (5) and (7). However, both equations (5) and (7) are the inverse supply function since the dependent variable on the left-hand side of the equation is the price level. For simplicity sake, the coefficients from equations (5) and (7) are converted back to the original supply function, based on equations (3) and (2). The corresponding coefficients are presented in Table 9.4. For example, in relation to industry SITC77 of Singapore, the coefficient in Table 9.4 ($\pi_1 = 1.06$) comes from $1/\beta_1$ (1/0.37), according to the relationship between π_i and β_i in equation (3). The other coefficients in Table 9.4 are calculated in the same fashion (additional information for the estimation of β_i can be obtained from the author upon request).

The first column on the left-hand side of Table 9.4 shows the price elasticity of export supply from both ASEAN and the U.S. The coefficients are statistically significant in every industry, except telecommunications and sound-recording equipment (SITC76) for the Philippines, general industrial machinery and equipment (SITC74) for Singapore and telecommunications and sound-recording equipment (SITC76) for the U.S. as an export competitor of Singapore.

For products related to general industrial machinery and equipment (SITC74) from Thailand, an increase of 1 percent in price will raise exports from Thailand by 1.59 percent while U.S. exports will increase by 1.12 percent. The findings in this column also indicate that the size of the price elasticity is substantially large, in general. The lagged price also plays a role on export quantities of both countries, although it is statistically insignificant in certain industries. The impact of the exchange rates also complies with the prediction.

In relation to the role of wage rates on the quantity of exports, the quantity of exports from ASEAN countries to the EU market is not very responsive to increases in wage rates compared to the case of the U.S. This might be explained through the fact that the general wage rates in ASEAN countries are much lower than the U.S. rates. Therefore, increases in wage rates in ASEAN countries may have a slight impact on comparative advantage in exports. This is not the case of the U.S., where the general wage rates are already high. Hence, only small increases in wage rates can have a significant impact on U.S. exports.

In terms of the most crucial point of the study, Table 9.5 shows that three ASEAN countries (Malaysia, the Philippines and Singapore)

Table 9.4 Value of coefficient (π_i) in the original supply equations: (2)

Variable	p_{it}^{as} p_{it}^{us}	p_{it-1}^{as}	p_{it-1}^{us}	e_{it}^{as-eu} e_{it}^{us-eu}	w_{it}^{as} w_{it}^{us}	R^2
Malaysia						
SITC-74						
q_{it}^{as}	2.38*	0.57**	−1.40	−0.48**	−2.95	0.63
	(0.23)	(0.10)	(0.41)	(0.09)	(0.95)	
q_{it}^{us}	1.30***	−0.84	0.36**	−0.55*	−0.62**	0.71
	(0.23)	(0.58)	(0.12)	(0.23)	(0.20)	
SITC-75						
q_{it}^{as}	3.45**	−3.55	−1.90*	−3.34	−1.48*	0.52
	(0.12)	(0.79)	(0.25)	(0.88)	(0.24)	
q_{it}^{us}	1.52*	−0.26*	1.64	1.94	−0.55***	0.66
	(0.36)	(0.09)	(0.83)	(1.08)	(0.17)	
SITC-76						
q_{it}^{as}	2.08*	1.81	−0.67**	−0.29***	1.81	0.56
	(0.26)	(0.64)	(0.13)	(0.04)	(0.71)	
q_{it}^{us}	1.14**	−0.55**	−0.09	−1.53	−0.40*	0.67
	(0.38)	(0.21)	(0.06)	(1.09)	(0.20)	
SITC-77						
q_{it}^{as}	2.04**	1.27**	−0.33*	3.22	−0.57**	0.48
	(0.21)	(0.25)	(0.07)	(1.46)	(0.15)	
q_{it}^{us}	1.37**	−0.71***	0.52*	−0.37**	2.08	0.62
	(0.31)	(0.15)	(0.22)	(0.11)	(1.22)	
SITC-78						
q_{it}^{as}	5.56***	−7.50	3.72	−0.78**	−5.06	0.41
	(0.05)	(1.12)	(0.50)	(0.06)	(0.68)	
q_{it}^{us}	1.16*	−0.45	0.55***	−0.43	−0.30*	0.69
	(0.48)	(0.35)	(0.12)	(0.35)	(0.14)	
Philippines						
SITC-74						
q_{it}^{as}	3.45*	0.90*	−5.28	−0.31***	−1.86**	0.50
	(0.16)	(0.15)	(1.27)	(0.02)	(0.23)	
q_{it}^{us}	1.28**	−0.55**	0.78*	−0.19*	−1.71	0.75
	(0.35)	(0.19)	(0.25)	(0.08)	(0.95)	
SITC-75						
q_{it}^{as}	2.94**	0.32***	−2.18*	−2.74	−4.65	0.61
	(0.14)	(0.03)	(0.41)	(0.70)	(1.11)	
q_{it}^{us}	1.39**	−0.38	0.10***	−0.36*	−0.99*	0.74
	(0.31)	(0.22)	(0.01)	(0.13)	(0.39)	
SITC-76						
q_{it}^{as}	1.15	0.13*	−0.17**	−0.83*	1.83	0.83
	(0.62)	(0.06)	(0.06)	(0.40)	(1.39)	
q_{it}^{us}	2.13*	−2.47	−1.57	−0.53***	−0.57*	0.67
	(0.26)	(0.89)	(0.59)	(0.06)	(0.15)	

Table 9.4 (continued)

Variable	p_{it}^{as} p_{it}^{us}	p_{it-1}^{as}	p_{it-1}^{us}	e_{it}^{as-eu} e_{it}^{us-eu}	w_{it}^{as} w_{it}^{us}	R²
SITC-77						
q_{it}^{as}	1.92**	0.12**	−0.69*	2.38	−0.12*	0.68
	(0.23)	(0.02)	(0.15)	(0.96)	(0.03)	
q_{it}^{us}	2.86*	−1.37**	0.51**	−1.06**	3.26	0.58
	(0.19)	(0.19)	(0.07)	(0.16)	(0.85)	
SITC-78						
q_{it}^{as}	1.20**	1.83	−0.25*	−0.30***	−0.69**	0.76
	(0.37)	(1.19)	(0.09)	(0.06)	(0.27)	
q_{it}^{us}	1.15***	−0.34**	0.74*	−1.20	−0.87	0.72
	(0.24)	(0.14)	(0.27)	(0.94)	(0.68)	
Singapore						
SITC-74						
q_{it}^{as}	3.70	1.37*	−3.78	−0.63**	1.93	0.43
	(0.24)	(0.20)	(0.91)	(0.07)	(0.36)	
q_{it}^{us}	2.63*	−1.08**	0.97*	2.26	−2.74	0.54
	(0.21)	(0.18)	(0.20)	(0.73)	(0.73)	
SITC-75						
q_{it}^{as}	1.56**	2.09	−0.08	−0.22***	−1.27	0.77
	(0.28)	(0.95)	(0.03)	(0.05)	(0.66)	
q_{it}^{us}	1.96*	−0.65***	0.96*	−1.33	−1.00**	0.68
	(0.29)	(0.12)	(0.26)	(0.51)	(0.21)	
SITC-76						
q_{it}^{as}	1.54***	0.22*	−0.69	1.78	−0.75*	0.73
	(0.17)	(0.07)	(0.31)	(0.81)	(0.28)	
q_{it}^{us}	0.80	−0.41**	0.22*	−0.51	−0.35**	0.82
	(0.96)	(0.24)	(0.18)	(0.45)	(0.18)	
SITC-77						
q_{it}^{as}	1.06**	−0.98	−0.33**	−0.20***	−1.30	0.76
	(0.39)	(0.70)	(0.14)	(0.06)	(0.93)	
q_{it}^{us}	2.44**	0.76*	−1.15*	−0.61	−3.02**	0.61
	(0.32)	(0.19)	(0.29)	(0.57)	(0.15)	
SITC-78						
q_{it}^{as}	1.49*	−2.03**	0.37***	−0.40*	1.21	0.74
	(0.23)	(0.14)	(0.14)	(0.14)	(0.86)	
q_{it}^{us}	1.14*	0.53	1.15**	−0.20	−0.23	0.69
	(0.36)	(1.13)	(0.11)	(0.20)	(0.73)	
Thailand						
SITC-74						
q_{it}^{as}	1.59**	−0.30*	0.60	−1.10*	−0.40	0.63
	(0.37)	(0.21)	(0.75)	(0.10)	(0.17)	
q_{it}^{us}	1.12*	−0.24*	−0.48***	1.88	−0.67*	0.73
	(0.34)	(0.09)	(0.12)	(0.51)	(0.14)	

Table 9.4   (continued)

Variable	p_{it}^{as} p_{it}^{us}	p_{it-1}^{as}	p_{it-1}^{us}	e_{it}^{as-eu} e_{it}^{us-eu}	w_{it}^{as} w_{it}^{us}	R^2
SITC-75						
q_{it}^{as}	1.47*	−0.49	0.32***	−1.21	−0.31***	0.68
	(0.50)	(0.17)	(1.86)	(1.31)	(0.18)	
q_{it}^{us}	1.96***	1.12*	−1.90*	−0.73	2.65**	0.62
	(0.17)	(0.19)	(0.12)	(0.55)	(0.09)	
SITC-76						
q_{it}^{as}	1.49**	1.10**	0.91	−0.43*	−0.49	0.74
	(0.20)	(0.23)	(0.73)	(0.19)	(0.89)	
q_{it}^{us}	1.33*	0.41	−0.19*	−0.45***	−1.57*	0.69
	(0.38)	(0.61)	(0.35)	(0.09)	(0.17)	
SITC-77						
q_{it}^{as}	1.85*	−0.50**	−2.76*	−0.52	−0.76	0.57
	(0.40)	(0.14)	(0.08)	(0.30)	(0.92)	
q_{it}^{us}	2.38**	2.83*	−0.64	−1.79**	0.17***	0.46
	(0.24)	(0.15)	(1.31)	(0.11)	(0.12)	
SITC-78						
q_{it}^{as}	2.22**	−0.82	1.58***	3.02	−0.82	0.50
	(0.18)	(0.91)	(0.07)	(0.62)	(0.05)	
q_{it}^{us}	1.15***	−0.34	0.74*	−1.20	−0.87**	0.65
	(0.12)	(0.32)	(0.39)	(1.13)	(0.18)	

Note: The value of coefficient in Table 9.4 (π_i in equation (2)) is calculated from the coefficient of the inverse supply function (β_i, λ_i), based on equation (3). Statistical significance is denoted as *** 1%, ** 5%, * 10%. (Standard errors are in parentheses.)

encounter the displacement effect, and Thailand does not. The exports from the Philippines have been displaced by exports from the U.S. in two industries: SITC74 – general industrial machinery and equipment, and SITC78 – road vehicles (including air-cushion vehicles). Both Malaysia and Singapore have encountered a displacement effect in exports of road vehicles (including air-cushion vehicles) (SITC78).

The degree of displacement effect is obtained from equation (9). Accordingly, an increase in 1 percent of exports of road vehicles (including air-cushion vehicles) (SITC78) from the U.S. reduces exports of the same product from Malaysia, Philippines and Singapore to the EU market by 0.05, 0.12 and 0.01 percent respectively. The degree of displacement effect in the products of general industrial machinery and equipment (SITC74) is 0.02 percent for exports from the Philippines. The cause of the displacement effect can be elaborated on based on equation (9) and the statistics

Table 9.5   Displacement effect

SITC	Industry	α_2	γ_2	λ_1	γ_1	α_1	β_1	Ω
	Malaysia							
74	General industrial machines	ins	0.51	0.77	ins	0.93	0.42	n/a
75	Office automatic and data-processing machines	0.35	0.81	0.66	0.48	0.33	0.29	0.67
76	Telecommunications and sound-recording equipment	0.21	0.69	0.88	0.32	0.27	0.48	0.56
77	Electrical machinery and apparatus	0.29	0.82	0.73	0.83	0.21	0.49	0.47
78	Road vehicles	0.12	1.35	0.86	0.61	0.29	0.18	−0.05
	Philippines							
74	General industrial machines	0.21	1.53	0.78	0.47	0.24	0.29	−0.02
75	Office automatic and data-processing machines	0.22	0.91	0.72	0.69	0.32	0.34	0.44
76	Telecommunications and sound-recording equipment	0.74	0.39	0.47	0.23	ins	ins	n/a
77	Electrical machinery and apparatus	ins	ins	0.35	0.17	ins	0.52	n/a
78	Road vehicles	0.23	1.54	0.87	0.31	0.18	0.83	−0.12
	Singapore							
74	General industrial machines	0.71	ins	0.38	0.74	0.85	ins	n/a
75	Office automatic and data-processing machines	0.44	0.67	0.51	0.49	0.22	0.64	0.75
76	Telecommunications and sound-recording equipment	0.82	0.34	ins	ins	0.71	0.65	n/a
77	Electrical machinery and apparatus	0.33	0.98	0.74	0.77	0.33	0.94	0.36
78	Road vehicles	0.09	1.61	0.67	0.42	0.25	0.41	−0.01
	Thailand							
74	General industrial machines	0.28	0.67	0.63	0.58	0.40	0.88	0.65
75	Office automatic and data-processing machines	0.30	0.91	0.68	0.85	0.31	0.89	0.39

Table 9.5   (continued)

SITC	Industry	α_2	γ_2	λ_1	γ_1	α_1	β_1	Ω
	Thailand							
76	Telecommunications and sound-recording equipment	0.35	0.96	0.67	0.74	0.36	0.51	0.49
77	Electrical machinery and apparatus	0.65	0.83	0.54	0.62	0.32	0.75	0.73
78	Road vehicles	ins	0.34	0.45	ins	0.68	0.42	n/a

Notes:
Displacement effect is defined as Ω which has a negative value. It is calculated according to equation (9).
The coefficients are in absolute value terms to calculate for Ω.
ins = statistical insignificance.

provided in Table 9.5. All of the four affected industries exhibit three common findings, regarding the magnitude (absolute value) of elasticities.

First, the size of cross-price elasticity of export demand for q_{it}^{as} with respect to p_{it}^{us} (or α_2) is small. This implies that the increase in quantity of exports from the ASEAN countries to the EU market does not respond well to increases in U.S. export prices.

Second, the value of price elasticity of export demand for q_{it}^{us} with respect to p_{it}^{us} (or γ_2) is substantially high. This indicates that the increase in the quantity of exports from the U.S. to the EU is considerably high even though the reduction in price is small.

Third, the size of cross-price elasticity of export demand for q_{it}^{us} with respect to p_{it}^{as} (or α_1) is bigger than the price elasticity of export demand for q_{it}^{as} with respect to p_{it}^{as} (or γ_1). This indicates that a small increase in the ASEAN price leads to substantial increases in demand for U.S. exports, while a small decrease in the ASEAN price leads to a tiny increase in demand for ASEAN products.

By comparing the findings with the previous studies, there is inconsistency in the estimated results due to the difference in studied cases. The empirical results revealed that the displacement effect was detected on exports of products of SITC74 and SITC78 between ASEAN countries (Malaysia, the Philippines and Singapore) and the U.S. in the EU market, while the displacement effect was not found on exports of machinery and transport equipment (SITC7) between ASEAN countries and China in the world market (Athukorala, 2009). Besides the difference in the case study, nonetheless, this study is different from theirs in two main ways. First, the export variable is treated as an exogenous variable in their studies. There is no interaction between two exporting countries in their framework. However, this study allowed two exporting countries to have interaction in their competition by endogenizing the export variable into the model. Second, this research provided the explanation for determining the factor of displacement effect explicitly, which has never been provided in previous research. This study adds to previous literature in that it provides a preliminary idea to understand the determinant factor and the cause of displacement effect.

6. CONCLUSION

Due to the fact that the EU is a significant export destination for ASEAN countries and that similar trade structures exist between ASEAN and the U.S., fierce export competition in the product group of machinery and transport equipment (SITC7) between ASEAN and the U.S. in the EU market is inevitable. In addition, the size of exports of SITC7 products from ASEAN is approximately three times smaller than U.S. commodities. This may also lead ASEAN to be confronted with the displacement effect.

The existing research on the displacement effect usually employs the gravity model as a study framework. The volume of exports of the larger country, such as China, is typically treated as an exogenous variable for the smaller country, such as Sudan, in the model. This notion is reasonable for the above-mentioned case because exports from China are 605 times bigger than exports from Sudan. The degree of displacement is captured through the coefficient of exports from the larger country. The research argues that such a framework may not be applicable to the study on export competition and the displacement effect in the case of ASEAN and the U.S. This is because the size of exports from the U.S. is just twice bigger than that of ASEAN in machinery and transportation equipment in the EU market. Thus, the study endogenizes the export variable in the framework. A simultaneous equations model is employed in the study and it also attempts to analyze the cause of the displacement effect through various elasticities which are derived from the model.

A system of simultaneous equations of export demand and export supply is estimated using the 2SLS technique for five industries at the 2-digit level of SITC7 industries on exports from four ASEAN countries and the U.S. The empirical findings affirm that the displacement effect occurs in two industries on exports from ASEAN countries to the EU – road vehicles (including air-cushion vehicles) (SITC78) for Malaysia, the Philippines and Singapore, and general industrial machinery and equipment (SITC74) for the Philippines. There is no displacement effect on exports from Thailand. One of the explanations for the cause of the displacement effect facing ASEAN countries is that the value of price elasticity of export demand for q_{it}^{us} with respect to p_{it}^{us} (or γ_2) is substantially high. This indicates that the increase in quantity of exports from the U.S. to the EU is considerably high even though the reduction in the U.S. price is small. This finding has meaningful policy implications for ASEAN, especially regarding the potential negative impact of the EU-U.S. FTA on ASEAN exports. As of 2016 the U.S. and the EU are negotiating to establish the EU-U.S. FTA. The current tariff barriers in the manufacturing sector of the EU are already low, while the existing non-tariff barriers are substantially high. It is expected that the non-tariff barriers between the U.S. and the EU would be removed significantly after the FTA comes into force. Elimination of non-tariff barriers would lead to a lower cost of production of U.S. business units. This would enable U.S. exporters to lower the price of their commodities when they export their product to the EU market.

Based on the findings of this research that the price elasticity of export demand for q_{it}^{us} with respect to p_{it}^{us} (or γ_2) is substantially high, it is expected that three ASEAN countries (Malaysia, the Philippines and Singapore) would suffer from a serious reduction of their exports in certain groups of products to the EU market due to the displacement effect, emanating from U.S. exports. Although the EU-U.S. FTA does not lower the export competitiveness of ASEAN on an absolute basis, the reduction in exports from ASEAN owing to the displacement effect requires ASEAN to improve its competitiveness on exports in order to maintain its market share. Hence, these three ASEAN countries need to increase the level of export competitiveness of their industries to compete with U.S. products in the EU market, especially in the two industries where the displacement effect is found: SITC74 and SITC78.

REFERENCES

Abbott, A.J. and G. De Vita (2002), 'Long-run Price and Income Elasticities of Demand for Hong Kong Exports: A Structural Cointegrating VAR Approach', *Applied Economics*, **34** (8), 1025–1032.

Anderson, J.E. (1979), 'A Theoretical Foundation for the Gravity Equation', *American Economic Review*, **69** (1), 106–116.

Anderson, J.E. and E.V. Wincoop (2003), 'Gravity with Gravitas: A Solution to the Border Puzzle', *American Economic Review*, **93** (1), 170–192.

Athukorala, P.C. (2009), 'The Rise of China and East Asian Export Performance: Is the Crowding-Out Fear Warranted?', *The World Economy*, **32** (2), 234–266.

Athukorala, P.C. and J. Riedel (1994), 'Demand and Supply Factors in the

Determination of NIE Exports: A Simultaneous Error-correction Model for Hong Kong: A Comment', *Economic Journal*, **104** (427), 1411–1414.

Baak, S.J. (2014), 'Do Chinese and Korean Products Compete in the Japanese Market? An Investigation of Machinery Exports', *Journal of the Japanese and International Economies*, **34**, 256–271.

Berger, B. and R.F. Martin (2013), 'The Chinese Export Boom: An Examination of the Detailed Trade Data', *China & World Economy*, **21** (1), 64–90.

Bhattacharya, A., S. Ghosh and W.J. Jansen (2001), 'Has the Emergence of China Hurt Asian Exports?', *Applied Economics Letters*, **8**, 217–221.

Constant, N.Z.S. and Y. Yue (2010), 'An Econometric Estimation of Import Demand Function for Cote D'Ivoire', *International Journal of Business and Management*, **5** (2), 77–84.

Durmaz, N. and J.H. Lee (2012), 'An Empirical Analysis of Import Demand Function for Turkey', Economics & Finance Working Paper Series UHV-WP 2012-01, University of Houston–Victoria.

Edwards, L. and P. Alves (2006), 'South Africa's Export Performance: Determinants of Export Supply', *South African Journal of Economics*, **74** (3), 473–500.

Eichengreen, B., Y. Rhee and H. Tong (2004), 'The Impact of China on the Exports of Other Asian Countries', NBER Working Paper No. 10768, National Bureau of Economic Research.

Eichengreen, B., Y. Rhee and H. Tong (2007), 'China and the Exports of Other Asian Countries', *Review of World Economics*, **143** (2), 201–226.

Fosu, O.E. and F.J. Magnus (2008), 'Aggregate Import Demand and Expenditure Components in Ghana', *Journal of Social Sciences*, **4** (1), 1–6.

Geda, A. and A.G. Meskel (2008), 'China and India's Growth Surge: Is it a Curse or Blessing for Africa? The Case of Manufactured Exports', *African Development Review*, **20** (2), 247–272.

Giovannetti, G. and M. Sanfilippo (2009), 'Do Chinese Exports Crowd-out African Goods? An Econometric Analysis by Country and Sector', *European Journal of Development Research*, **21** (4), 506–530.

Goldstein, M. and M.S. Khan (1978), 'The Supply and Demand for Exports: A Simultaneous Approach', *Review of Economics and Statistics*, **60** (2), 275–286.

Goldstein, M. and M.S. Khan (1985), 'Income and Price Effects in Foreign Trade', in R.W. Jones and P.B. Kenen (eds.), *Handbook of International Economics*, Amsterdam: Elsevier, pp. 1041–1105.

Greenaway, D., A. Mahabir and C. Milner (2008), 'Has China Displaced Other Asian Countries' Exports?', *China Economic Review*, **19** (2), 152–169.

Gujarati, D. and D. Porter (2008), *Basic Econometrics*, 5th edn., New York: McGraw-Hill/Irwin.

Khan, S.A., S. Khan and K.U. Zaman (2013), 'An Estimation of Disaggregate Import Demand Function for Pakistan', *World Applied Sciences Journal*, **21** (7), 1050–1056.

Koukouritakis, M. (2006), 'EU Accession Effects on Export Performance: The Case of Greece', *South-Eastern Europe Journal of Economics*, **4** (2), 147–166.

Levin, A., C.F. Lin and C. Chu (2002), 'Unit Root Tests in Panel Data: Asymptotic and Finite-Sample Properties', *Journal of Econometrics*, **108**, 1–24.

Módolo, D.B. and C. Hiratuka (2012), 'Chinese Competition's Impact on Third Markets: An Analysis by Region and Technological Category', Discussion Paper No. 003, Estudos Econômicos, Ministério da Fazenda.

Montinari, L. and G. Prodi (2011), 'China's Impact on Intra-African Trade', *The Chinese Economy*, **44** (4), 75–91.

Muscatelli, V.A., T.G. Srinivasan and D. Vines (1992), 'Demand and Supply Factors in the Determination of NIE Exports: A Simultaneous Error-correction Model for Hong Kong', *Economic Journal*, **102**, 1467–1477.

Narayan, S. and P.K. Narayan (2010), 'Estimating Import and Export Demand Elasticities for Mauritius and South Africa', *Australian Economic Papers*, **49** (3), 241–252.

Rahmaddi, R. and M. Ichihashi (2012), 'How Do Foreign and Domestic Demand Affect Exports Performance? An Econometric Investigation of Indonesia's Exports', *Modern Economy*, **3**, 32–42.

Riedel, J. (1988), 'The Demand for LDC Exports of Manufactures: Estimates from Hong Kong', *Economic Journal*, **98** (389), 138–148.

Silgonera, M., S. Katharina, J. Wörza and C. Schitterb (2015), 'Fishing in the Same Pool: Export Strengths and Competitiveness of China and Central, Eastern and Southeastern Europe at the EU-15 market', *China Economic Review*, **32**, 68–83.

Tang, T.C. (2005), 'Revisiting South Korea's Import Demand Behavior: A Cointegration Analysis', *Asian Economic Journal*, **19** (1), 29–50.

Wang, Z. and S. Wei (2008), 'What Accounts for the Rising Sophistication of China's Exports?', NBER Working Paper No. 13771, National Bureau of Economic Research.

10. Innovation performance in the small and medium enterprises of India – evidence from the food processing industry

Bhumika Gupta and Jeayaram Subramanian

INTRODUCTION

In most developing countries, small and medium-sized enterprises (SMEs) constitute the bulk of the industrial base and contribute significantly to their exports as well as to their gross domestic product (GDP) and/or gross national product (GNP). For instance, India has nearly three million SMEs, which account for almost 50 percent of industrial output and 42 percent of India's total exports. It is the most important employment-generating sector and is an effective tool for the promotion of balanced regional development. These SMEs account for 50 percent of private sector employment and 30–40 percent of value-added in manufacturing. The SME sector produces a diverse range of products, including consumer items, and capital and intermediate goods (Kharbanda, 2001).

As countries integrate into the global village, these SMEs will have to respond accordingly and thus deserve special attention. To enable SMEs to mitigate problems of technological backwardness and enhance their access to new technologies, it is imperative to give them a conducive environment, which in the present context of globalization calls for a human-centered approach with tacit knowledge playing a predominant role. As knowledge resides only in the human mind, it can only be harnessed by focusing on increasing human capabilities through the process of increased communication, cooperation and linkages, both within enterprises as well as across enterprises and knowledge-producing organizations (Kharbanda, 2001).

This chapter sets out to answer the important questions as to how SMEs manage innovation, given their limitations in terms of resources, and as to what are the factors which affect innovation performance, given the resource constraint. To get a meaningful answer to the research questions, the study considers the case of a medium-sized enterprise in the south Indian state of Kerala called 'Canning Industries – Cochin' (CAICO).

Three main research objectives of the study are: (1) To investigate details of the food processing industry in India. (2) To investigate the nature of innovation activity, its associated discourse, sources of innovation and factors which affect innovation performance in Indian food processing SMEs. (3) To explore the major factors that affect innovation performance in a selected SME from Kerala, a state located in south India. The purpose of this chapter is to report on the preliminary findings of the study.

1. STATE OF THE ART

The State of the Art, also known as the *Literature Review* (or Foundations), serves an extremely important function of enabling understanding of existing research carried out in this particular area. In this section we review the existing literature in terms of what is innovation in SMEs, their sources of innovation, innovation performance and factors affecting innovation performance in SMEs.

From Invention to Innovation

In basic terms, innovation is more than mere invention. An invention is a new product, process or service that has been developed after a process of analysis and experimentation. Innovation, on the other hand, goes beyond this definition and includes the act of successfully introducing that product, process or service to the marketplace. The difference between invention and innovation is use and acceptance. Innovation also differs from improvement. An improvement is the same thing that works better. An innovation, on the other hand, may be used for the same purpose as a previous device or process, but does so in a way that changes the way in which people do the thing (Wienclaw, 2008).

Innovation and Performance

The traditional model of firms' behavior postulates that innovations can have only a transitory effect on firms' performance as the new knowledge will soon be diffused and imitated by rivals. Hence, in the long run all firms will converge to the steady-state equilibrium (Knight, 1921). However, there is a vast amount of evidence about some firms in different industries and in different institutional settings remaining superior to their rivals for a considerable period of time, irrespective of the measurements of firm performance used – employment, sales, productivity or profitability (Hashi and Stojcic, 2010). Studies from the early period of research on innovation have typically reported a positive relationship between innovation and measurements of firm performance. Most of these studies used innovation expenditure as the principal measurement of innovation at the firm level. Using cross-sectional data for US firms between 1972 and 1977, Griliches (1986) finds that higher R&D investment leads to higher rates of productivity growth among firms (Hashi and Stojcic, 2010).

How is Innovation Performance Measured?

Having described what innovation is, the study investigates how innovation is considered as a performance criteria and how companies measure innovative performance.

Innovation measurement is an ongoing concern at most companies. Most companies currently do not have a systematic or standard way of measuring either investments in, or returns from, innovation. As a result, measurement of innovation performance tends to be ad hoc, with considerable variation in the measurements used from year to year (Mankin, 2007). Eric Mankin, President of Innovation and Business Architectures, Boston, suggests four kinds of measurements, as preferred ways to evaluate innovation performance.

1. *Number of ideas funded:* The focus of this measurement is on the front end of innovation – the number of new ideas that can generate enough interest to result in formal resource commitment on behalf of the company.
2. *Return on investment (ROI) or project net present value:* These are familiar project-based measurements of financial return. As companies invest in new ideas, they need to generate attractive returns from those investments; these kinds of measurements track that anticipated level of return.
3. *Innovators in senior positions/CEO commitment:* How many of the senior executives in a company or division attained these positions by implementing new ideas that created value? Does the CEO spend a significant amount of his or her time on innovation? These are measurements of a company's process and culture – a way of assessing a company's commitment to meeting the challenge of the new. They are quite different from the project-based measurements above. Here, the emphasis is on encouraging innovative thinkers for long-term success.

4. *Long-term customer adoption:* This is one of a set of results-based metrics that evaluate innovation success by the success of a company's new products and services. The intent of customer-based measurements is to stimulate an organization to focus on ways of cementing and increasing customer loyalty. In other words, create fans – not just customers. For firms using these measurements, innovation is successful when existing customers eagerly anticipate a company's new offerings, waiting in line to buy them. According to Mankin (2007), measuring innovation performance is a challenge and there are various tools and approaches for measuring the same, but not one of them is perfect. Dashboards or scorecards are one often-mentioned solution to this problem of too much variety. A dashboard is a set of measurements, updated in real time, that displays a range of different performance measurements for a company.

This idea leads us to the next question, as to what kinds of measurements are to be incorporated into the dashboard or scorecard. Mankin (2007) suggests the following measurements:

- *Results-based measurements:* These focus on business outcomes, such as sales or profits, stock price or market valuation. Rapid customer adoption and increases in customer loyalty are good examples of these results-based measurements, which track the pay-off from innovation investments.
- *Process measurement:* This is the leading measurement for innovation performance. Some of the aspects, according to Mankin (2007), that are included in a process measurement are the number of projects in the pipeline, the number of ideas that get funded, the average time to market, the number of patents applied per year and the CEO's commitment to innovation. The assumption underlying process measurement is that doing the right activities will lead to improved business results. The problem, however, is that it is difficult to find the right activities to measure as the right leading indicators. And putting too much emphasis on process measurement often leads to counter-productive business results. For example, measuring the number of patent applications per year will reward increased patent activity. Yet a number of recent studies have found that most patents have no business value, and the cost of obtaining them averages around US$10,000. So, for many companies, rewarding high patent output actually reduces profitability and increases clutter.
- *Project measurement:* Project measurements look at the returns and investments from specific innovation projects. Measurements such

as "time to cash" or ROI are calculated on a project-by-project basis. Project measurements are especially prevalent in industries such as pharmaceuticals, chemicals or consumer electronics, where innovative efforts are undertaken in large and discrete projects. In these situations, there are a number of tools that can provide a measurement of project-based innovation performance.

- *Portfolio measurement of innovation performance:* These kinds of measurements characterize the set of innovative efforts being undertaken rather than an individual project. Just as financiers create portfolios of different financial assets, and evaluate the performance of the portfolio, so too should companies investing in innovation spread their investments across a variety of different kinds of products. Portfolio measurements are the best way to measure the level of diversification in the innovation projects and to manage overall risk.

Significance of SMEs in India and an Overview of Innovation in Indian SMEs

In most developing countries, SMEs constitute the bulk of the industrial base and contribute significantly to their exports as well as to their GDP and/or GNP. For instance, India has nearly three million SMEs, which account for almost 50 percent of industrial output and 42 percent of India's total exports. It is the most important employment-generating sector and is an effective tool for promotion of balanced regional development. These account for 50 percent of private sector employment and 30–40 percent of value-added in manufacturing. It produces a diverse range of products, including consumer items and capital and intermediate goods (Kharbanda, 2001).

The Indian government realizes the role played by micro, small and medium enterprises (MSMEs) in the economic and social development of the country because employment potential and the overall growth in the MSME sector are much higher than in large industries. The government has fulfilled its mission by formulating policies and designing and implementing support measures in the field of credit, technological up-gradation, marketing and entrepreneurship development. This has resulted in an increasing rate of innovations within the MSME sector and most of the innovations in the MSME segment have been witnessed in these areas.

The areas for increasing the competitiveness of MSMEs have included technology (including technology for improving quality), procurement, skills development and finance. Innovation can manifest itself in several forms, from operational efficiency and business model optimizations to product- and service-related novelties. Innovation in India is increasingly becoming local, with end-user-friendly conditions considered at the forefront of the process. This increase in local emphasis is reflected in the availability of an increasing array of products and services. Traditional strengths, such as affordable medicines, have been expanded to underserved markets beyond India.

2.   THE INDIAN FOOD PROCESSING INDUSTRY – A SNAPSHOT

The food processing industry in India remains a sunrise industry, notwithstanding the global economic recession and its massive fallout for India's export oriented sectors. Despite strong growth in the secondary and tertiary sectors post-liberalization in 1991, agriculture continues to be the driver of the country's economy, generating around 25 percent of India's GDP and also providing employment to almost two-thirds of the country's population. And as farming is the resource base for the food processing industry there are endless possibilities of exploring and exploiting India's diverse range of agricultural products and other primary sector products including forestry and fisheries. It is not a surprise that the food processing industry in India has emerged as one of the most promising sectors, having acquired the unique distinction of being adaptive in terms of embracing the latest technology, cutting edge skills, professionalism and expertise. However, India has not been able to do justice to its immense potential in the processed food sector, primarily due to its weak backward and forward linkages, and massive wastage of agricultural produce driven by supply chain weakness and infrastructure bottlenecks. Added to this is the inability of the sector to cultivate and nurture world-class talent, which can drive the growth of food processing industries across the globe. Therefore, despite the impressive growth and huge potential, India is yet to be established as a major player in the global agricultural market because of the skill gap and the shortage of technically skilled manpower in all the domains of food processing technology. Recent trends in the global processed food industry have generated a massive demand for professionals and individuals with expertise and awareness of the latest issues and inventions in the field of food processing (MOFPI, 2010).

According to the Agricultural and Processed Food Products Export Development Authority (APEDA), the Ministry of Commerce and Industry, Government of India, the food processing sector is one of the largest sectors in India in terms of production, growth, consumption and export. India's food processing sector covers fruit and vegetables, spices, meat and poultry, milk and milk products, alcoholic beverages, fisheries, forestry, grain processing, and other consumer product groups like confectionery, chocolates and cocoa products, soya-based products, mineral water, and high-protein foods, etc. Since liberalization in August 1991, proposals for projects have been submitted in various segments of the food and agro-processing industry. Besides this, the Indian government has also approved proposals for joint ventures, foreign collaboration, industrial licenses and 100 percent export oriented undertakings. Out of this, foreign investment is over US$1.6 million (Rs.10,000 crores). The Indian food processing industry is primarily export oriented. India's geographical situation gives it the unique advantage of connectivity to Europe, the Middle East, Japan, Singapore, Thailand, Malaysia and Korea. One such example indicating India's location advantage is the value of trade in agriculture and processed food between India and the Gulf region. Retail, one of the largest sectors in the global economy (US$7 trillion), is going through a transition phase in India. One of the prime factors for the non-competitiveness of the food processing industry is because of the cost and quality of marketing channels. Globally, more than 72 percent of food sales occur through supermarkets. India presents a huge opportunity and is all set for a big retail revolution. India is the least saturated of global markets with a small organized retail sector and also with the least competitive of all global retail markets.

SMEs in the Indian Food Processing Industry

According to the SME Rating Agency of India, the food processing industry, due to its diverse nature and a policy of small-scale industry (SSI) reservations, is comprised largely of small enterprises. The organized sector mostly consists of large companies, and accounts for only 25 percent of the market while the remaining 75 percent of the market is divided between the small-scale and the unorganized sectors. The micro- and local community-based food processing enterprises have dominated the primary processing segment of the industry. Small and medium firms are mostly operating in niche markets. The food processing industry is among the sectors reserved for SSI. Though de-reservation of food products began during the 1990s, there are still around 12 products reserved for manufacturing in the small-scale sector. These products are bread, pastries, confectioneries, rapeseed oil (except solvent extracted), mustard oil, sesame oil, groundnut oil, sweetened cashew nut products, ground and processed spices other than spice oil and oleoresin spice, tapioca sago and tapioca flour.

Prominent food processing companies like Priya Foods, MTR, Surya Food & Agro Ltd, and Haldiram's have long been well-known names in their respective regions, with limited national presence. However, lately these companies have changed their strategy towards expanding their market reach. This phenomenon among food processing companies received impetus following the entry of large Indian business enterprises such as ITC, Godrej, Venky's India, Marico, etc., into the branded foods segment. Another factor has been the growth of retail stores, which are emerging as a driving factor for food processing, though they account for just 1 percent of food sales at present.

The United Nations Industrial Development Organization (UNIDO) has identified over 60 clusters of SMEs existing in the food processing sector across India. The state-wide distribution of the clusters shows the largest concentration of companies in Maharashtra and Gujarat followed by Andhra Pradesh, Punjab and Orissa. UNIDO's study of Indian food processing clusters identified some common deficits in these areas. These include:

- Inadequate knowledge of technical standards, packaging facilities, food laws and regulations.
- Quality raw material supply problems.
- Weak information channels with regards to price and quality.
- Lack of infrastructure facilities for testing and research.

For perishable food items, sub-contracting relationships among processing firms does not appear to be a satisfactory arrangement. As a result, cooperation among small units is limited. Further, linking with larger processing firms will be limited in its scale. Thus, unlike in the auto components and textile industries, where the supply chain plays a critical role in the development of the SME segment, it may not be very relevant to the food processing segment, especially in short shelf-life products. However, being part of the supply chain for retail outlets could be a driving factor for the growth of SMEs. In the light of these realities, the government will have to continue to play a critical role in supporting SMEs in the food processing sector.

3. METHODOLOGY

This study has employed a case embedded design. To control for industry effects and to enable comparability, the case has been drawn from the food products manufacturing/processing industry from the state of Kerala in south India. This firm has been selected from firms whose primary business is the manufacture of food additives, which includes food flavorings and taste enhancers, seasonings, colorings, processed herbs and spices, savory specialties, nutrients, and processing aids.

Three kinds of secondary data have also been used in our initial context analysis:

- Government and industry association statistics and reports related to SMEs innovations and the food processing sector.
- Content analysis of the websites of ten food processing SMEs in Kerala. These websites generally contain information about the history of the firms, their main customers, and in some cases, their suppliers. The list was derived from the website of the All India Food Processors' Association (AIFPA).
- Statistics and reports available from the websites of AIFPA, Dun & Bradstreet, India and the government of India.

We have also conducted an in-depth semi-structured interview with the general managers/proprietors of a leading food processing SME of the Kerala region. The interview was conducted face to face at the firm's premises by experienced researchers. The interview was tape-recorded and transcribed for ease of data analysis.

4. FINDINGS

Need for Innovation in the Food Processing Industry

We can broadly define the term innovation as doing something new or a new way of doing something old (Lele, 2013). The Indian food processing industry is not immune to change or innovation. Numerous factors such as changing lifestyles, the evolution of the concept of the nuclear family, women joining the workforce and spending less time in the kitchen, higher disposable income amongst families, and a focus on healthier diets, have influenced the players in this industry to come up with innovative products to satisfy these needs. The primary aims of the market players in this industry have been to increase the shelf life of perishable food products, to come up with new designs in packaging and also to come up with entirely new product ranges to cater to the needs of specific target markets. Some of the major food items that have been transformed recently include edible oils, soya, oats, processed meat and fish categories, and various fruit pulps. A lot of attention has started flowing towards sugar-free food items, low-calorie foods and artificial sweeteners, as India is slowly becoming the diabetes capital of the world. Even innovative packaging has gained a lot of momentum in recent years. According to a study, about 38 percent of the revenues of the packaging industry are sourced from the food processing industry. Similarly, as consumer preferences change over time, there has to be a drastic shift in the level of innovation in the processing of foods too. Some of the innovative techniques of processing foods are dehydration, osmotic drying, freeze-drying, spray drying, sterilization and pasteurization, to name but a few. Hence, the underlying concept here is, innovation comes into play during various stages of the food processing industry, whenever there is a change in consumer preferences, lifestyles and day-to-day food habits.

Canning Industries – Cochin

Established in 1947, Canning Industries – Cochin (CAICO) is a company situated in Thrissur in the south Indian state of Kerala. The company specializes in the production of various fruit pulps. In India, there are basically three ways in which businesses are run, namely partnership, private and public limited companies. CAICO falls under the public limited company category where members of the public hold the shares or the ownership of the company. The shareholders elect the board of directors, which comprises the top management. CAICO has distinct management teams that look into the financial, human resources, marketing, production and quality control aspects of the company. CAICO has around 80 to 85 employees in total, of which approximately 60 are food-handlers (workers in the food processing industry), and the remaining employees work in the quality control department. Hence, CAICO falls under the 'medium enterprise' segment of SMEs in India, based on the number of employees. (The range of employees count in India for the medium enterprises category is from 20 to 199.)

Innovation Dialogues

Tidd and Bessant (2009) in their popular book, *Managing Innovation: Integrating Technological, Market and Organizational Change*, identify several sources of innovation, of which the present chapter focuses on certain specific sources: recombinant innovation – ideas and applications in one world transferred to another; watching others – entrepreneurs observe how other entrepreneurs (they may be from the same segment or a different segment) provide solutions to similar problems and these entrepreneurs adapt and refine those ideas and finally develop solutions for the problems they face; users as innovators – this kind of innovation is propelled by the desire of an individual or a group to modify a product to meet their needs (Hippel, 1988).

During the interview the SME managers spoke at length about what innovation means to them, the various sources of innovation, and other factors which they feel affect the innovation performance of the firm. The following responses were provided:

"Innovation is more of doing existing things in a new or a different way, more than doing entirely new things – the phenomenon which the company calls 'Technology Shift'."

"The need for innovation comes like this . . . For the past 16 to 17 years, we've been the pioneers in canning in the entire southern India. But over a period of time, we had to shift from canning, owing to two major reasons: first, the cost of canning started skyrocketing, and the second, the technology of canning started becoming obsolete over a period of time."

". . . the main idea of canning had its seeds from *government institutions* like the Central Food Research and Technology Institute (CFTRI), Mysore and the Central Institute for Food Processing at Lucknow."

"There are numerous ways to develop capabilities. The question is not to merely develop the products, but it ultimately should result in sales. Stakeholders are looking at what is the bottom line. To achieve the bottom line you have to build volumes; to build volumes you have to fashion your product in such a way that it should be very cost effective in the market. This is where technology would play a key defining role."

"There are two major sources of funds: capital reserves and banks. The company has a long-term relationship of over 40 years with a reputable nationalized bank in India and because of this the bank understands the problems faced by the company from time to time and the corresponding requirements of the company too."

"Being the General Manager of the firm, I myself get actively involved in the entire process. I play the role of conceptualizing an idea and communicating its specifications and guidelines to the other respective departments and ensure its materialization. I also personally monitor the production data each day, in all the three production lines, the effectiveness of employees and its corresponding planning too."

"Customer suggestions and feedback form a significant part, since they are involved in testing of the products too. For instance, there was a suggestion from one of my customers for starting production of maple pulp. But due to logistical reasons (maple trees are grown only in Canada), the idea couldn't materialize. But the customer was after the company to somehow materialize the idea. Due to the regulations and law in India, however that was shelved, though it looked a good proposition."

". . . the company has a good rapport with a person who is in turn connected to more than 600 distributors across the state. Hence, it is easier to get contact details of distributors through him and push them to handle CAICO products."

"The marketing representatives closely work between the distributors and the retailers. Some advertisement back-up has to be given to the public, so that the awareness is created, which in turn facilitates the product to move from the shelf to the customer. Our company exports more than 30–35 percent, mainly to Gulf countries."

"The government should help food processors by subsidies. For example, in sales tax – value added tax for all the states for processed food is only 5 percent. In Kerala it is 14.5 percent. They are not ready to apply their mind. They are not ready to hear!"

"While the laborers are cooperative, the problem comes with the labor department. The department keeps harassing the company to a large extent but the laborers never complain against the company. None of my laborers have made any complaints to the labor department regarding our industrial relations for the last three four years!"

From the responses above it is very clear that innovation performance depends upon many factors. The emergent factors from our research are consolidated and presented in the following model (Figure 10.1).

Technology and Human Resources

Several researchers have noted that human resource management (HRM) leads to firms' sustainable competitive advantage and superior performance, and HRM is an important means of gaining these competitive advantages (Schuler and MacMillan, 1984; Barney, 1991; Wright et al., 1994). Technological innovation – the development of new products or new technologies – has an important influence on firm performance (Mumford, 2000). In practice, a firm's technological innovation mainly comes from internal innovation (Pavitt, 1990), and internal innovation mainly comes from employees with capabilities. Thus, there is a close relationship between HRM, technological innovation and firm performance. In the long run, efficient HRM can advance a firm's technological innovation, improve the company's competitive advantage and increase the company's performance (Huselid, 1995). It has also been seen that various aspects like employee training, motivation levels, effective appraisal and control play a vital role in improving the innovation performance of the firm. In the research, too, it is quite clearly established that technology

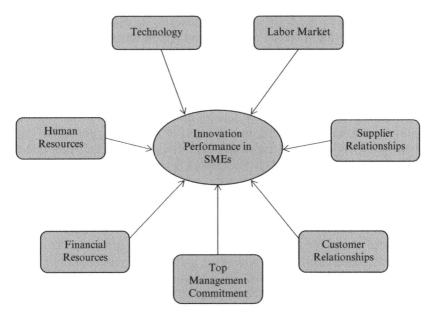

Figure 10.1   Factors affecting innovation performance in SMEs

and human resources play a very significant role with respect to successful innovation performance.

Availability of Financial Resources

The availability of financial resources on affordable terms and in a non-bureaucratic manner is yet another problem the SMEs confront, hindering access to new technologies. It is imperative, therefore, to influence existing financial networks and, if need be, to set up a separate mechanism for funding smaller enterprises, especially those categorized as micro-enterprises. One of the key ways to promote access to new technologies among SMEs in developing countries is to provide venture capital, which in a way helps in the indigenous development of technologies (Kharbanda, 2001).

Today in India there are numerous banking and financial institutions (both government and private), providing venture capitals, thus serving as a helping hand for SMEs to access the latest technology to enhance innovation and hence the firm's performance. Some of the banking and financial institutions include the Industrial Development Bank of India (IDBI), the Industrial Credit and Investment Corporation of India (ICICI), and the Industrial Finance Corporation of India (IFCI), etc. In the study too, it is very clear that financial resources and relationships with banks help greatly in the production of innovative products.

Top Management Commitment and Resources

The top management team (TMT) constitutes the dominant coalition of individuals responsible for the management of a company, particularly in formulating and implementing strategies for change (Chen et al., 2006). The composition of the TMT plays a key role in the innovation performance of the firm. Several researchers have been successful in finding a relationship between the education level of the top management people and the firm's innovation performance; however, the results of empirical research on the existence of any direct relationship between the TMT's characteristics and successful innovation are inconclusive. Previous research studies like those of Daellenbach et al. (1999) and Wally and Becerra (2001) did not find any relationship between innovation performance and higher educational levels of the TMT. Also, functional diversity plays a key role in making strategic decisions. Managers with different functional expertise possess different types and levels of knowledge as well as different perspectives and attitudes toward the issues requiring top management decisions (Camelo et al., 2010). In our study we have discovered that the managing director him-/herself assumes personal responsibility for monitoring all the key processes and issues in the firm, which in turn indicates the significance of the commitment of the top management.

Customer and Supplier Relationships

In today's business environment customers play an active role and they change the dynamics of the marketplace. Also, customers are co-creators of value for the firm. Customer co-creation during innovation involves activities in which customers take an active part during the development process of a new offering (Sjödin and Kristensson, 2012). Successful firms have understood the superiority of customer orientation over a firm's internal orientation. However, fostering customer orientation in order to guide the firm's innovative activities is not enough at a time when suppliers account for the largest portion of the value delivered to the customer, when the fragmentation of the supply chain has gone beyond the outsourcing of manufacturing and logistics tasks, and when suppliers have to bear more design and development responsibility than before (Wagner, 2009).

Wagner (2009) also suggests that the innovation performance of a firm lies in identifying and attracting innovative suppliers, assessing suppliers' downstream customer orientation and maintaining a truly collaborative supplier relationship. From a strategic point of view, the firm has to develop strategic alliances with suppliers, aimed at fostering the firm's competitiveness through innovation performance (Prajogo et al., 2004).

From the study, it is evident that customers, suppliers and distributors play a very significant role in successfully making a product realize its true value. Suggestions from customers, as highlighted by the research, indicate the good rapport the firm maintains with them and serve as a valid tool to identify the needs and demands of the market. Strong distributor and supplier relationships help the firm to take its product to the market successfully, which helps in the value delivery process.

Labor Market

Over the last few decades, research has been carried out to establish if a relationship exists between labor supply and its impact on the innovative activities of the firm. The skill-biased technological changes theory has largely analyzed the impact of the innovation performance of the firm on the wages and skills of the workforce. Theoretical and empirical results have dealt with the magnitude of the shift of the relative demand for skilled labor, yielding a new equilibrium characterized by a higher relative wage and a higher share of skilled employment. According to this point of view, wage inequality has been seen as a direct consequence of higher innovation activities (Pieroni and Pompei, 2008). From the study it is evident that the labor factor plays a significant role in the innovation performance of the firm. Since Kerala is a state which is prone to labor unrest, this factor assumes more significance.

5. CONCLUSION

The emergent theme from this study is that since India is predominantly an agriculture-driven economy, food processing is a very important industry. There are numerous factors which affect innovation performance in SMEs but this study has discussed only the predominant ones. Additional research into this area, with the investigation of an increased number of firms, may reveal further interesting factors which may directly affect innovation performance. This research should also be undertaken with other industries too, as these findings are limited only to the food processing industry in India. Additional research should also be undertaken to find out how innovation diffuses and transcends across the various levels of the firm, resulting in breakthrough products, processes and services.

REFERENCES

Barney, J. (1991), 'Firm resources and sustained competitive advantage', *Journal of Management*, **17** (1), pp. 99–110.

Camelo, C., Fernández-Alles, M. and Hernández, A.B. (2010), 'Strategic consensus, top management teams, and innovation performance', *International Journal of Manpower*, **31** (6), pp. 678–695. doi: http://dx.doi. org/10.1108/01437721011073373.

Chen, G., Tjosvold, D. and Liu, C. (2006), 'Cooperative goals, leader people and productivity values: their contribution to top management teams in China', *Journal of Management Studies*, **43** (5), pp. 1177–1200.

Daellenbach, U.S., McCarthy, A.M. and Shoeneker, T.S. (1999), 'Commitment to innovation: the impact of top management team characteristics', *R&D Management*, **29** (3), pp. 199–209.

Griliches, Z. (1986), 'Productivity, R&D and basic research at the firm level in the 1970s', *American Economic Review*, **76** (1), pp. 141–154.

Hashi, I. and Stojcic, N. (2010), 'The impact of innovation activities on firm performance using a multi-stage model: evidence from the community innovation survey', *CASE Network Studies and Analyses*, **410**, 0_1, 3–38. Accessed at http://search.proquest.com/docview/763168786?accountid=38661.

Hippel, E.V. (1988), *Sources of Innovation*, New York: Oxford University Press.

Huselid, M. (1995), 'The impact of human resource management practices on turnover, productivity, and corporate financial performance', *Academy of Management Journal*, **38**, pp. 635–672.

Kharbanda, V. (2001), 'Facilitating innovation in Indian small and medium enterprises – The role of clusters', *Current Science*, **80** (3), p. 344.

Knight, F.H. (1921), *Risk, Uncertainty and Profit*, Boston, MA: Hart, Schaffner & Marx/Houghton Mifflin Co.

Lele, N. (2013), 'Food & Beverage News: F&B specials – innovations in the food processing industry', *Food & Beverage News*. Accessed 27 August 2013 at http://fnbnews.com/article/detnews.asp?articleid=34101&sectionid=32.

Mankin, E. (2007), 'Measuring innovation performance', *Research Technology Management*, **50** (6), pp. 5–7. Accessed at http://search.proquest.com/docview/2 13800437?accountid=38661.

MOFPI (Ministry of Food Processing Industries) (2010), Data Bank on Economic Parameters of the Food Processing Sector. Accessed 21 September 2013 at http://www.mofpi.nic.in/H_Dwld.aspx?KYEwmOL+HGqTrhLeUJv1qtnM1 Ayq/Q4OmzDNdfKzvW4D2rHvYa8L+w==.

Mumford, M.D. (2000), 'Managing creative people: strategies and tactics for innovation', *Human Resource Management Review*, **10** (3), pp. 313–351.

Pavitt, K. (1990), 'What we know about strategic management of technology', *California Management Review*, **33**, pp. 17–126.

Pieroni, L. and Pompei, F. (2008), 'Labour market flexibility and innovation: geographical and technological determinants', *International Journal of Manpower*, **29** (3), pp. 216–238. doi: http://dx.doi.org/10.1108/01437720810878897.

Prajogo, D.I., Power, D.J. and Sohal, A.S. (2004), 'The role of trading partner relationships in determining innovation performance: an empirical examination', *European Journal of Innovation Management*, **7** (3), pp. 178–186. Accessed at http://search.proquest.com/docview/211767643?accountid=38661.

Schuler, R.S. and MacMillan, I.C. (1984), 'Gaining competitive advantage through human resource management practices', *Human Resource Management*, **23** (3), pp. 241–255.

Sjödin, C. and Kristensson, P. (2012), 'Customers' experiences of co-creation during service innovation', *International Journal of Quality and Service Sciences*, **4** (2), pp. 189–204. doi: http://dx.doi.org/10.1108/17566691211232918.

Tidd, J. and Bessant, J. (2009), *Managing Innovation: Integrating Technological, Market and Organizational Change*, 4th edn. Hoboken, NJ: John Wiley and Sons.

Wagner, S.M. (2009), 'Getting innovation from suppliers', *Research Technology Management*, **52** (1), 8–9. Accessed at http://search.proquest.com/docview/2137 99456?accountid=38661.

Wally, S. and Becerra, M. (2001), 'Top management team characteristics and strategic changes in international diversification', *Group & Organization Management*, **26** (2), pp. 165–188.

Wienclaw, R.A. (2008), 'Product innovation', *Product Innovation – Research Starters Business*, 1–6.

Wright, P.M., McMahan, G.C. and McWilliams, A. (1994), 'Human resources and sustained competitive advantage: a resource-based perspective', *International Journal of Human Resource Management*, **5** (2), pp. 299–324.

11. The emergence of Samsung as a global ICT player

Nigel Callinan

1. SAMSUNG'S EARLY ROOTS

Samsung began business in the late 1930s, while Korea was still under Japan's colonial rule, as a small operation trading in dried seafood, produce and noodles (McNamara, 1990). The following decade was a turbulent time to try to run a business on the Korean peninsula as Japan soon became embroiled in wars, first in East Asia and then in Southeast Asia. The hostilities culminated in the Second World War, which was then followed almost right away by the Korean War. As with most other companies, Samsung struggled to keep its operations going during the wars, but it did manage to relocate and re-emerge as a successful textile company in the 1950s when Korea regained its independence, even though the country had been split into a North-South divide.

In the 1960s, Samsung's direction as a company underwent a dramatic change of direction, when Korea's President Park Chung-Hee began a strategy of steering companies into specific industries that his Government considered to be of importance to the country's goals and direction. As part of this move, Samsung began working in the Semi-Conductor and Electronics area in 1969, initially making use of technology and government-controlled soft loans from Japan given in reparation for wartime activities (Eckert, 1991). Its primary target market was exclusively Korean customers at the time, but plans were put in place early to try to turn its sights towards exporting its products and components as soon as possible. Throughout the 1970s, Samsung gradually diversified its range of businesses into construction, shipbuilding, paper and retail in conjunction with a series of five-year governmental economic plans that sometimes shifted focus to encourage the development of specific business areas (Lim, 2002).

In the mid-1970s, Samsung took its first steps towards internationalization by exporting a series of low-cost televisions that sold well in emerging economies like Panama. In order to expand their supply chain and minimize production costs, the company then began to open assembly plants outside Korea in the early 1980s, starting off in Portugal before expanding to the U.S. (Kim, 1997). This also signaled the start of another initiative, as Samsung began to develop its research and development (R&D) capability domestically in Korea, especially in the semi-conductor area. This period also saw the company take a few tentative steps into the telecommunications hardware business, when it acquired a company called Hanguk Jeonja Tongsin that made switchboards (Lee and Lee, 2009). This coincided with some changes inside Korea that helped to create some business opportunities as will be seen in the next section.

2. DOMESTIC TELECOMMUNICATIONS IN KOREA

In 1981, a series of restructuring decisions were made in Korea's telecommunications area to drive progress (Antonelli, 1991). This began with the creation of a new law on the establishment of the Korea Telecommunications Authority (KTA), paving the way for a government-owned monopoly carrier. The KTA was launched in January 1982 with support from a governmental '*Information Welfare Society*' project that aimed to provide telecommunications services throughout the country. This started out with the construction of Korea's first digitally switched network using a fiber optic backbone. Other important moves made by the Korean Government to support the new market structure were the creation of The Framework Act on Telecommunications and the Telecommunications Act in 1983. These laws decreed that all telecommunication services could only be provided by carriers approved by the Ministry of Communications (Amsden, 1989).

As communication systems were all government-owned in South Korea at the time, the creation of mobile phone networks was managed in the same way. In 1984, a new organization called Korea Mobile Telecom (KMT) was formed as an offshoot of the KTA. The aim of the KMT was to provide a first generation (1G) analogue cellular service using Advanced Mobile Phone Service (AMPS) (Choi, 1990). Most of the network equipment was brought over from AT&T and Motorola in the U.S. In 1987, the government took its first step away from a monopoly by announcing a plan to privatize the KTA and it also invited private companies to offer database and data processing solutions (Kim, 1993).

The KTA achieved full nationwide coverage in 1991. One driver during this period was that the Korean government earmarked mobile telecommunication as one of the country's pivotal strategic industries to drive exports (Kim, 1992). A significant decision taken at this time was on which technology emerging mobile providers should use. A very influential body in the decision-making process was a government-owned telecommunications research institute known as the Electronics and Telecommunications Research Institute (ETRI). The Korean Government initially set up ETRI in 1976 and they created a digital switching system called TDX, which was transferred to Samsung, LG, Daewoo and Hanhwa for production in the early 1980s (Lee and Gomez, 1992). The KTA financed the entire project and permission to manufacture the technology was split equally between the four companies.

In 1989, ETRI started to work on mobile networks using TDX along with a technology known as Code Division Multiple Access (CDMA) that was first used with phones in the USSR during the 1950s (Skylar, 2001). In order to commercialize CDMA, ETRI worked with an American company called Qualcomm who had recently made a number of technology breakthroughs using CDMA. Qualcomm owned the core technologies but they were searching for partners to test and implement their new systems (Lee and Gomez, 1992).

The first phase of the CDMA project in Korea was launched in 1989, supervised by ETRI with project management provided by the KTA. They worked with 63 researchers and a budget of 4.5 billion Korean Won (KRW). From 1990 to 1995, four more companies joined the initiative as Designated Manufacturers (DMs): Samsung Electronics, LGIC (which later became LG Electronics), Hyundai Electronics and Maxon (Chang, 2003).

3.   GSM VS CDMA

With Samsung, Korea's other major companies and the government behind the CDMA project, the South Korean Government decided to approve CDMA as the only permitted mobile network standard in the Korean domestic market in 1993 (Wang and Kim, 2007). However, the decision to exclusively use CDMA placed Korea at odds with the majority of global phone networks. Internationally, the emerging dominant technology standard was the Global System for Mobile Communications (GSM). This was a standard developed by the European Telecommunications Standards Institute (ETSI) to establish protocols for the second generation (2G) digital cellular networks utilized by mobile devices (Mouly and Pautet, 2002).

In contrast to Korea, 13 European countries worked together and agreed to adopt GSM as their mandatory standard in 1987 (Funk, 2001). Mobile phones could not roam between CDMA and GSM networks, so that meant that phones from outside Korea could not be used within

Korea and Korean-made CDMA phones could not be used in Europe. One effect that this had was that it kept Nokia and Ericsson, which went on to become some of the global handset leaders in subsequent years, out of the Korean market and partially protected the sales of products from domestic handset manufacturers (Haug, 2002). In contrast, the U.S. took a different approach and allowed the use of both GSM and CDMA at the same time by different carriers (Funk, 2002), creating competing network technologies. For example in 2013, five of the biggest seven mobile networks in the U.S. used CDMA: Verizon Wireless, Sprint, MetroPCS, Cricket, and U.S. Cellular, accounting for almost 60 percent of the market. Conversely, only AT&T and T-Mobile used GSM, representing approximately 40 percent of the user base (GSM Association, 2013). With its dominance in Europe and a significant presence in the U.S., GSM became the closest thing to a global standard for mobile communications at the time, reaching over 80 percent market share at its peak (Funk and Methe, 2001).

4. MOVING TOWARDS PRIVATIZATION

In 1991, the Korean Government began taking steps towards reducing its monopoly over the domestic market, and Korea Mobile Telecom (KMT) began a privatization process. At this time, KMT rebranded its company as the Hankuk Idong Tongshin Corporation. The privatization project meant that Korea's large *Chaebol* companies started to show an interest in telecommunications. The Sunkyong Group (now known as SK) decided to branch off from their core business of petrochemical and energy processing into communications, so they invested in the privatization of the Hankuk Idong Tongshin Corporation. While this privatization was taking place, Samsung created their first mobile phone operating system in 1992, bringing them closer to having a viable product that could be used with KMT's networks.

By June 1994, the Sunkyong Group had become the largest shareholder in the former KMT (Kim et al., 2013). As Samsung and KMT (initially as KTA) had worked closely together to commercialize both TDX and CDMA with technologies that were mutually interdependent, this immediately created a link between Sunkyong and Samsung. The Sunkyong Group began to be strongly involved in the CDMA development process. They organized a special taskforce to carry out various field tests using Samsung's handsets that provided essential feedback to the commercialization process. This was the beginning of a close relationship between Samsung Electronics and Sunkyong that eventually resulted in Samsung offering handset models exclusively to Sunkyong (SK) in Korea.

However, the Korean Government wanted to introduce competition into the mobile market. Therefore, in 1994, they allowed a second mobile service provider into the market. A company called Shinsegi was awarded the license to operate. When the Sunkyong Group launched the world's first 2G digital CDMA service in January 1996, Shinsegi Telecom quickly followed them into the marketplace using the same technology just three months later (Yun et al., 2002). In June 1996, the Korean Government moved to further deregulate the market by selecting three more approved Personal Communication Service (PCS) providers. Korea Telecom Freetel (a subsidiary of KT), LG Telecom and Hansol PCS were chosen, and they began operating in October 1997 (Kushida and Oh, 2006).

However, this all took place just over one month before South Korea's economy suddenly crashed in 1997, along with a number of other countries in the region. Korea required International Monetary Fund (IMF) intervention to save its ailing economy. One of the IMF's demands was that major public service organizations must be privatized, so a movement began to restructure KT. Despite these moves, the Korean Government continued to be heavily involved in the mobile telephone business. The Government established a research fund for CDMA technologies using a license fee gathered from the five main mobile network operators calculated by their market share (Lyytinen and King, 2002). A body called The Institute of Information Technology Assessment (IITA) controlled this fund. By taking this approach, the government ensured that collaboration continued between SK Telecom, Samsung, ETRI and KT. The official reason for this was so that any delays between technology development and commercialization could be minimized, but of course it also allowed the Government to steer the direction of technology development.

5.   THE RISE OF SAMSUNG

It was also around this time that the rise of Samsung and LG began to be apparent in the Korean mobile handset market. In the final days of 1G analogue phones in 1995, U.S.-based Motorola was the market leader with domestic Korean consumers, holding a 52 percent share of the handset business. In 1996, Samsung opted to try to compete with Motorola both inside and outside of Korea at the same time by selling their phones through Sprint, a U.S.-based CDMA network. Sprint agreed a US$600 million deal with Samsung, whereby Samsung would offer their handsets to U.S. consumers with Sprint for three years under the co-branded name Sprint-Samsung (Lee and McNulty, 2002). This paved the way for Samsung to expand into Hong Kong in 1997, and then into Brazil in 1998.

Meanwhile back in Korea, the relationship between the networks and handset providers created virtually exclusive sales channels. Therefore in the 2G roll-out, Samsung handsets were sold for use with SK Telecom networks while LG handsets were bundled with LG Telecom. An ecosystem evolved where the Korean Government, National Research Centers, network providers and the Korean handset manufacturers were all working closely together on the development, sale and distribution of mobile phones. This meant that by 1999, domestic manufacturers had taken in excess of 90 percent of the market share within Korea (Steinbock, 2003). Moreover in 1999, Samsung also moved into first place in the global CDMA market where they accounted for more than 50 percent of the market share in this sector. However, the global CDMA market was much smaller than the GSM market, which constituted 70 percent of the total global mobile communications market (Rapporteur, 2002).

In parallel with the above changes, the Korean mobile operators began to introduce data service functions in late 1998 using 14.4kbps connections, before upgrading to 64kbps in 1999 (Forge and Bohlin, 2008). This was when short messaging services (SMS) became the most in-demand service, and the three main domestic Korean players agreed to make the system interoperable across their networks (MIC, 1999). For 2G, Wireless Application Protocol (WAP) and iMode were the only two available standards. To take advantage of the popularity of the new services, a race began to provide the best possible network. In 2000, this led to the launch of Korea's first broadband mobile service (2.5G) by SK Telecom using CDMA2000 technology (Han, 2007). There was an agreement between the Korean network operators that when a company launched a new service, they would have exclusive rights to it for six months and then others could use it. This also applied to this new broadband service, so KTF LG Telecom also launched a 2.5G service right on cue in May 2001. This period saw a consolidation of minority network operators. SK Telecom acquired Shinsegi in January 2001 and Hansol PCS was merged into KTF in May 2001 (Park and Lee, 2002).

As high-volume data transmission traffic increased, the bandwidth of 2G mobile phone networks began to struggle with multimedia broadband Internet services so 3G started to emerge as a possible solution. The International Telecommunication Union (ITU) sought to establish a set of global standards for 3G wireless communications called International Mobile Telecommunication-2000 (IMT-2000). Both wCDMA (wideband CDMA) and CDMA2000 were officially included in the IMT-2000 standards (Chandler, 2003).

The Korean Government adopted a multi-standard approach for their next-generation 3G regulations. There were two types of standard for 3G services available at the time. CDMA2000 was an upgrade to QualComm's 2G CDMA technology. wCDMA was a European standard that was not dependent on GPS satellites owned by the U.S. government (Chen, 2007). As wCDMA was not compatible with either GSM or CDMA2000, handset manufacturers predicted that a large new market would quickly emerge for both network and terminal equipment. In October 2001, the Japanese company DoCoMo launched the world's first 3G service using FOMA technology, which is a variant of wCDMA (Kushida, 2008).

For 3G, the Korean Government decided on a multiple-standard policy, allowing both wCDMA and CDMA2000 1x (Kim, 2003). The Government awarded licenses for wCDMA to SKT and KTF, and a license for CDMA2000 to LG Telecom. In May 2002, KTF launched the world's first CDMA2000 service in Korea. Again, using the six-month rule mentioned earlier, SK Telecom followed them into the marketplace using the same technology in November 2002. Both companies were also awarded licenses for wCDMA, but they postponed deployment of this technology, which again kept the European handset manufacturers out of Korea. By June 2003, SKT had 800,000 new subscribers, while KTF had about 470,000. Moreover, around 40 percent of the new phones sold at that time had cameras included. These new features and systems made it possible for emerging applications to thrive including Multimedia Messaging Services (MMS), ringtone downloads, character animations, media downloads and location-dependent services. For example, SKT received 9 percent of their revenue from multimedia data services during the first quarter of 2003 (Kim, 2003).

Two significant organizations whose influence diminished at this time were Qualcomm and ETRI. Qualcomm continued to be an important company in the CDMA2000 area, but some of their competitors, including Samsung and Nokia, started manufacturing comparable chipsets, which affected their business. In addition, Qualcomm's strategic development path diverged from some of their Korean partners when it came to CDMA2000 (Mock, 2005). Moreover, ETRI, which was a leading group in the development and commercialization of 2G CDMA, decreased its profile significantly at this time. It acted in a supporting position only in the development of 3G. Meanwhile, KT invested KRW10.5 billion in a number of 3G development initiatives (Jho, 2007b). When KT was awarded a 3G business license from the government they used it to start up a service called KT ICOM, but they failed to establish a central role during this time. The non-Korean manufacturers (Ericsson, Motorola and Nokia) elected to not take part in the development of 3G CDMA services in Korea, and instead focused on IMT2000 projects.

6. CREATION OF THE WIPI STANDARD

As interactive multimedia content grew in Korea, a problem began to emerge. When service and content providers started to sell increasingly sophisticated data services, the three main operators in the Korean market each developed their own platforms to run Internet applications on mobile devices. The technology used to make these applications diverged. SK Telecom used their own Virtual Machine (VM), KTF chose Qualcomm's Brew and LG Telecom went for Java. Therefore, a content provider would have had to develop and test applications for all three platforms to serve all mobile customers in the market (WIPI Association, 2005). To address the problem, the Korea Wireless Internet Standardization Forum (KWISF) created a Mobile Platform Special Subcommittee (Lee and Oh, 2008). The three main operators, the Telecommunications Technology Association (TTA) and ETRI worked together to make a new standard for mobile Internet applications. It was called the Wireless Internet Platform for Interoperability (WIPI).

WIPI was a middleware platform developed in Korea that officially aimed to allow mobile devices, irrespective of manufacturer or carrier, to run applications. Most of the code behind WIPI was built on Java, but it also had the capability to download and execute compiled binary applications. Therefore, WIPI was able to run both Java- and Brew-based applications. The South Korean Government then created a mandatory rule that all mobile devices sold through the nation had to use the WIPI platform. As WIPI was developed in Korea only, this new rule essentially blocked certain phones from being sold in the Korean market (Ramstad and Woo, 2009).

As a result of the introduction of WIPI and other mandatory regulations, the telecommunications area became a bone of contention for trade between the U.S. and Korea (Suh and Chen, 2007). For example, a dispute began in 2004 over the Korean Ministry of Information and Communication's (MoIC) plan to set a mandatory standard in the 2.3 gigahertz (GHz) bandwidth spectrum for wireless Internet (i.e. Wi-Fi). U.S. companies and officials made accusations that the Korean Government was making decisions under the influence of ETRI, and the standards were being developed to deliberately block foreign importers in order to help Samsung and LG (Mahlich and Pascha, 2007). These moves led a U.S. Trade Representative (USTR) organization to label South Korea as a '*key country of concern*' in its 2004 report, which assessed U.S. trading partners' compliance with international trade agreements (Jho, 2007a). For almost two years, the USTR argued with the South Korean government about the MoIC's requirement to stipulate that all mobile devices must use WIPI only to transfer data over the Internet (Lee, 2009).

7.   THE EMERGENCE OF SMARTPHONES

In 2002, a revolution was on the horizon for mobile phones and their operating systems. This was the emergence of smartphones. A smartphone is a convergent mobile device with more advanced computing capability, features and connectivity than previous phones (Falaki et al., 2010). The earliest smartphones merged the functionality of personal digital assistants (PDAs) and mobile phones. Then, more advanced smartphones added features from portable media players, digital cameras and GPS navigation devices to create multi-use phones (Moon, 2009).

One of the first commercially successful smartphones was the BlackBerry from a Canadian company called Research in Motion (RIM). When it was released in 2003, the BlackBerry phone signaled a technology convergence by supporting push email notifications, mobile calls, text messages, Internet browsing, fax and Wi-Fi information services. BlackBerry initially got a strong foothold in the market by focusing on email functions and targeting business customers (Cowhey and Aronson, 2009). The first BlackBerry phone used a monochrome screen with a built-in QWERTY keyboard that was designed for '*thumbing*', i.e. needing just the thumbs to type.

This convergence also opened up a massive opportunity for Apple, the U.S. technology company. They decided to leverage their hugely successful personal media player (PMP), the iPod, and their experience in user interface design from their personal computer products in order to make a smartphone. Development on the iPhone began in 2004 and the iPhone was officially unveiled on January 9th, 2007 at the Macworld 2007 convention in San Francisco (Apple, 2013). The two initial iPhone models went on sale in the U.S. in June 2007, in the UK, France and Germany in November 2007, and in Ireland and Austria during the spring of 2008. Samsung provided flash memory and components for both the iPod and iPhone so they also stood to benefit somewhat from the emergence of their new competitor (Frommer, 2008).

The iPhone had a profound effect on how people perceived smartphones because Apple marketed the idea of using these devices for leisure, general communication and business through a touchscreen input. The iPhone was a huge hit, and just over a year later it had already caught up on the BlackBerry sales figures internationally. However, in Korea neither the BlackBerry nor the iPhone were released at the time because they did not develop products that complied with Korea's WIPI compatibility legislation.

Even though they were protected domestically in Korea due to legislation barriers, the emergence of smartphones posed a very big challenge to both LG and Samsung internationally. By 2007, Samsung had become the world's leading CDMA phone manufacturer and sat in second place in the overall global phone market behind Nokia. LG Electronics had also expanded its business quickly. Together, Korean companies held more than 60 percent of the worldwide CDMA phone market in 2007. Between 2000 and 2007 Samsung's market share almost doubled (from 10 percent) in the second quarter of 2002, while LG had a larger share than Motorola (5 percent) and Sony Ericsson (5 percent) combined. In 2007/2008 Nokia was the global handset leader with more than 40 percent of the market share, but Samsung was second at over 15 percent and LG was not far behind at around 10 percent (Virki, 2011). Samsung's business strategy was to sell its phones based on its hardware features such as the megapixel ability of its cameras, along with handset size and weight. However, it now faced smartphones marketed on functionality, with an emphasis on user interactivity design and applications. Many Samsung phones at the time included operating systems that were not even branded. This shift was further illustrated when Apple unveiled its App Store in order to sell native and third-party apps on its devices in July 2008 (Apple, 2013).

One reaction to the emergence of the iPhone and the BlackBerry phone was the creation of the Open Handset Alliance in November 2007 (Kim, 2008). This group of technology businesses included Google, HTC, Sony, Samsung, Sprint Nextel, T-Mobile, Qualcomm and Texas Instruments. They announced that they planned to work together to develop open standards for mobile devices. As part of this initiative, Google unveiled the Android Mobile operating system. Android was initially a separate company partly financed by Google, but Google then bought the company outright in 2005 (Google, 2013). This new mobile operating system was built on open source code, meaning that the software could be adapted and used by any device manufacturer, wireless carrier or even hobby programmers.

Within Korea, Samsung and LG continued to enjoy domestic handset dominance with more than an 80 percent market share throughout 2008 (Bicheno, 2013). One side effect of the exclusion of international competitors was that Korean handset makers were able to charge a premium price for their products within their home country. Criticism from Korean consumers grew, as many people wanted to get access to the kind of user experience offered by the BlackBerry and iPhone systems. This led to a large debate among the commissioners of the Korea Communications Commission (KCC). Essentially, there were two barriers to foreign smartphones in Korea. The first was the mandatory WIPI platform as discussed earlier. The second was that the integrated mapping functionality of certain smartphones violated a South Korean regulation stipulating the usage of domestic Korean software for location-based services on mobile devices.

Amid the consumer pressure, the KCC opted to retire the WIPI specification. They made the decision in late 2008 and set the expiration date for the rule as April 1st, 2009 (Oliver and Jung, 2009). They also created an exemption to the map regulation for the iPhone that allowed Apple to include Google Maps as an integrated app as they did on all iPhones at that time. The first mobile provider to announce that they would sell the iPhone in Korea was KT. It had recently merged the KTF and KT brands to try to catch up on SK Telecom which then controlled more than 50 percent of Korea's wireless customers (Lee, 2010). SK decided to sell HTC, RIM's BlackBerry phones and Nokia instead of the iPhone (McInnes, 2011). This left the number three carrier, LG Telecom, in trouble, because they were still using the CDMA EV-DO standard to provide mobile data services, so they still could not accommodate smartphones at all (Churchill, 2011).

Meanwhile, by late 2008 Apple had eaten into the global business of both Nokia and Samsung, jumping ahead of the Korean company in global market share for smartphone handsets. The market positions of Nokia, Samsung, Motorola and LG were all severely threatened and they needed to make major changes to adapt to emerging customer expectations. These companies quickly needed to find a way to compete with Apple's user interface and its industrial design approaches. With its new smartphone model, Samsung decided to focus its engineering work on the physical design of handsets and use Google's Android operating system as the user interface. They called this phone the Samsung Galaxy (also known as the i7500). It was announced in April 2009 and first went on sale in June 2009 (Rowinski, 2012).

Other mobile companies, including Motorola, HTC, Sony Ericsson and LG, also opted to use Android with some of their models. In contrast, Nokia decided to stick with the Symbian operating system and their sales began to plummet. By the second quarter of 2009, Android held a 2.8 percent share of the global smartphone market and use of the operating system was accelerating quickly (Canalys, 2013). However, Apple still forged ahead globally in 2009, controlling over 14 percent of this emerging market compared with 3.3 percent for Samsung and an even smaller share for LG. One significant mistake during this period was LG's decision to only use Android in its low-medium end phones. Its sales figures went into a sharp decline and the LG Electronics CEO resigned suddenly in October 2010, explaining that he had to take responsibility for the company's recent poor management and performance in the mobile area (Miller, 2010).

In 2010, more convergent products started to appear. These products were called tablets and they combined features of mobile phones and laptop computers in flat touchscreen devices. Again, Apple used its experience with laptops, phones and the app ecosystem to enter the market in this new area with the release of the iPad in April 2010. The iPad was available as both a Wi-Fi only device and a mobile device using existing networks (Apple, 2013). This product was another success for Apple and it signaled a global shift towards larger-screen mobile devices. Samsung also opted for a larger screen size in the mobile phone area when they released a 4-inch Galaxy S phone in June 2010. This decision helped the Galaxy S to become the flagship model for Android. By the fourth quarter of 2010, Android smartphones had taken 33 percent of the market, becoming the most widely used smartphone operating system with the Galaxy S, and later the SII, at the forefront. One huge breakthrough was that all three of the major carriers in China decided to sell the Samsung Galaxy S in 2010, opening up the largest consumer market in the world (Hyers, 2013).

Although the switch over to Google's Android system allowed Samsung phones to compete and eventually surpass Apple's phones in sales, the move was seen as an example of the weakness of Korean companies' user interface design ability when competing internationally. To address this problem and decrease its reliance on Google, Samsung began to develop its own operating system called Bada (literally meaning sea in Korean) in 2010. Samsung launched a range of Samsung Wave phones using the new mobile operating system but the phones were not a success (Byford, 2013). They then canceled the development of Bada and merged it into a new operating system development project called Tizen being worked on together by Samsung and Intel. The group working on the Tizen operating system is hoping it will become the system of choice for smart televisions, a new convergence of televisions, PC and mobile technologies (Kim and Cheng, 2013).

The year 2011 can be seen as the year when Samsung really started to dominate the global smartphone scene. Nokia had been the market leader for 15 years and many analysts expected that Apple's iPhone would be the product that would topple Nokia from its position. However, sales of the Galaxy Series with its Android operating system accelerated very quickly to jump into the lead. This led Apple to begin a massive patent lawsuit campaign against Motorola Mobility and Samsung (and some other Android device manufacturers) to try to block sales of the devices. Samsung reacted by countersuing Apple in the patent area. By July 2012, both companies were embroiled in over 50 legal battles all over the world, with billions of dollars in compensation sought by each side (Zeman, 2013). Some of the cases made it all the way to rulings, resulting in products being banned and fines being administered to both companies at varying levels. Other cases were resolved by settlements and updated licensing agreements.

By the third quarter of 2012, Android held a 75 percent share of the global smartphone market based on a report by the IDC research company. By the second quarter of 2013, Android accounted for 67 percent of worldwide tablet shipments and 80 percent of shipments for smartphones, placing them in a dominant position globally (Hyers, 2013). However, this was not necessarily good news for Samsung because many new Android-based products were arriving on sale at cheaper prices than its models. In addition, Apple managed to tie up a deal with the main Chinese networks in 2014 to enter the world's largest consumer market, allowing it to compete directly on the same footing as Samsung globally.

Staying at the forefront of a market is often equally as hard as getting to the top and this will also be the case for Samsung. Its smart devices seem likely to be squeezed by competitors at the premium end of the market in high-income economies, while lower-cost rivals eat into its market share from below in emerging markets. Its only possible defense will be to try to keep modifying its products with new software and hardware features in the hope that it identifies a key innovative change that consumers are willing to pay for before its rivals get to it first. The fate of Korea itself is now closely tied to Samsung as its sales network spans 80 countries, employing over 370,000 staff, while providing 20 percent of Korean exports and revenue that represents 17 percent of the national economy.

8.   SUMMARY

This study is a good example of how a domestic environment can influence the ability of a multinational corporation to expand beyond its own borders. Samsung was part of a group of private and public organizations that formed a group and worked together on the development of ICT devices, standards and networks within Korea. The Korean Government steered and supported the industry using legislation mandating the use of certain technology, effectively excluding international businesses from competing against Korean companies. The chapter began by looking at how the Government made a series of decisions in the early 1980s that allowed the telecommunications area in Korea to develop, albeit under a monopoly.

Then, when mobile technologies began to emerge, the Korean Government opted to tread its own path instead of waiting to see what became a dominant global standard. As development of the CDMA standard progressed, the relationship between the Korean Government, the handset makers and the network providers deepened. The Government even asked the five operators to pay a license fee and contribute to CDMA development. Therefore, they all had a vested interest in commercializing the system successfully. This relationship was kept in place even when the Government started to deregulate the industry and allow additional carriers to operate.

To illustrate the effect that the creation of this ecosystem had, the example of Motorola was included in this chapter. In 1995 it had a significant 52 percent market share in Korea's domestic handset business, but just four years later Korea's own handset manufacturers held a 90 percent market share. It was a dramatic shift in a very short time that clearly illustrated how the barriers raised by the collaboration agreements made by the Government affected Motorola. The strength of the collusion between handset makers was also shown by the six-month rule used by the Korean companies each time a new technology or service became available.

The creation of the WIPI mobile connectivity standard again provided a significant barrier to international handset manufacturers. The official reason for creating the standard was to allow all the Korean carriers to run the same applications. This may well be true, but as a by-product it created yet another barrier to international handset manufacturers. It was considered enough of a problem by the U.S. Government to flag South Korea as a key country of concern when it came to telecommunications trade. The implementation of WIPI coincided with the decline of U.S. company Qualcomm's involvement in the domestic Korean market. It also happened at a time when Samsung's chips were ready for use with handsets. The other example of a trade barrier that the U.S. protested about around that time was a Wi-Fi spectrum requirement for laptops.

When smartphones, specifically the iPhone and the BlackBerry, went on sale around the world, they caught a lot of the feature phone handset makers off guard because both of the new players came from outside the established group of phone companies. The success of these new handsets affected the sales of both LG and Samsung internationally but had no initial effect inside South Korea as the new products were blocked by WIPI and the domestic Korean mapping requirement. Samsung reacted quickly (within just over a year) by taking the decision to abandon their own phone operating system in favor of Google's Android. It also tried to change its design philosophy to directly compete with Apple. In contrast to Samsung, LG were much slower to react, which negatively affected their business very significantly for the next few years. It eventually decided to emulate Samsung's approach to try to catch up.

Samsung's decision saw it come back into the market strongly with high-end, large-screen smartphones that went on sale at a lower price than its competitors. The biggest losers in the industry were Nokia and Motorola which did not react quickly enough to the smartphone revolution. One downside of Samsung's change in strategy was that it started benchmarking Apple as the standard it wanted to reach. This resulted in a convergence of designs and features that set them on a direct collision course with Apple, resulting in a prolonged series of intellectual property legal battles.

In summary, this chapter shows how the Korean Government protected and nurtured both Samsung and LG by helping them in the country's domestic market. This took place via collaborative development efforts, technical trade barriers and exclusive sales relationships. The relationships between the companies and the Government were very strong because of deeply rooted family and business connections in Korea. In this study, it can be said that the government's strategy paid dividends as Samsung managed to use the opportunities it was given to rise to the very top of the international mobile handset industry.

REFERENCES

Amsden, A.H. (1989), *Asia's Next Giant: South Korea and Late Industrialization*, New York: Oxford University Press.

Antonelli, C. (1991), 'The Diffusion of Advanced Telecommunications in Developing Countries', Development Centre of the Organisation for Economic Cooperation and Development, Paris.

Apple (2013), 'Apple reinvents the phone with iPhone'. Apple homepage. Accessed 14 August 2013 at http://www.apple.com/pr/library/2007/01/09Apple-Reinvents-the-Phone-with-iPhone.html.

Bicheno, S. (2013), 'South Korea and Japan Smartphone Markets are Dominated by the Premium Price Tier', *Strategy Analytics*, 25 July. Accessed 2 August 2013 at http://www.strategyanalytics.com/default.aspx?mod=reportabstractview er&a0=8747.

Byford, S. (2013), 'Samsung Finally Folding Bada OS into Tizen', *The Verge*, 25 February. Accessed 26 April 2013 at http://www.theverge.com/2013/2/25/4026848/bada-and-tizen-to-merge.

Canalys (2013), 'Android Overtakes iOS with 53 Per Cent Market Share in Tablets'. Canalys website, 1 August 2013. Accessed 9 August 2013 at http://www.canalys.com/newsroom/small-tablets-drive-big-share-gains-android.

Chandler, C. (2003), *CDMA 2000 and CDMA 450*. International Telecommunication Union. Accessed 19 January 2013 at http://www.itu.int/ITU D/tech/events/2003/slovenia2003/Presentations/Daypercent203/3.3.1_Chandler.pdf.

Chang, S.J. (2003), *The Internet Economy of Korea*, Boston, MA: MIT Press, pp. 263–291.

Chen, H.H. (2007), *The Next Generation CDMA Technologies*, New Jersey: John Wiley and Sons, pp. 105–106.

Choi, B.I. (1990), 'Information Technology-led Development: Its Past, Present and Future in the Republic of Korea', *Information Technology Policy and*

International Cooperation in Asia, Tokyo: Asian Productivity Organization, pp. 73–83.

Churchill, S. (2011), 'LG Telecom: CDMA & LTE Handover', *Daily Wireless*, 5 July. Accessed 3 May 2013 at http://www.dailywireless.org/2011/07/05/cdma-lte-roaming-via-lg-telecom/.

Cowhey, P.F. and Aronson, J. A. (2009), *Transforming Global Information and Communication Markets: The Political Economy of Innovation*, Boston, MA: MIT Press, p. 45.

Eckert, C.J. (1991), *Offspring of Empire: The Koch'ang Kims and the Colonial Origins of Korean Capitalism, 1876–1945*, Seattle, WA: University of Washington Press.

Falaki, H., Mahajan, R., Kandula, S., Lymberopoulos, D., Govindan, R. and Estrin, D. (2010), 'Diversity in Smartphone usage', in *Proceedings of the 8th International Conference on Mobile Systems, Applications, and Services* (pp. 179–194). ACM, June.

Forge, S. and Bohlin, E. (2008), 'Managed Innovation in Korea in Telecommunications – Moving Towards 4G Mobile at a National Level', *Telematics and Informatics*, **25**, November.

Frommer, D. (2008), 'Apple, RIM Get Easier Entry to Korean Market', *Business Insider*, 11 December 2008. Accessed 2 June 2013 at http://www.businessinsider.com/2008/12/apple-rim-get-easier-entry-to-korean-market-aapl-rimm.

Funk, J.L. (2001), *The Mobile Internet: How Japan Dialed up and the West Disconnected*, Bermuda: ISI Publications Limited.

Funk, J.L. (2002), *Global Competition Between and Within Standards: The Case of Mobile Phones*, New York: Palgrave.

Funk, J.L. and Methe, D.T. (2001), 'Market- and Committee-based Mechanisms in the Creation and Diffusion of Global Industry Standards: The Case of Mobile Communication', *Research Policy*, **30**, 589–610.

Google (2013), 'Company Timeline', Google homepage. Accessed 10 May 2013 at https://www.google.com/intl/en/about/company/timeline/.

GSM Association (2013), '2013 GSM Statistics', *GSM World*, March 2013. Accessed 28 March 2013 at http://www.gsmworld.com/newsroom/market-data/market_data_summary.htm.

Han, I.S. (2007), 'Success of CDMA Telecommunications Technology in Korea: The Role of the Mobile Triangle', *Innovation and Technology in Korea: Challenges of a Newly Advanced Economy*, Heidelberg: Physica-Verlag, p. 290.

Haug, T. (2002), 'A Commentary on Standardization Practices: Lessons from the NMT and GSM Mobile Telephone Standards Histories', *Telecommunications Policy*, **26** (3–4), pp. 101–107.

Hyers, K. (2013), 'Android Captures Record 80 Per Cent Share of Global Smartphone Shipments in Q2 2013', *Strategy Analytics*, 1 August. Accessed 7 August 2013 at http://blogs.strategyanalytics.com/WSS/post/2013/08/01/Strategy-Analytics-Android-Captures-Record-80-percent-Share-of-Global-Smartphone-Shipments-in-Q2-2013.aspx.

Jho, W. (2007a), 'Global Political Economy of Technology Standardization: A Case of the Korean Mobile Telecommunications Market', *Telecommunications Policy*, **31**, 129.

Jho, W. (2007b), 'Liberalization as a Development Strategy: Network Governance in the Korean Mobile Telecom Market', *Governance: An International Journal of Policy, Administration and Institutions*, **20** (4), 636.

Kim, D.H. (2003), 'Korea Takes Bold Risks to Become IT Powerhouse', *The Korea Times*, 30 April. Accessed February 2012 at http://times.hankooki.com/lpage/tech/200304/kt2003043017080611790.htm.

Kim, E.J. (1992), 'Changing Telecommunications Policies and Infrastructure in the Republic of Korea', *Telecommunications Journal*, **59** (12), 574.

Kim, E.J. (1993), 'Telecommunications Development in the Republic of Korea: An Alternative Model?', *Telecommunications Policy*, **17**, 2 March.

Kim, K.B., Jung, S.D., Lee, C.J. and Hwang, J.S. (2013), 'Structure of Technology Evolution: The Way on Which ICT Industry Emerged in Korea', 24th European Regional Conference of the International Telecommunication Society, Florence, Italy, 20–23 October 2013. Accessed 3 February at http://www.econstor.eu/bitstream/10419/88508/1/774032391.pdf.

Kim, K.M. and Cheng, R. (2013), 'Samsung Co-CEO: We Want Tizen to be on Everything', *Cnet News*, 5 August. Accessed 10 August 2013 at http://news.cnet.com/8301-1035_3-57597026-94/samsung-co-ceo-we-want-tizen-to-be-on-everything/.

Kim, L. (1997), *Imitation to Innovation: The Dynamics of Korea's Technology Learning*, Boston, MA: Harvard Business Press.

Kim, T.H. (2008), 'Goodbye WIPI, Hello iPhone', *The Korea Times*, 10 December. Accessed 18 March 2013 at http://www.koreatimes.co.kr/www/news/nation/2008/12/133_35873.html.

Kushida, K.E. (2008), 'Wireless Bound and Unbound: The Politics Shaping Cellular Markets in Japan and South Korea', BRIE Working Paper 179a, 1 February 2008, p. 26. Accessed June 2012 at http://brie.berkeley.edu/publications/wp179A.pdf.

Kushida, K.E. and Oh, S.Y. (2006), 'Understanding South Korea and Japan's Spectacular Broadband Development: Strategic Liberalization of the Telecommunications Sectors', BRIE Working Paper 175, June 2006.

Lee, C.S. and Gomez, E.D. (1992), 'The Contribution of the Information Sector to the Industrial Growth of Korea', *Media Asia*, **19** (3), 156–164.

Lee, H. and Oh, S. (2008), 'The Political Economy of Standards Setting by Newcomers: China's WAPI and South Korea's WIPI', *Telecommunications Policy*, **32** (9), 662–671.

Lee, H.C. and McNulty, P. (2002), 'Korea's Information and Communication Technology Boom, and Cultural Transition After the Crisis', Washington, DC: World Bank. Accessed 2 December 2013 at http://www.esri.go.jp/jp/prj/seminar/seminar058b.pdf.

Lee, S. (2009), 'ICT Co-Evolution and Korean ICT Strategy – An Analysis Based on Patent Data', *Telecommunications Policy*, **33** (5–6), 253–271.

Lee, S.J. and Lee, E.H. (2009), 'Case Study of POSCO – Analysis of its Growth Strategy and Key Success Factors', KDI School of Public Policy & Management, Paper No. 09-13.

Lee, Y. (2010), 'S. Korea's iPhone Users Surpass 1 Million in 9 Months', *Yonhap News*, 19 September. Accessed 22 January 2013 at http://english.yonhapnews.co.kr/techscience/2010/09/19/8/0601000000AEN20100919001600320F.HTML.

Lim, Y. (2002), 'Hyundai Crisis: Its Development and Resolution', *Journal of East Asian Studies*, **2** (1), 185–240.

Lyytinen, K. and King, J. (2002), 'Around the Cradle of the Wireless Revolution: The Emergence and Evolution of Cellular Telephony', *Telecommunications Policy*, **26** (3–4), 97–100.

Mahlich, J. and Pascha, W. (eds.) (2007), *Innovation and Technology in Korea: Challenges of a Newly Advanced Economy*, Berlin: Springer Science & Business Media.

McInnes, K. (2011), 'An Interview with a BlackBerry User from South Korea', BlackBerryCoolwebsite, 19 January. Accessed 19 July 2013 at http://www.blackberrycool.com/2011/01/19/an-interview-with-a-blackberry-user-from-south-korea/.

McNamara, D.L. (1990), *The Colonial Origins of Korean Enterprise, 1910–1945*, New York: Cambridge University Press.

MIC (1999), *The Establishment of Cyber Korea 21*. Ministry of Information and Communication. Korea Communications Commission.

Miller, R. (2010), 'LG Electronics CEO Resigns in Wake of Waning Mobile Phone Sales', *Engadget*, 16 September. Accessed 17 February 2013 at http://www.engadget.com/2010/09/16/lg-electronics-ceo-resigns-in-wake-of-declining-mobile-phone-sal/.

Mock, D. (2005), *The Qualcomm Equation: How a Fledgling Telecom Company Forged a New Path to Big Profits and Market Dominance*, New York: AMACOM Division of American Management Association.

Moon, I. (2009), 'Apple Envy Drives Samsung Shakeup', *Business Week*, 15 December. Accessed 9 February 2013 at http://www.businessweek.com/global-biz/content/dec2009/gb20091215032027.htm.

Mouly, M. and Pautet, M.B. (2002), *The GSM System for Mobile Communications*, Paris: Telecom Publishing.

Oliver, C. and Jung, S.A. (2009), 'S. Korean Regulators Relent on iPhone Sales', *Financial Times*, 23 September. Accessed 25 January 2013 at http://www.ft.com/cms/s/0/d268d778-a80f-11de-8305-00144feabdc0.html?nclick_check=1.

Park, J. and Lee, J. (2002), 'The Prospect and Policy Directions of the Broadband Internet Market', *Telecommunication Market*, **40**, 73–88.

Ramstad, E. and Woo, J. (2009), 'South Korea Clears Way for iPhone Sales', *The Wall Street Journal*, 24 September. Accessed 4 March 2013 at http://online.wsj.com/article/SB125367616595333125.html.

Rapporteur, T.S. (2002), *Wireless Communications, Principles and Practice*, New Jersey: Prentice-Hall, Inc.

Rowinski, D. (2012), 'A Brief History of the (Samsung) Galaxy', *Readwrite*, 26 April. Accessed 8 July 2013 at http://readwrite.com/2012/04/26/a-brief-history-of-the-samsung-galaxy#awesm=~oe5OstM9NW7JrC.

Skylar, B. (2001), *Digital Communications: Fundamentals and Applications* (2nd edn.), New Jersey: Prentice-Hall PTR.

Steinbock, D. (2003), 'Globalization of Wireless Value System: From Geographic to Strategic Advantages', *Telecommunications Policy*, **27**, 207–235.

Suh, J. and Chen, D.H.C. (eds.) (2007), *Korea as a Knowledge Economy: Evolutionary Process and Lessons Learned*. Washington, DC: World Bank.

Virki, T. (2011), 'Samsung, Apple to end Nokia's Smartphone Reign', *Reuters News Agency*, 13 June. Accessed 4 March 2012 at http://www.reuters.com/article/2011/06/13/us-nokia-smartphones-idUSTRE75C18O20110613.

Wang, J. and Kim, S. (2007), 'Time to Get In: The Contrasting Stories About Government Interventions in Information Technology Standards (The Case of CDMA and IMT-2000 in Korea)', *Government Information Quarterly*, **24** (1), 115–134.

WIPI Association (2005), 'Wireless Internet Platform for Interoperability', The Australian Government Department of Communications, Information

Technology and the Arts archive website. Accessed 2 December 2012 at http://www.archive.dcita.gov.au/__data/assets/pdf_file/0014/30362/Session_III_2_Hyun_Gwang_Rib_InnoAce_WIPI_050531.pdf.

Yun, K., Lee, H. and Lim, S.H. (2002), 'The Growth of Broadband Internet Connections in South Korea: Contributing Factors', Asia/Pacific Research Center, Stanford University. Accessed 2 February at http://iis-db.stanford.edu/pubs/20032/Yun.pdf.

Zeman, E. (2013), 'Apple Dealt Setback in Samsung Lawsuit', *Information Week*, 27 June. Accessed 5 July 2013 at http://www.informationweek.com/hardware/handheld/apple-dealt-setback-in-samsung-lawsuit/240157420.

12. Epilogue: labour mobility and human resources

Robert Taylor

Emerging Asian economies, especially those of China and members of the Association of Southeast Asian Nations (ASEAN), with a growing middle-class clientele, offer potentially vast commercial opportunities for local and Western multinational corporation (MNC) investors. Penetration of these markets, however, through both trade and investment, is still hampered by protectionist tariff and non-tariff barriers together with restrictions on labour mobility. National governments in the region have been reluctant to change domestic legislation to accord with the blueprint set for the ASEAN Economic Community (AEC), the body briefly referred to in the Introduction. The fact is that governments have been at the mercy of sectoral interests, less competitive industries, which stand to lose if they have to operate in an open market.

It is essential, however, that such dissension be silenced if regional economic integration is to be achieved. A solution lies in the pressure being exercised by the middle class, with increasing discretionary income and rising expectations. Thus less competitive firms in ASEAN countries could take advantage of a discerning consumer taste for diversified products and services by targeting niche markets like those for highly nutritious food, health products and environmentally friendly goods. Such businesses will no longer engage in markets where, for instance, MNCs have a cost advantage, and the former's production facilities can be adapted to the creation of niche products. On these terms a division of labour could emerge (Pitakdumrongkit, 2013).

In fact, in another sense, specialization is already in existence in the region. Lower logistics costs and advanced technologies have facilitated the extension of supply chains over large distances, with components being sourced in one country and assembled in another, an example being iPhone production where parts are produced in five countries – China, Korea, Japan, Germany and the United States – with final assembly in China. In this way, supply chain production, involving China and ASEAN countries, is set to contribute to regional economic integration (Rana and

Chia, 2013). This division of labour reflects differing levels of economic development and technological advancement among the nations of the region, reflecting in part Akamatsu's 'flying geese' theory, discussed by Andreosso-O'Callaghan in her chapter. There will, however, need to be accelerated moves to value-added production if Asian countries are to avoid the middle-income trap, recently highlighted by the International Monetary Fund (IMF). Thus a premium should be placed on innovation and its vehicle, research and development (R&D), promoted by both companies and governments, en route to a knowledge-based economy. In summary, specialization can help to eliminate protectionism and promote free trade (Pitakdumrongkit, 2013).

Economic integration, however, demands not only the free movement of goods, services and investment but the mobility and effective deployment of skilled labour. Such migration is already taking place in the region, with Singapore having the highest ratio of foreign labour to the local population. In Malaysia about a quarter of the workforce consists of migrant workers in areas like manufacturing and agriculture. Nevertheless there remain legal barriers at both national and community levels, with labour flows amounting to less than 2 per cent of total ASEAN employment. This is because at community level only eight Mutual Recognition Agreements (MRAs) have been signed, allowing only certain professionals such as engineers, accountants and medical practitioners to move freely to work in foreign enterprises, while failing to liberalize the mobility of unskilled labour. Additionally, individual member states have also been reluctant to permit labour mobility: migrants paid less are seen by host countries' populations as threatening the livelihood of higher-cost local employees; exporting states fear that their nationals will be exploited or underpaid. In an age of concerns about terrorism, security issues also come to the fore.

In the past, apprehension has focused on migrants taking low-paid work in labour-intensive manufacturing industries and the service sector. But as services move up the value-added chain, there is a premium placed on the advanced technical and foreign language skills possessed by, say, university graduates, whether native or foreign, even though host country nationals are more conversant with local culture. Migration is in the interests of further economic integration which the Asian Development Bank (ADB) estimated in 2014 would raise the region's gross domestic product (GDP) by about 7 per cent and create 14 million new jobs by 2025. A precondition is greater liberalization of labour mobility, particularly of the highly skilled (Pitakdumrongkit, 2015).

As the countries of the region move towards a knowledge-based economy, a capacity for innovation together with local and expatriate employee motivation will prove crucial. This will require more sophisticated control of the workforce, and to this end MNCs especially will introduce induction into a corporate culture in order to inculcate loyalty and prevent movement of employees to competitors. While such managerial practices have long been present in some form, their elaboration is now subsumed under the term human resource management, a Western concept and the parlance used in American and European business schools. Since the economic reforms of the 1980s MNCs in China have introduced and adapted human resource management to the local environment. Similarly, certain managerial techniques introduced during the American occupation of Japan have now come to be seen as uniquely Japanese. Moreover other Western free market influences have been apparent in Asia. In China and Vietnam, where a state industrial sector formerly predominated, there has been a transition from a seller's market to the profit motive which necessitates material incentives for the workforce. Throughout Asia, family and other private businesses have thrived on personal relationships between employer and employee as a control mechanism, but expansion must surely lead to the appointment of a more specialist managerial cadre.

In contrast with such state sector and traditional private businesses, Asian and Western MNCs can develop more structured approaches in areas like recruitment, remuneration and training. As the media fuel rising expectations and a consumer culture emerges, demand for higher living standards will grow. Selection criteria in recruitment will become more rigorous, with attractive remuneration packages offered in order to retain highly qualified managerial cadre. Similarly, there will be pressures to institute a minimum wage, now being enforced in China. In high-technology industries and services training should be designed to ensure a competitive edge in a changing market as well as provide in-house opportunities for promotion and advancement.

These facets of human resource management will become *de rigueur* as both local and Western MNCs advance across the region. The corporate cultures which emerge will only be effective if they adapt successfully to indigenous cultural values and norms. While China's MNCs may benefit from the presence of the Chinese diaspora, other conglomerates must also utilize both expatriates and local managers in their quest for competitiveness. In summary, this trajectory suggests the emergence of various hybrid systems of management in MNCs as the region moves towards further economic integration.

REFERENCES

Pitakdumrongkit, K. (2013), '"Going Niche" for ASEAN Economic Community', accessed 6 May 2013 at www. rsispublication@ntu.edu.sg/rsis086/2013.
Pitakdumrongkit, K. (2015), 'ASEAN Economic Community: Slow Progress on Labour Issues', accessed 18 March 2015 at www.rsispublication@ntu.edu.sg/rsis058/2015.
Rana, P.B. and Chia, W.M. (2013), 'LEP2: Phase Two of South Asia's "Look East" Policies?', accessed 21 March 2013 at www.rsispublication@ntu.edu.sg/rsis047/2013.

Index

Printed and bound by CPI Group (UK) Ltd, Croydon, CR0 4YY

23/04/2025

14660985-0001